Cambridge Studies in Social Anthropol

General Editor: Jack Goody

65

Kinship and class in the West Indies

For a list of other titles in this series, see p. 203

Kinship and class in the West Indies

A genealogical study of Jamaica and Guyana

RAYMOND T. SMITH
University of Chicago

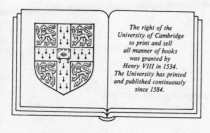

The right of the
University of Cambridge
to print and sell
all manner of books
was granted by
Henry VIII in 1534.
The University has printed
and published continuously
since 1584.

CAMBRIDGE UNIVERSITY PRESS
Cambridge
New York   Port Chester   Melbourne   Sydney

Published by the Press Syndicate of the University of Cambridge
The Pitt Building, Trumpington Street, Cambridge, CB2 1RP
40 West 20th Street, New York, NY 10011, USA
10 Stamford Road, Oakleigh, Melbourne 3166, Australia

First published 1988
First paperback edition 1990

Printed in Great Britain at the University Press, Cambridge

British Library cataloguing in publication data

Smith, Raymond T.
Kinship and class in the West Indies: a
genealogical study of Jamaica and Guyana.
– (Cambridge studies in social anthropology; 65).
1. Kinship – West Indies
I. Title
306. 8'3'09729   HQ576

Library of Congress cataloguing in publication data

Smith, Raymond Thomas, 1925-
Kinship and Class in the West Indies.
(Cambridge studies in social anthropology; 65)
Bibliography.
Includes index.
1. Kinship – Jamaica. 2. Kinship – Guyana.
3. Jamaica – Social life and customs.
4. Guyana – Social life and customs.
5. Jamaica – Genealogy. 6. Guyana – Genealogy.
I. Title. II. Series: Cambridge studies in social anthropology; no. 65.
GN564.J25S53 1988   306.8'3'097292   87-11662

ISBN 0 521 34522 7 hardback
ISBN 0 521 39649 2 paperback

For Flora

Contents

Preface

This book is the first of a projected three-part work that examines West Indian kinship, and the studies that have been made of it, over the past thirty or forty years. In this initial volume I present the findings of a number of genealogical studies carried out in Jamaica and Guyana, using them to question certain orthodox assumptions about class differences in West Indian kinship. In order to interpret these data adequately it has been necessary to consider some aspects of the historical development of kinship, and of kinship studies, in the West Indies, and to touch upon a number of theoretical issues that underly the direction taken by this analysis. In the second part of the projected work I shall present material derived from a twenty-five-year longitudinal study of two villages in Guyana – one Afro-Guyanese and one Indo-Guyanese – a study that also leads to a reconsideration of many accepted ideas about lower class kinship in the Caribbean and elsewhere. The final work will review the development of kinship studies in the Caribbean over the period since the ending of World War II and suggest some of its implications for kinship theory generally, and for the study of Afro-American kinship in particular.

I am indebted to many people who have contributed to the making of this book. To the National Science Foundation, the John Simon Guggenheim Foundation and the Lichtstern Memorial Fund Committee who provided funds at various stages that made possible the field research and writing. To the University of the West Indies and the University of Guyana who provided hospitality, practical assistance and intellectual stimulation. To the colleagues who worked with me on the broader study at various stages: Jack Alexander, Patricia Anderson, Diane Austin, Dalton Davis, Christopher Davis, Michael Fischer, Nancy Foner, Derek Gordon, Jacqueline Mayers, Barbara Miller, Allen Roberts, and Don Robotham. Lois Bisek, Kathryn Barnes and Molly Carrington have, over many years, provided the kind of assistance without which research would be impossible, and Joy Pilgrim gave invaluable help in this study as in others. My thanks also to Colin Smith who prepared the maps at short notice. I owe a special debt of gratitude to David Schneider, both for his own work that

has stimulated so many scholars even when they could not wholly agree
with him, and for the always provocative comments he has made on mine.

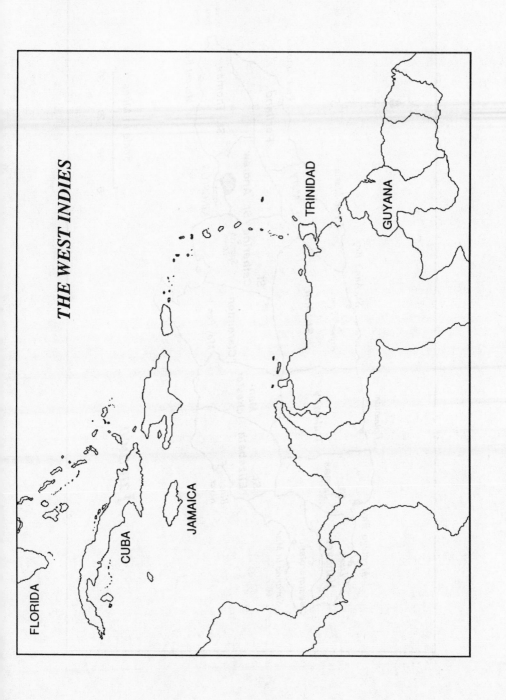

THE WEST INDIES

FLORIDA

CUBA

JAMAICA

TRINIDAD

GUYANA

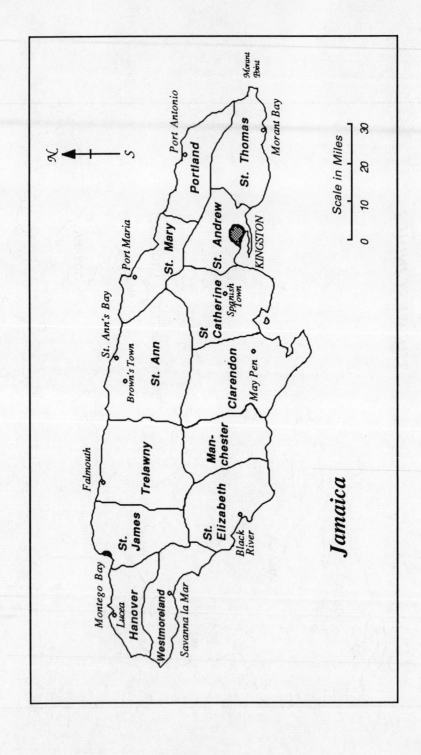

Jamaica

1

Introduction: assumptions, procedures, methods

If there is one point I have consistently tried to make throughout this book, it is that psychology, anthropology, and the social sciences in general, have repeatedly falsified their 'observations' by unrecognized epistemological and ideological closures imposed upon the system under study.

Anthony Wilden 1972

West Indian family life has always interested social scientists, but few have understood it. Like other aspects of Caribbean ethnography, it is difficult to grasp in terms of accepted social theory, and because of this the study of West Indian kinship assumes a wider significance. Even in the eighteenth century West Indians discussed the peculiarities of their kinship arrangements. One Jamaican-born writer published, in 1793, in German, an essay on 'The Nair system of gallantry and inheritance,' subsequently expanded into a romantic novel preoccupied with love and marriage (or the absence of it), entitled *Das Paradies der Liebe*. The author, James Henry Lawrence, used the Nayar of Malabar as the model on which to construct a utopian system of perfect equality of the sexes, in which children would be affiliated only to their mothers (Lawrence 1976 [1811]). Eighteenth-century West Indians were prolific writers, and they rightly felt themselves to be an integral part of the modern world in which egalitarian ideas were increasingly common, but one wonders how much of Lawrence's inspiration came from his Jamaican background. The Caribbean has its own history, with social and cultural systems that must be studied in their own right. For all their appeal to advocates of free love, and other social reforms, the kinship systems of the Nayar and the West Indian slave societies were rooted in the soil of hierarchy – not egalitarianism.[1]

This book looks at the effect of hierarchy in West Indian societies before and after the abolition of slavery, attempting to show the interaction of various ideologies with a persistent system of social practice, and the particular manifestations of that interaction in the domains of family and kinship. The broad outlines of West Indian kinship are well known, and

[1] See Dumont 1980 for a discussion of hierarchy.

1

have been for several hundred years, but the social science literature on this topic has developed a peculiar myopia that is, it will be argued, a by-product of theory. Hence the statement by Wilden at the head of this chapter.

Contrary to commonsense ways of thinking there is no reason for the Caribbean as a whole, or any of its constituent territories, to possess the bounded system of social relations and integrated culture that social scientists have generally assumed to be 'the unit of study,' or, even more erroneously, the unit of empirical existence. On the contrary, this has always been a region of open frontiers, shifting populations, vast cultural heterogeneity, complex economic relations and unstable political authority. Caribbean history has been turbulent, bringing together peoples from every part of the globe in a swirling vortex of greed, lust, and striving reminiscent of the destructive hurricanes that sweep through the region every year. It is remarkable that Caribbean peoples have constructed for themselves a social and cultural existence that defies the contingent aspects of history, defining, delimiting and giving meaning to experience, even determining what that experience shall be. The social and cultural systems so created are far less closed than some social scientists would have us believe. Stable enough so that cultural assumptions outlive novel experiences, they are neither completely consistent nor well-integrated, 'logico-meaningful' wholes.

To study the West Indian family one has to understand the relation between what people say is correct behaviour and what they actually do. This requires reexamination of accepted ideas about the boundaries between classes, races, cultures and societies. It is comparable in many ways to the study of creole languages. A great deal has been known about the form and content of such languages but new theoretical perspectives, relating language to the context of its use, have led to new insights and understandings – but not to agreement (Hymes 1971; Labov 1972; Silverstein 1972; Bickerton 1975; Sankoff 1980). So, in the study of Caribbean kinship the issues are theoretical and not factual. There is general agreement that illegitimacy rates are high, marriage unstable and that women play an unusually prominent role in the domestic and kinship domains. There is much disagreement as to why this should be so. The most general aim of this work is to recognize the coexistent opposition between open and changing social processes and the relative stability of the cultural conceptions through which those processes are mediated and, to a considerable extent, constituted. Some kind of picture, or model, of the culture of kinship has to be made for purposes of analysis, but the primary aim is to remain sensitive to the complexities of the historical process itself.

Introduction

1. Cultural diversity, anthropological method, and historical process

What does it mean to say that a study of the West Indies is significant beyond the concerns of Caribbean studies? Throughout the Americas, and for 500 years, Europeans and 'natives' have been jointly engaged in productive enterprises ranging from fur trapping to timber extraction, mining and plantation agriculture. The first kinship links were forged between Europeans and Indians or Africans in the context of these joint activities. The links were not legally recognized, and the subject peoples were treated as being less than human, but the first attempts to incorporate non-Europeans into European offshoot societies were made here. This was the formative stage of a worldwide phenomenon; the creation of multiracial, multicultural societies – sometimes called 'plural societies' (see pages 5-7 below for a fuller discussion of plural society theory). The habits of mind, understandings, and systems of classification resulting from these first efforts at social incorporation continue to influence social action; their formation is seen most clearly in the colonies of the Caribbean and South America. Anthropology, with its preference for the primitive isolate, for the 'pre-contact situation,' has not been a useful guide to this kind of study (notable exceptions include Tambiah 1973, El Zein 1974 and some recent works reviewed in R.T. Smith 1984c). Anthropology has tended to obscure and mystify understanding. In the process of European expansion sharp contrasts were drawn between cultures. Europeans created images of 'exotic' or 'primitive' cultures, always in contrast to their own; anthropology became the emergent science through which such images were given a spurious precision. Real cultural diversity exists, of course, and there is some heuristic value in comparing that diversity through mental experiments exaggerating differences. But these experiments place culture outside history, and are often confused with reality. Lévi-Strauss has defended the procedure with characteristic eloquence in explaining why he concentrates on 'primitive' societies. At the same time he recognizes that:

The circumstances of its [anthropology's] appearance are comprehensible only in the context of a particular social and economic development: one suspects then that they are accompanied by a seizure of conscience – almost of remorse – that humanity could have remained alienated from itself for such a long time, and above all, that that fraction of humanity which produced anthropology should be the same fraction of humanity which has made so many other men the objects of execration and contempt. (Lévi-Strauss 1966, p. 122)

This attempt to rescue anthropology as the conscience of an exploitative Europe is less than convincing. The distinctive product of European expansion was not the juxtaposition of 'civilized' and 'primitive,' of 'hot' and 'cold' societies, nor even the creation of plural societies; it was the formation of colonial societies with properties all their own.

3

After two centuries or more of treating Africans as property, totally lacking in civil rights and assumed to be more like beasts than men, the British in the West Indies deliberately changed course in the 1830s. They decided to civilize the ex-slaves and make them part of a new society based on the principles of philosophical radicalism and dissenting Christianity. This recognized a process already begun, but was nonetheless self-conscious and organized. Even though it adapted to the realities of power and the interests of British capital, it stands as the most sustained deliberate effort at social change and cultural transformation in recent history. It is a paradigm of western efforts to do good in the world in the name of progress. Of course, it was a failure. It failed because it equated civilization with European racial superiority, with European economic interests and with European culture, thus contradicting its own universalistic intentions. It encapsulated the anthropological view of profound differences among cultures and overlooked the realities of its own environment. Instead of producing a smooth transition from tradition to modernity, a transition that takes place only in the imagination of modernization theorists, it produced colonial society with all its complex and quite distinctive systems of economic organization, status differentiation, racism, religious complexity and ceremonial symbolism. Many aspects of colonial society exist in the modern world long after the formal ending of colonial rule.

2. Kinship as a special field of investigation

The study of kinship and family life by anthropologists has been particularly sensitive to the observer's intellectual assumptions. Some of those assumptions were the unexamined premises of European culture; others were generated in colonial societies themselves.

Since the eighteenth century (at least), the family of man, woman and their children has been pictured as a universal form of human grouping, appearing with the emergence of man himself and constituting the simplest mode of association out of which more complex structures were built. Sociologists and anthropologists have clothed these old ideas in all kinds of glamorous theoretical dress, but most kinship theories are based on unexamined assumptions that distort observation (see pp. 8-10 below). In the Caribbean, where the evidence showed the functional viability of a wide range of family forms, elaborate theories have been developed to explain why the nuclear family should exist and what forces have inhibited its proper development. Most of these theories assume that the lower classes have 'deviant' families and then attempt to explain why. Explanations vary: some describe transformed versions of West African polygyny; some relate different forms of family to varying modes of socio-economic

4

adaptation; one author invented something called the 'lower class value stretch' (Rodman 1963. See R.T. Smith 1978a, 1984b for a fuller discussion). All these theories assume that the West Indian lower class has a family system different from that of the middle class. Only Braithwaite has questioned this orthodoxy (Braithwaite 1953).

3. Plural society theory

These anthropological assumptions are the product, partially at least, of the ideology of colonial society itself, being close to the historically generated myths of the dominant groups. Among those myths the concept of 'plural society' has played a prominent role.

Plural society *theory* (as opposed to the concept of pluralism used by political scientists, or the more diffuse idea of pluralism as cultural diversity) was developed early in the twentieth century by an English colonial administrator, J.S. Furnivall, in an attempt to understand the complexity of the South-East Asian societies in which he worked (Furnivall 1948). A more rigid form of Furnivall's ideas was introduced into Caribbean studies by M.G. Smith (1953, 1956); since then the concept of plural society has been incorporated into various ideologies and stimulated an amount of controversy disproportionate to its intellectual significance, though it has not been widely used in actual social analysis.

Furnivall was struck by the extent to which European capitalism brought together disparate groups of people in places like Burma and Java, setting them to work in economies driven by the profit motive and in the process corroding their customs, religions and values. What concerned him most was the fact that these multiracial, multilingual colonies left intact the social boundaries of their constituent groups, drained away the content of intra-group morality and did nothing to create a wider sense of nationhood. M. G. Smith borrowed much of Furnivall's phraseology about the boundedness of the constituent groups within colonial society, while ignoring his observations about the erosion of culture and the need to create a national 'religion' to replace the several 'cultures' that had been lost. On the contrary, Smith asserted that in societies such as those in the West Indies each 'social segment' preserves (or develops) its own institutions and distinctive culture, so that the totality is held together, and *can* be held together, only by the power of the dominant unit (see Braithwaite 1960 and R. T. Smith 1966 for critical discussions of these ideas).

Over time M. G. Smith has modified his theory to take account of the obvious; such as the potent effects of education upon all segments of the population, and the equally obvious pervasiveness of government institutions. But he still clings to the idea that each segment of West Indian society has its own institutions of marriage, family, child-rearing, inheri-

5

tance and so forth. (Although he says that 'segment' is not 'race,' the units are the black lower class, the brown middle class, the white upper class, East Indians, Chinese and so forth.) By treating these entities as though they are to be understood in terms of their diverse 'substances,' rather than in terms of the relations between them, Smith reverts to the crudities of a functionalism unmodified by the refinements of the 1950s and 1960s. In a previous publication I noted the similarity between M.G. Smith's concept of 'institution' and that of Bronislaw Malinowski (R. T. Smith 1966). There also seems to be a marked similarity between some of M. G. Smith's formulations and those put forward by Malinowski for understanding 'culture contact' in Africa.

In a now classic symposium on *Methods of study of culture contact in Africa* (published as Memorandum XV of the International Institute of African Languages and Cultures), Malinowski objected to Meyer Fortes' proposal to treat the 'contact situation' as if it were any other social situation, using the functionalist method developed by Malinowski himself. He acknowledged Fortes' wisdom in emphasizing functionalist methods, and termed himself the 'Arch-Functionalist' in mocking reference to his critics, but pointed out that the functionalist method had been worked out 'with the purpose of describing and analysing one culture, and a culture at that, which through age-long historical development has reached a state of well-balanced equilibrium. These two main presuppositions of functionalism in its simple form break down in contact studies. We have to deal not with one culture alone, but with two cultures and a *tertium quid*' (Malinowski 1938, p. xxxvi). This creates, or recreates, the theoretical foundation of a 'plural society theory' that is closer to M. G. Smith's ideas than to Furnivall's more sophisticated views. Malinowski argues that functionalism in these situations must be a method 'in which the mutual relations and the functional variations of the dependent factors is studied, not within one culture, but with regard to three mutually dependent phases' (p. xxxvii). Change for Malinowski is now an 'interaction between the European and African cultural phases, from which there emerges a third one, wherein the two worlds interpenetrate, achieve a co-operation or a compromise, or remain in the grip of conflict' (p. xxxvii).

This formulation fits M. G. Smith's view of Caribbean kinship where each of his three 'segments,' black, white and brown, is alleged to have its own institutional forms of family, kinship and marriage, with the brown segment being the result of mixture in a way that the others are not. In his 1940 Presidential Address to the Royal Anthropological Institute, entitled 'On Social Structure,' A.R. Radcliffe-Brown had some sharp criticisms of this kind of theory, calling it 'simply a way of avoiding the reality' (Radcliffe-Brown 1952, p. 202). He went on, 'For what is happening in South Africa, for example, is not the interaction of British culture,

Afrikander (or Boer) culture, Hottentot culture, various Bantu cultures and Indian culture, but the interaction of individuals and groups within an established social structure which is itself in process of change' (p. 202). The rigidities of Radcliffe-Brown's structural-functionalism are no more useful than Malinowski's version of pluralism, but in this instance his criticism is appropriate.[2]

In the period after World War II, when so much research was linked to the British Government's programme of Colonial Development and Welfare, it was easy for social scientists to accept the definition of socially significant problems presented to them by the more influential sections of West Indian societies. The poverty of the masses seemed to set them apart from the affluent in every way, reinforcing the old colonial assumption that the lower classes are culturally distinct, have different social institutions, and may not be capable of total assimilation to civilized society. The anthropologist's predisposition to treat the unit being studied – be it village, region, ethnic group, race or class – as if it were a closed system, introduced further distortion (see R. T. Smith 1982b). By avoiding these biasses, this study documents the extent to which culture and social relations span income and status differences, and the extent to which the family structure of different classes and racial groups can be understood as variations on a common structural scheme.

4. The matrifocal family

I have continued to use the term 'matrifocal family' in this work even though it has come to be surrounded by a dense fog of misunderstanding, and in spite of some shifts in the meaning I now attach to it. As I used the term in the 1950s, it meant the following:

A form of family life bounded by formal parameters of legal and moral expectation of coresidential marriage as the basis for child-bearing and child-rearing, but actually structured in terms of an array of types of conjugal union – legal, non-legal and extra-residential – associated with variable forms of domestic grouping. The analysis of field data from Guyana emphasized (a) the pattern of variation in household composition over time as households changed from something approximating the 'nuclear family' to more complex forms as daughters brought into the domestic group children conceived outside wedlock, and as more households became female headed in the later stages of their development; (b) the association of this variation with the progression from a phase of relative stability of coresidential unions to a phase of increasing salience of the relations of mother and children within the domestic domain, and (c) the relation between this pattern of domestic group developmental cycle and the low social status of the population group studied, with a consequent effect upon the role performance of male heads of

---

[2] For an informed discussion of plural society theory as ideology see Robotham 1980, 1985; see also M. G. Smith's vitriolic rejoinders in M. G. Smith 1983, 1984.

households. Thus, the term 'matrifocal family' referred NOT to a system of female-headed families, nor to a matriarchal family system, but to a social process in which there was a salience of women – in their role as mothers – within the domestic domain, correlated directly with the class position of the population involved, and focussing on the articulation of kinship and class. (See R. T. Smith 1956)

There is no dispute over the accuracy of the 'facts,' broadly conceived. Vast amounts of survey data have been collected, both in the Caribbean and in North America, and all show the prevalence of high illegitimacy rates, relatively unstable unions, and complex domestic relations in which women play a prominent part. What is lacking is adequate understanding of the meaning of these data.

I believe that there is value in retaining the term 'matrifocal family,' and I also believe that its genesis and reproduction in the West Indies is closely related to the hierarchical structure of these societies. But it is not peculiar to the lower class, nor is it simply the consequence of certain functional problems within an ideally conceived nuclear family. It is part of a complex of meaning and action that constitutes the West Indian creole kinship system, a complex that necessarily involves all classes and status groups.

If differences in family structure between classes and status groups are so much less than had been supposed, how could misperceptions have persisted through many years of careful investigation?

5. Quantitative analysis and the refinement of error

To discover the nature and extent of variation, social scientists generally make quantitative analyses of selected variables and measure their covariance to determine functional and causal relations. In the case of family structure this has meant the collection of census and survey data in standardized form.

The sampling unit has almost always been the household. Everyone knew that household units are difficult to define, but in the interests of practicality an attempt had to be made. The relationship between household and family is another difficult issue dealt with at some length in the report of the British Guiana census of 1960. It began by defining a Private Household as 'one or more persons living together and sharing at least one daily meal. In general a household comprises a father, mother, children, other relatives, as well as other persons sharing in their household arrangements' (Trinidad and Tobago Central Statistical Office 1964, p. ix). A family, by contrast, was defined as consisting 'of two or more persons living together in the same household and bound together by ties of marriage or kinship.' It continued: 'Those members of a household who in general comprise a family are a man, his wife (or common law wife), their

8

own or adopted children together with any close relatives of theirs . . . A parent with an unmarried child or children living together in the same household thus comprise a family. However, if a son or daughter marries or forms a common law relationship and brings his or her partner to live in the parents' household, then another family is established within that household' (ibid.). These definitions are arbitrary but they must correspond in some way with the common sense categories of those who planned the census, and indeed we see a gradual shift over time as the categories are questioned. By 1970 the *Jamaica Population Census: Preliminary Report* defines a household as comprising 'a person who lives alone or a group of persons who live together and who may or may not eat together' (p. 6). Whether born of despair or a sense of definitional economy is not known, but it is as good a definition as that found in a sophisticated treatise on kinship theory: 'Operationally households can be defined as "that set of relationships which describes the associations of an individual over a 24 hour period"' (Buchler and Selby 1968, p. 21). The authors express their indebtedness to R. N. Adams for the personal communication on which this definition is based, but they never explain what they mean by saying that 'only one set of relationships is activated throughout the 24-hour period, and consistently enacted, and that is the household' (Buchler and Selby 1968, p. 21). The problem with these definitions is that they are neither native categories nor rooted in a theory where 'households' are a category in a system of abstractions. They are just put together out of the observer's own assumptions. It is impossible to conduct a census or survey without establishing rules for the inclusion and exclusion of household members, and good survey research recognizes the arbitrary nature of these rules. Still, it is tempting to treat the final distributions as representations of social reality; why collect the material in the first place if it is not to be subjected to analysis? (See Kruskal 1981 for an excellent discussion of these problems.)

Having isolated households for enumeration the next step is to establish the exact relationship between members. These relationships, once again, must be specified in a list of categories drawn up by the survey designer. Most usually one individual is designated 'head' of the household, a procedure often surrounded by uncertainty and ambiguity, compounded as the relationship of other members is arrived at. It is not necessary to continue listing the crucial points at which arbitrary decisions must be made in the interest of precision. The categories are predetermined in the survey design and cannot be varied without disturbing the whole structure of data collection, processing and analysis – particularly in large and expensive censuses and surveys.

The analysis of West Indian family structure has also depended on such information as conjugal status, child-bearing history, income, land holding, race, education, age, sex and place of residence. Only the data on sex is reasonably free of uncertainty and ambiguity. Even so, large quantities of material are collected and subjected to ever more sophisticated analytical procedures, a process that too often results in the refinement of error.

6. Procedures used in this study

The data presented in this book were collected in Jamaica and Guyana. Though reference is made to 'West Indian' or even 'Caribbean' kinship, these are *case studies*; detailed genealogical material collected from just a few individuals over a series of interviews lasting from about 20 up to perhaps 150 hours per individual. The reasoning behind this choice of method will be discussed in Chapter 2. Here I shall just explain how we went about things.

To avoid the inherent disadvantages of the *a priori* definitions required for survey research it was decided to find out what concepts are embedded in West Indians' kinship behaviour and family life, and to make a careful record of the whole range of variation, and even ambiguities, in those concepts. One method of doing this is to get people talking about kinship in general and their own familial experience in particular, though we were well aware of the difference between what people say and what they actually do. That relationship was central to our interest, but the emphasis in data collection was on paying careful attention to what people are saying.

Apart from the author, who directed the study as well as interviewing, eight investigators participated in the project. Each one had extensive background knowledge of the West Indies (five were West Indians) and all were familiar with the theoretical aims of the study. All except one were graduate students in anthropology or sociology at the University of the West Indies or the University of Chicago; except for the late Dalton Davis, all are now professional social scientists. The quality of the interviewing was excellent.

The main vehicle for data collection was the extended case study based on multiple interviews organized around the collection of a complete genealogy. The idea was to provide data comparable to those collected by Firth and his associates in London, and by Schneider and his co-workers in Chicago (Schneider 1980 [1968]; Schneider and Cottrell 1975; Firth, Hubert and Forge 1970). The aim of the interviews was to get informants talking freely, with a minimum of interviewer stimulus, about family life, kinship relations, and associated aspects of social life. The genealogy, containing the informant's knowledge of all individuals related in any way through consanguinity, conjugal unions or kinship links created in other ways (to be discussed in Chapter 2), was used as a framework on which the

10

informant was expected to hang a great deal of general comment. This comment would, it was hoped, reveal basic assumptions about the nature of kinship and status.

Even with nine people working full time it was impossible to interview more than a few individuals. Each interview took about two hours, and to write up a full account occupied many more hours. One investigator, Jack Alexander, transcribed all his interviews verbatim from tape recordings – as well as entering a great deal of the material on genealogical charts. Other interviewers used tape recordings only as an aid to memory in writing abbreviated accounts.

Since we knew that only a small number of individuals could be interviewed, they were selected to represent a sufficient range of social types, at least wide enough to draw some conclusions about race and class differences. Before explaining the techniques used to select informants a brief overview of the relevant aspects of West Indian society in general, and Jamaica and Guyana in particular, is necessary.

7. Class and race in West Indian societies

For clarity of exposition the data have been divided along three main dimensions: class, race, and an urban-rural distinction. Jamaica and Guyana differ from each other and neither represents the Caribbean as a whole, though some features of both societies are common throughout the region. Class and race have much the same configuration from one end of the Caribbean to the other, partly because of their uniformly dependent economies (see Jefferson 1972; Stone 1973; R.T. Smith 1967, 1976, 1982b; Post 1978; Rodney 1981; Lewis 1983).

The lower class is descended from African slaves and East Indian indentured immigrants; descendants of Europeans form a significant part of the lower class only in the Hispanic Caribbean and a few small islands. The plantation, and particularly the sugar plantation, has impressed its peculiar influence upon most Caribbean societies.

Jamaica is a small, mountainous island (approximately 144 miles long and 49 miles wide, and rising to 7,360 feet at Blue Mountain Peak) with a population in 1970 of 1,848,512. Acquired by Britain from Spain in 1655, it grew rapidly as a plantation colony and by the mid-eighteenth century had a complex social life at a time when Guyana was little more than a Dutch trading post. Modern Guyana was formed by the coalescence of three extensive colonies – Demerara, Essequibo and Berbice – with a combined area of 83,000 square miles and drained by three major river systems. Most of the country is densely forested and the 1970 population of 701,718 was mainly concentrated in the low-lying coastal region which is about 270 miles long and 10 to 40 miles deep. This is the area of most intense cultivation, where both sugar and rice are grown on drained and irrigated lands. The only British colony on the South American mainland, British Guiana was formed in 1831 out of the three colonies ceded to Britain by the Dutch in 1814. During the early nineteenth century, once the fertile coastal soils were drained and irrigated, the three colonies became areas of expanding cultivation; their production of sugar increased while that of Jamaica declined. The abolition of slavery in 1838 ruined many planters, but the demand for labour on the highly productive soils of the Guyana coastland was so great that it was feasible to import large numbers of workers from China, India and Madeira. Because of declining production Jamaica had a surplus of labour and imported few new workers. This accounts for the differing racial composition of the two countries today. In 1967 (the last year for which official figures were available) Guyana's population of 692,780 comprised 49.3 percent East Indians, 29.7 percent African, 11.8 percent Mixed, 4.5 percent Amerindian, 0.6 percent Chinese, 0.9 percent Portuguese, and 0.2 percent Other Europeans (Guyana Handbook 1975). In the same year Jamaica's population was enumerated as being 91 percent African, 6 percent Mixed, 2 percent East Indian, 0.5 percent Chinese and 0.5 percent White, which includes a small population of Middle Eastern origin (Commonwealth Caribbean 1970). Jamaica's Chinese, Syrian, and Lebanese population is descended from free immigrants, most of whom came to engage in trade, and only a part of the small Indian population entered as indentured labour.

In the nineteenth century Jamaica turned increasingly to crops other than sugar, particularly banana, developing in the process a rural middle class of farmers with medium sized holdings whose counterparts did not appear in Guyana until the emergence of a rice industry during and after World War I. Today both countries are major producers of bauxite (though production has declined precipitously during the 1980s); Guyana also produces gold, diamonds and manganese as well as timber. All these factors have made both countries dependent upon volatile world markets, a dependence that shapes their class structure.

The rural lower class consists of plantation workers and small farmers along with petty traders, small craftsmen (carpenters, masons, shoe-makers, tailors, seamstresses and the like), and landless labourers who make the best living they can by casual work. In spite of attempts at industrialization and the development of new economic sectors such as tourism and mining, the proportion of the labour force engaged in agriculture remains high. However, the urban areas are heavily populated by rural migrants, forced to live in substandard housing and to subsist by the process known in Jamaica as 'scuffling.'

Until the mid-twentieth century all the West Indian colonies were controlled by an elite of white planters and administrators, few of whom became a permanent part of the society. However, they – along with the larger number of whites in lesser positions on the plantations, in the military, and in clerical positions – fathered a growing population of mixed racial origin that constituted a 'coloured middle class' as early as the eighteenth century (see Chapter 4). Thus, in the formative stage of the development of these societies an association was formed between economic class and a hierarchy of racial groups. Even today, when all the British Caribbean territories are independent, the term 'upper class' is rarely used to refer to local elites. In Guyana the enterprises formerly owned by foreign firms have been nationalized and converted into state-owned 'cooperatives.' The Jamaican government acquired partial interest in some economic concerns, but a local business elite, often working in partnership with outside capital, is an important social and political element. Leaving aside the foreign investors and the foreign governments on whom the local leaders are dependent, who constitutes the local elite and what is their social origin?

i. Composition of the elites

By the end of the nineteenth century a class of 'intelligentsia' had emerged in all the British Caribbean colonies. Its core was the old coloured middle class, descendants of white men and black or coloured women originally, but by now a self-perpetuating group. This class was the peculiar creation of colonial society itself; composed of doctors, lawyers, journalists, clergymen, teachers and civil servants who were vital to the maintenance of the colonial regime and enjoyed high social status on that account (see R.T. Smith 1967, 1970, 1982b). But this class also embodied the contradictions of the colonial regime. Highly 'civilized' in its possession of English culture but excluded on account of race, it became the spearhead of a growing demand for national self-determination and its members now constitute the ruling elite – or contend among themselves for the right to lead.

The composition of this class is considerably changed since the late nineteenth century. Blacks, East Indians, Chinese, Portuguese and other elements (such as Syrians and Lebanese in Jamaica), have been absorbed into the creole elite, and in Jamaica a small Jewish population has also played an important part (see Campbell 1976; Heuman 1981; Nicholls 1985; Holzberg 1977). The processes by which these groups were able to become upwardly mobile tells a lot about the dynamics of the society.

Sephardic Jews migrated to Jamaica as early as the seventeenth and eighteenth centuries, becoming closely allied with the Free Coloured group during the slavery period, and sharing many of their civil disabilities. After emancipation they followed the racially mixed, fair-skinned creoles into the professions, though many Jewish families concentrated on business activities of one kind or another. A few Jewish families formed part of the late nineteenth- and early twentieth-century immigration of 'Levantines,' as David Nicholls calls them (Nicholls 1985). Most were Syrians, Palestinians and Lebanese, engaged initially in petty trade or itinerant peddling, often with family ties spread across a number of Caribbean islands, but over the years the families have come to constitute a sizeable sector of the business elite. Although members of all these groups have, like the earlier Jewish immigrants, intermarried with coloured or black families, they remain, even today, socially distinct, partly because of religion and extensive intra-group marriages. One author has tried to document their concentration in business, in the control of corporations and in financial institutions (Reid 1977); a subsequent study has emphasized the minority status of Jews and Levantines in the control of corporations, but confirms the fact that they do have a substantial share of economic power (Holzberg 1977).

Chinese monopolized the retail grocery trade in Jamaica before the development of supermarkets, and today they remain prominent in retail trade. In Guyana the Portuguese played much the same specialized role as the Chinese Jamaicans, while Sino-Guyanese – though active in shopkeeping – intermarried much more with the rural black and Indian population. All these groups were able to use the income generated by business and trade to propel some of their children into the ranks of the educated. In the West Indies the possession of wealth alone was not sufficient to secure entry to the elite; it had to be accompanied by command of that 'English culture' dispensed by the secondary schools. This condition is changing rapidly, especially in Jamaica where more ostentatious styles of living with luxurious houses, expensive cars and extravagant spending have become status credentials in themselves.

Upward mobility into the elite was difficult, but not totally impossible, for the children of the black and East Indian lower class. In Jamaica the rural lower middle class, referred to above (see page 12), was tightly integrated into the churches and ambitious to secure education for its children. Practically the only avenues for enhanced occupational status were entry to teaching, the police and nursing. In both countries, Jamaica and Guyana, racial prejudice made it difficult for blacks to progress beyond this level of the occupational system until well into the twentieth century. For East Indians in Guyana even these avenues were blocked unless Indians became Christians, and the few Indians who succeeded in entering the professions did so with difficulty.

In the period after World War II there was a sharp increase in the rate of upward social mobility; the expansion of education and social services triggered by the passing of the Colonial Development and Welfare Acts, the upsurge in economic growth based on the development of the bauxite

14

industry, expansion of rice farming and the favourable prices for sugar and other tropical produce, all contributed to a mood of optimism that was not broken until the mid-1970s. Emigration to Britain, the United States and Canada drained off some needed talent, but increased opportunities for those left behind. The expansion of home building, the growth of medical services, the improvement of transport and recreational facilities all contributed to higher levels of living for everyone. In Guyana improvements in rice agronomy and the mechanization of agriculture eliminated the drudgery of hand operations, while the stabilization of agricultural prices encouraged farmers to send their children to primary and secondary schools, and to universities, in unprecedented numbers. Many of these changes, desirable though they were, increased the vulnerability of the region to movements in the world economy – as became painfully evident when inflation took hold in the 1970s. Most of the interviews on which this analysis is based were carried out between 1967 and 1972, a period seen by most Jamaicans and Guyanese as one of expanding opportunity unlike anything in the past.

This brief account of West Indian class and racial distinctions is necessarily simplified; to select informants it was simplified yet again. The broad divisions used in the presentation of most of the material are: 'Established or Old Middle Class'; 'New Middle Class'; and 'Lower Class' further distinguished between urban and rural, East Indians and others. The distinction within the 'middle class' is really between those who had been born into families of middle-class status, and those who had become upwardly mobile into it. This proved to be a most important distinction. At first it seemed desirable to make a similar division within the lower class, between a more stable, fully employed working class and an economically depressed lower class, but it soon became evident that such a division does not exist.

8. The selection of cases

In Jamaica a series of rural field sites – in St. Thomas, St. Ann and Trelawny – were chosen for their access to scattered farm communities within easy reach of sugar plantations, thus enabling us to sample families ranging from middle farmers to landless labourers.

St. Thomas has the reputation of being both poor and backward with considerable land hunger, though the area in which Michael Fischer worked during the summer of 1968 was not markedly poorer than other parts of rural Jamaica. It is close to a sugar plantation providing seasonal employment, and not far from the sugar and banana wharves of the port of Bowden. Fischer characterizes the population of the area as follows:

The majority of . . . residents fluctuate . . . between being a 'Lumpenproletariat' and a 'working class.' The access which almost all have to small bits of food-producing land means that they have a greater security than a true Lumpen-proletariat. On the other hand, most cannot support themselves on this land alone as a true peasantry. Most are unskilled or semi-skilled laborers and tradesmen dependent on a seasonal plantation wage economy which hires almost exclusively on a task or piece-work basis, and which itself operates in an insecure world market. Above this 'mass' of . . . residents there exists a lower middle class of clerks, teachers, postmistresses, and one or two others who have managed to move upwards (e.g., through veterans' pensions from the world wars, employment abroad, etc.). (Fischer 1974, p. 27)

The community chosen for study in St. Ann was more differentiated than this. Situated on a ridge overlooking the north coastal plain, it too has a sizeable population of marginal peasants dependent on seasonal work on the adjacent sugar plantations, but it also supports a more prosperous group of cash crop farmers, and has been greatly influenced by the bauxite and tourist industries. Nancy Foner worked in this community for more than a year and has documented its social structure in her book *Status and Power in Rural Jamaica* (1973).

That part of Trelawny studied by Don Robotham shares many of the characteristics of the other two communities except that it is more affected by the bauxite industry. Robotham draws a contrast between old and new aspects of life in the area. The old community is:

Based on (1) the classic relation between peasant 'mountain' hinterland and coastal sugar plantation, a relation which exists between upper Trelawny and the Low-lands; (2) the export of minor crops such as coffee and pimento; (3) local production for the internal marketing system; (4) the consumption of bread, flour and saltfish, khaki and 'blue-drill' cloth and 'good shoes' from small shops and stores; (5) a pattern of living in wooden, or in a few cases, wattle and thatch homes. The 'new' town is based on post World War II developments such as banana production, and the bauxite and tourist industries, which have brought concrete homes, a gas station and supermarkets, and which have drawn the community into a closer, and increasingly disadvantageous, integration with the national, and therefore the international economy and society. (Robotham 1970, pp. 39-40)

Finally, Jacqueline Mayers worked in an extensive settlement on the edge of the city of Kingston. These lands had been owned by the Water Commission and reserved as a catchment area, but gradually became filled with squatters moving down from the hills of St. Andrew to be in closer contact with the urban job market. Ten years before the study began the lands had been sold to the settlers, who were then able to build more permanent houses. As they began to replace temporary structures with concrete block buildings, generally working as and when money was available, the size and form of the houses reflected their own social needs and preferences rather than the ideas of some planner, architect or builder of mass housing. Buildings clustered around a common yard, instead of lining up in the orderly rows of the official housing schemes. By the late 1960s the population of this area was quite large, and although most people worked in the city the community had a definite rural atmosphere and many residents retained active ties to hill communities within walking distance across the Hope River.

Within the city of Kingston proper two neighbourhoods were chosen; neither was a slum but both are declining middle-class residential areas with families ranging from those with minimal incomes to some with skilled occupations and others with small businesses such as hairdressing or dressmaking. Interviewing in these areas was done by Patricia Anderson and Barbara Miller.

The initial procedure was to carry out a 'locating survey' using a short questionnaire dealing mainly with occupational and family matters. The technique of a locating survey had been used by Schneider in his study of middle-class families in Chicago; in Jamaica we adapted questions from the Guyana Mobility Survey, which had been developed by Sara Graham in consultation with R.T. Smith (see Graham 1973). The aim was to locate good informants for the more extensive interviews used in genealogy collection, but the survey data were interesting in themselves. Fischer, Foner and Robotham all used them in their accounts (Fischer 1974; Foner 1973; Robotham 1970). From these samples, of fifty or so families in each area, a smaller number of individuals was chosen for intensive interviewing based on their willingness, and on a judgement as to their suitability. One interviewer could handle about six informants at a time, interviewing each one perhaps twice a week. Attempting more interviews than this resulted in the accumulation of untranscribed notes and tapes.

Jack Alexander used a different method of selection of informants for his year-long study of middle-class families in Kingston, Jamaica. Names of potential informants were suggested by people he consulted, such as clergymen, or he contacted informants at meetings of civic organizations, or they were introduced to him by mutual friends. His sample was not random; informants were selected to cover all the relevant cultural domains. The core group consisted of seven men and four women, all but two of whom were between thirty and fifty-five years old. Some 178 interviews were tape recorded and transcribed verbatim. Fourteen subsidiary informants provided valuable and extensive information but their genealogies were not complete enough for inclusion in the tables (see Alexander 1973, 1976, 1977).

In Guyana work was concentrated in the city of Georgetown since a great deal of information on rural kinship already existed (R.T. Smith 1956; Smith and Jayawardena 1959; Jayawardena 1962). However, the opportunity arose for me to work with a woman I had known in rural Guyana in 1951, as well as with an East Indian man born in the rural areas, who had lived there for most of his life. These are the only two cases from rural Guyana to be included in the tabulations, but other studies of East Indian kinship – carried out before and after the genealogical research – have been drawn upon in the general discussion (see R.T. Smith 1978b, 1984d for an account of those studies).

Other Guyanese informants were all resident in Georgetown and were interviewed by Dalton Davis, Donald Robotham and me during the summer of 1967. They included individuals born into the middle class, some who had come from poor families but had become teachers or white-collar workers, and some skilled workers and poor people. Neither time nor resources permitted the inclusion of informants of all races, but the genealogies cover the whole racial spectrum in the sense that informants have relatives of every race and degree of racial mixture.

The social characteristics of the informants whose genealogies were complete enough to be tabulated are listed in Table 1. The cases are grouped following the broad model of class development laid out previously, and this is shown abbreviated in Table 2. In later chapters the data are sometimes aggregated into simpler divisions for ease of presentation. All names have been changed to protect the privacy of informants, and possible identifying characteristics such as age or occupation have sometimes been modified. No claim is made for the representativeness of these data in a statistical sense; the aim is to establish a mode of analysis and to explore the extent to which quantitative data can be made more meaningful by a detailed study of informants' – rather than observers' – categories. From that point of view, Chapter 4, which presents a series of tables summarizing the results of the genealogical analysis, is included to provide a reference point for other discussions and for comparison with the North American and English studies (Schneider 1980 [1968]; Schneider and Cottrell 1975; Schneider and Smith 1978; Firth et al. 1970). Readers with less interest in genealogical analysis will find most of the results embodied in other chapters.

TABLE 1: SOCIAL CHARACTERISTICS OF PRINCIPAL INFORMANTS

Case No.	Pseudonym	Sex	Occupation	Age	Born	Race	Marital Stat	Gen. Size
OLD UPPER MIDDLE CLASS								
Jamaica: Urban								
202	C. Cook	F	None	Old	Rural	Fair	Widowed	733
206	B. Sears	F	None	Mid	Rural	Fair	Married	730
256	R. Sears	M	Business (High)	Mid	Rural	Fair	Married	116
209	O. Wagner	M	Business (Med)	Mid	Rural	Fair	Married	427
Guyana: Urban								
106	B. Fowler	M	White Coll. (H)	Yng	Urban	Brown	Married	262
110	Esther Brown	F	White Coll. (L)	Yng	Urban	Brown	Married	335
OLD LOWER MIDDLE CLASS								
Jamaica: Urban								
204	P. Morris	M	Profession (M)	Yng	Urban	Brown	Married	119
205	B. Johnson	M	Profession (M)	Mid	Rural	Brown	Married	369
207	W. Stern	M	Profession (L)	Old	Rural	Brown	Never Married	349
Guyana								
105	Walter Grey	M	Profession (L)	Old	Rural	Black	Widower	80
NEW UPPER MIDDLE CLASS								
Jamaica: Urban								
251	A. Benton	M	Profession (M)	Old	Urban	Black	Married	125
201	C. Benton	F	Profession (L)	Mid	Rural	Black	Married	96
203	N. Garner	M	Profession (M)	Mid	Rural	Brown	Married	182
253	R. Garner	F	Profession (L)	Mid	Rural	Brown	Married	249
259	P. Wagner	F	None	Mid	Rural	E.Ind.	Married	41
Guyana: Urban								
101	R. Singh	M	Profession (H)	Old	Urban	E.Ind.	Married	206
112	R. Ramdan	M	White Coll. (L)	Mid	Rural	E.Ind.	Married	465
NEW LOWER MIDDLE CLASS								
Jamaica: Urban								
303	V. Cramer	F	Own Account (L)	Mid	Rural	Dark	Married	475
Guyana: Urban								
109	C. Jordan	M	White Coll. (L)	Yng	Rural	Black	Never Union	187
111	R. Bayley	M	Profession (L)	Mid	Rural	Black	Married	186
151	M. Bayley	F	Profession (L)	Mid	Urban	Black	Married	213
Jamaica: Rural								
506	A. Frost	F	Own Account (L)	Yng	Rural	Black	Visiting	121
605	R. Jackson	F	Profession (L)	Mid	Rural	Brown	Married	362
LOWER CLASS								
Jamaica: Urban								
301	G. Bascom	F	None	Mid	Rural	Brown	Married	123
302	Alice Smith	F	Low Manual	Mid	Rural	Dark	Visiting	448
304	Bertha Small	F	Low Manual	Yng	Urban	Black	Common Law	113
305	W. Campbell	F	Low Manual	Mid	Rural	Black	Married	240
306	Clara Monroe	F	Own Account (L)	Yng	Rural	Fair	Married	219
307	Nancy Rogers	F	Own Account (L)	Old	Rural	Brown	Widow	343
401	Elizabeth David	F	Domestic	Yng	Urban	Black	Common Law	108
402	Stanley Williams	M	Unemployed	Yng	Urban	E.Ind.	Visiting	318
403	Cybelline Brooks	F	None	Mid	Rural	Black	Married	176
404	Esther Fyfe	F	None	Old	Urban	Syrian	Married	79
405	Elva Lawrence	F	Own Account (L)	Old	Rural	Black	Widow	/606
406	Myrtle Gentles	F	None	Mid	Rural	Black	Common Law	210
456	James Gentles	M	Skilled Manual	Old	Urban	Black	Common Law	52
Jamaica: Rural								
501	H. Williams	M	Manual (Low)	Old	Rural	E.Ind.	Common Law	178
502	H. Best	F	Higgler	Mid	Rural	E.Ind.	Common Law	205
503	E. Jones	F	Small Farmer	Mid	Rural	Black	Never Marr.	422
504	V. Price	F	None	Old	Rural	Black	Married	150
505	F. Tate	F	None	Old	Rural	Black	Married	276
601	Jewel Green	F	Small Farmer	Old	Rural	Black	Married	581
602	J. McGregor	M	Medium Farmer	Old	Rural	Black	Married	661
603	Agnes Murray	F	Own Account (L)	Old	Rural	Brown	Widow	235
604	Nerissa Daley	F	Higgler	Mid	Rural	Black	Married	350
Guyana: Urban								
102	H. Roberts	M	Manual (L)	Yng	Urban	Black	Married	222
103	James Murray	M	Manual (L)	Old	Urban	Brown	Married	289
104	F. Albert	F	Own Account (L)	Mid	Rural	Black	Visiting	142
107	Ethel Hunt	F	Own Account (L)	Old	Rural	Black	Widow	136
108	Lester Chase	M	Manual Skilled	Yng	Urban	Black	Common Law	84
Guyana: Rural								
888	Eugenie Black	F	Profession (L)	Mid	Rural	Black	Never in a Union	1106

19

SUMMARY OF TABLE 1

Total Number of Cases   51
Male Informants   20
Female Informants   31

Old Middle Class Informants
Male: Number=7; Mean Age=42; Mean Size Genealogy=246 (Range 80-427)
Female: Number=3; Mean Age=44; Mean Size Genealogy=599 (Range 335-733)

New Middle Class Informants
Male: Number=6; Mean Age=44; Mean Size Genealogy=225 (Range 125-465)
Female: Number=7; Mean Age=41; Mean Size Genealogy=222 (Range 41-475)

Lower Class Informants
Male: Number=7; Méan Age=45; Mean Size Genealogy=258 (Range 52-661)
Female: Number=21; Mean Age=46; Mean Size Genealogy=299 (Range 79-1106)

TABLE 2: CASES BY CLASS AND COUNTRY CATEGORIES

Description	Case Numbers
Old Upper Middle Class: Kingston	202;206;256;209
Old Upper Middle Class; Georgetown	106;110
Old Lower Middle Class; Kingston	204;205;207
Old Lower Middle Class: Georgetown	105
New Upper Middle Class: Kingston	201;203;251;253;259
New Upper Middle Class; Georgetown	101;112
New Lower Middle Class: Kingston	303
New Lower Middle Class: Georgetown	109;111;151
Rural Middle Class: Jamaica	506;605
Urban Lower Class: Jamaica	301;302;304;305;306; 307;401;402;403;404; 405;406;456
Urban Lower Class: Guyana	102;103;104;107;108
Rural Lower Class: Jamaica	501;502;503;504;505; 601;602;603;604
Rural Lower Class: Guyana	888

20

2

Kinship, culture and theory

The objectivity aimed at by anthropology is on a higher level [than other social sciences]: The observer must not only place himself above the values accepted by his own society or group, but must adopt certain definite methods of thought; he must reason on the basis of concepts which are valid not merely for an honest and objective observer, but for all possible observers.

Lévi-Strauss 1963

The theoretical issues raised by this study are not new, but their implications for the analysis of Caribbean kinship have not been explored except in a few brief publications (Alexander 1976, 1977; Drummond 1980; Fischer 1974; R.T. Smith 1973, 1978a, 1978b, 1982a, 1984c, 1984d). This short chapter provides interested readers with a fuller, but not exhaustive, explanation of the concepts and theoretical principles only touched upon in the first chapter. There we established the following: (1) the study of kinship has been profoundly influenced by assumptions about the empirical, or necessary, universality of the nuclear family; (2) the perception of lower-class social life in the Caribbean has been conditioned by the ideological structure of colonial society; (3) the quantitative analysis of 'family structure' raises serious problems of definition which are often resolved to the detriment of understanding. These issues come to a focus in the meaning of 'normal' (see R.T. Smith 1973).

1. Ideal norms and behavioural norms

The concept 'norm' has two major referents in the social science literature: it can refer to regularities in observed behaviour which may be expressed in a normal distribution curve or as a statement of average or modal regularities; or it can refer to the ideal patterns, or models, toward which behaviour is oriented. The dualism inherent in these different meanings of 'norm' leads to statements such as, 'Most studies find little or no correlation between an individual's attitudes or normative beliefs and his

21

behavior' (Cancian 1975, p. 112). An example of this would be the apparent disjunction between West Indians' belief in legal Christian marriage as the proper framework for sexual relations and child rearing, and behaviour that results in illegitimacy rates of up to 73 percent of live births. We saw that definition and observation is part of the problem – understanding what people are really saying when they talk about marriage – but there is also a theoretical issue involved. Cancian's solution is to substitute collective for individual 'normative belief.' After a tendentious interpretation of Talcott Parsons' ideas, norms are defined as collective perceptions and become consistent with action (Cancian 1975, p. 147).

Nadel put the issue of statistical versus ideal norms clearly when he said:

> In one respect, however, the statistical ideal, even if it can be achieved, offers to the anthropologist only inconclusive data; for it produces only half the knowledge at which he must aim. Since we are concerned with intended and task-like behaviour, we must require its standardization in a statistical sense to have also a 'subjective' significance. This lies in the expectations by which the actors are guided when behaving in a standardized fashion. Unless these, too, are given, the statistically regular and probable modes of acting remain for us meaningless. (Nadel 1951, p. 115)

Nadel was one of the first anthropologists to pay serious attention to the work of Max Weber and he footnotes this passage with a reference to Weber's discussion of 'adequacy on the level of meaning.' The difficulty of translating Weber's expression *sinnhafte Adäquantz* has been discussed by Talcott Parsons (1947, p. 99, n. 20). Parsons himself adopted Weber's solution of making the actor's subjective orientation one analytically separable element in the theory of action: we must not only observe what people do, but also understand what they intend their actions to be (see Parsons 1949). This creates more problems since one must now determine the meaning as well as the exterior form of behaviour. Weber was most insistent that this did not involve psychological analysis to find out what each particular individual thinks he is up to. Instead, we must find ways to study *systems of concepts*. His comparative study of religion is an extended attempt to study systems of this kind and the way in which they become embodied in behaviour, affecting it in areas which seem remote from religion – such as economics. Before considering Weber's ideas further let us examine the way in which this problem has been dealt with in recent anthropology.

2. Culture and social action

Parsons, in elaborating on Weber's schema, developed two distinguishable theories: one theory took individual action as its point of departure but generalized the categories of the theory to wider spheres of collective

22

behaviour; the other dealt with societies as structured and integrated totalities with little reference to the components of individual action (see Dubin 1960; Bendix 1960, pp. 265-86; Jeffrey Alexander 1983, Vol. 4, pp. 170-5). In his later work Parsons asserted that the cultural system is the high order subsystem that maintains the 'governing,' or controlling, patterns of the system of action in which it is found. Culture provides a 'highly stable structural anchorage quite analogous to that provided by the genetic materials of the species-type, focussing on the learned elements of action just as the genes focus upon the heritable elements' (Parsons 1966, pp. 6-7). In this view, culture is related to the normative structure of social systems as a 'legitimating' mechanism. Normative order within a social system becomes regularity of purposive behaviour which has to meet the functional requirements of collective organization. Since conflicts of interest are inevitable, social order has to be maintained by a system of compatible and integrated rules of behaviour. These rules, and the behaviour that follows them (with a normal range of deviation) is the very stuff of the social system, internalized as part of the individual's perso-nality.

Parsons has understood clearly the need to study culture as a system of patterns of, and for, action – as Kluckhohn once put it – while at the same time taking careful note that social action must be limited by organizational needs. Things must get done in a reasonably orderly fashion regardless of what people think. However, Parsons provides few directions for using these analytical distinctions in sociological practice, and has succeeded in eliminating from consideration much of the real action involved in economic and political life by assuming a congruence between ideal patterns and behavioural norms.

3. Anthropology as the study of abstracted culture

Anthropologists have been influenced by Parsons in different ways. Some, like Lloyd Fallers, have pursued leads provided for the comparative study of politics and social stratification (Fallers 1956, 1973). Others found the idea of the analytic separability of 'culture' to be compatible with an older tradition of social science specialization in which anthropology claimed culture as its special preserve. Anthropology could now be redefined as a discipline specialized in the study of culture as a system of symbols and meanings, rather than an all-embracing study of man and his works. Archaeology and physical anthropology could be reassigned to history and biology. This development had some rewarding consequences, even if it did not lead to a wholesale reorganization of the profession, but some less useful developments also took place. One such is the tendency to divorce cultural analysis from any concern with social context and social process. It can be intellectually satisfying to provide a 'cultural account' of the system of symbols and meanings embedded in social action, particularly since it requires creative as well as analytical ability, but there are severe limitations. A good example is Schneider's work on American kinship.

Schneider insists that the cultural system, defined almost precisely as Parsons defined it, should be treated 'in its own right' as a nonreducible aspect of concrete systems of social action. Cultural anthropology should specialize in understanding the systems of ideas that are embedded in, and presumably guide, social action. For many years he has carried out an extended critique of previous work in comparative kinship studies, showing that the elaborate edifice of comparative categories is built on basic, and unexamined, assumptions of Euro-American culture. Consequently it fails to grasp the meaning of the phenomena it purports to describe (see Schneider 1972). It has been assumed, complains Schneider, that for the whole human race 'kinship' is just what it is for Europeans – a matter of blood and marriage. This is because anthropologists have failed to pay attention to the precise statements of their informants, carelessly translating them into the familiar terms of European kinship. The European assumption that kinship arises from 'biology' is just a belief system like any other, with no more claim to scientific validity than the belief in ghosts (Schneider 1965; 1984).

Perhaps the most interesting part of Schneider's analysis of middle-class American kinship concerns role theory, attempting a novel definition of the way in which roles are constructed (Schneider 1980 [1968]). The usual view of social roles is that they are like parts in a play learned by social actors, each role being appropriate to an activity in a particular social institution. Since each individual has to play many roles over the course of his life, especially in complex societies, it becomes a problem to make sure that the parts are kept sufficiently separate so that they do not interfere with each other. 'Role conflict' might cause problems for the social system as well as the individual. Schneider is not concerned with that particular problem because he is not interested in how things get done. He concentrates on the cultural counterpart of the social role; on what he calls 'the person.' The person is, by definition, capable of action in society, but is to be understood first as a composite figure put together from parts taken from different 'pure' cultural domains. This needs some explanation.

4. Pure and conglomerate levels

Schneider thinks of culture as a system of symbols and meanings with its own logic and mode of integration, distinct from any problem of social order and indeed distinct from any part it might play in social action. The meaning of each unit in a system of cultural symbols derives from its relation to other symbols in the system, and not from the way it is used in the give and take of everyday life. If we consider the concept 'father' we find that in American kinship, according to traditional role theory, 'father' is a role in the family system, along with the roles mother, husband, wife, son, daughter, brother, and sister. Attached to each role are rules specifying what an individual occupying that role should or should not do. Fathers should support their children and normally should live with them, discipline them, see that they go to school, set a good example, teach them how to play games and so forth. They should love their children in a fatherly way and that precludes sexual intimacy, excessive physical punishment or economic exploitation. All these features specify proper behaviour and, according to Schneider, indicate the social system aspects of social role. The father as a person in American culture has to be seen in somewhat different terms.

Let us ask, says Schneider, how the father as a 'person,' a cultural construct, is put together. What is the 'distinctive feature' of the father as a person? The notion of 'distinctive feature' is taken from linguistics and is discussed more fully in Schneider (1980, pp. 134-5) and Yanagisako (1978, pp. 25-7). For our purposes suffice it to say that the minimal definition of father in American culture is that he is the genitor – the man whose seed joined in biomystical union with that of the mother to produce the child. At 'the pure cultural level' it does not matter whether the father had any contact with, or even knowledge of, his offspring; what makes him a father is being the genitor. In addition to this 'pure' level of cultural meaning Schneider creates another. Whereas purity demands that cultural domains be kept separate, at the 'conglomerate' level of cultural meaning the units are made up of pieces from different pure domains. The distinctive feature of father is taken from the kinship domain; he is the genitor. At the conglomerate level the father as a person in American culture is also a male. As such, certain aspects of the cultural system of sex roles will apply to him. He is of a certain age and race, features which also carry cultural assumptions from their respective domains, and he has a class component. Taken together all these cultural elements are combined to create an image of the father located at a particular position in social space.

This appears to be a different and fruitful way of approaching the understanding of social roles. Instead of trying to write a script from a close observation of what the actors are doing, or gathering all the possible prescriptions that attach to a particular social position, he is trying to understand the 'model' or image that people have in mind when they think of 'father' as a potential actor; that image is defined only by its relation to other images such as mother, son or daughter in a *system* of images. No individual will just act out the model; it is a shared image that is part of a symbol complex. Since the 'conglomerate' image is made up of parts from the 'pure' domains, persons who are situated at different points in social space will embody different combinations of elements. In the early 1970s, using these theoretical concepts, Schneider and I showed that class differences in family structure in the United States are due primarily to differences in sex roles, and not to differences in the kinship elements (Schneider and Smith 1978).

A major difficulty with this kind of analysis is to understand the relation between culture and actual behaviour. Schneider has tried to explain the difference between the pure and conglomerate systems and suggest how they are related to norms.

The conglomerate system is oriented toward action, toward telling people how to behave, toward telling people how-to-do-it under ideal circumstances. It is thus much closer to the normative system. The pure system, however, is oriented toward the state-of-being, toward How Things Are. It is in the transition from How Things Are and How Things Ought To Be to the domain of If That Is So, How Then Should One Act that the pure systems come together to form the conglomerate systems for action. (Schneider 1972, p. 42)

This is an almost classic case of the assumption that there is a radical distinction between systems of thought and systems of action. What is the point of making such a sharp distinction between the conglomerate level of culture and the normative level of the social system? It radically separates culture from social structure and makes it difficult to put them back into conjunction other than by some device such as the assumption that culture is a 'controlling code' comparable to the genetic code; an idealist solution favoured by Talcott Parsons in his later work.

5. Culture and practice

The problem was recognized and dealt with by Max Weber a long time ago. In setting out the basic definitions of sociology and social action he began by saying that 'Sociology . . . is a science concerning itself with the interpretive understanding of social action and thereby with a causal explanation of its course and consequences' (Weber 1968, p. 4). At no subsequent point does he permit a disjunction between understanding at the level of meaning and understanding at the level of causal relations. For example, he says: 'A correct causal interpretation of a concrete course of action is arrived at when the overt action and the motives have both been correctly apprehended and at the same time their relation has become meaningfully comprehensible' (Weber 1968, p. 12). This insistence on understanding both levels, cultural and action, is important, but so is Weber's caution in constructing and using 'models.'

Action in the sense of subjectively understandable orientation of behavior exists only as the behavior of one or more individual human beings . . . it may . . . be convenient . . . to treat social collectivities, such as states, associations, business corporations, foundations, as if they were individual persons . . . but for the subjective interpretation of action in sociological work these collectivities must be treated as solely the resultants and modes of organization of the particular acts of individual persons, since these alone can be treated as agents in a course of subjectively understandable action. (Weber 1968, p. 13)

These warnings against reification have been taken as an indication that Weber is interested only in individual motivation at the expense of cultural understanding, but this is a false interpretation. Weber outlines a whole methodology for arriving at the understanding of concrete courses of action, in both its 'objective' and 'subjective' aspects, and the constructs he employs correspond to the 'cultural' and 'social system' levels of later sociology. He argues that it is useful to employ devices such as the idea of the functional integration of social systems, so long as one realizes that this is just a first step toward understanding the meaning of social action. Equally we must recognize that:

The theoretical concepts of sociology are ideal types not only from the objective point of view, but also in their application to subjective processes. *In the great majority of cases actual action goes on in a state of inarticulate half-consciousness or actual unconsciousness of its subjective meaning.* The actor is more likely to 'be aware' of it in a vague sense than he is to 'know' what he is doing or be explicitly self-conscious about it. In most cases his action is governed by impulse or habit. Only occasionally and, in the uniform action of large numbers, often only in the case of a few individuals, is the subjective meaning of the action, whether rational or irrational, brought clearly into consciousness. (Weber 1968, pp. 21-2) (My emphasis)

Returning to Weber's discussion of these problems makes us realize that the construction of 'normative' and 'conglomerate' levels of analysis is unnecessary and confusing. Cultural analysis is nothing more than an ideal type, or model, of the subjective meaning that is so unclear in the consciousness of individual actors. Its purpose is to contribute to 'the interpretive understanding of social action and thereby [arrive at] . . . a causal explanation of its course and consequences' (ibid., p. 4).

Within this framework Schneider's insistence on the methodological priority of cultural analysis has some validity. Not because culture constitutes a controlling code and thereby assumes causal priority in the understanding of social action, but because without adequacy at the level of meaning the other dimensions of the analysis are all too likely to be rooted in the unexamined assumptions of the observer's own culture. The history of anthropology is full of examples of this difficulty. There have been long disputes over whether there are societies without 'law'; arguments about whether bride price constitutes the 'purchase' of women; and more recently attempts to interpret all behaviour as 'market relations.'

Schneider has also argued that complexes of cultural symbols cut across social institutions and advanced this as another reason for keeping cultural analysis separate from institutional and normative enquiry (Schneider 1976). That seems to be a minor point once it is realized that 'social institutions' are themselves analytical constructs. An adequate understanding of the cultural assumptions of one's informants is an essential part of the social reality with which one is dealing. Whether that adequate understanding can come from the construction of a 'cultural account' or requires the development of a more adequate theory of practice, a process begun by Weber and more recently carried forward by Bourdieu (1977), is the key question.

6. Kinship ideology and Caribbean family structure

What does all this have to do with the study of West Indian kinship? A great deal. It is surprising to find that little attempt has been made to pay close attention to the ideas, the concepts, of the people being studied – even at the rudimentary level required for creating a cultural account.[1] The emphasis has been on 'objective' data gathering (using predetermined categories), or on the premature interpretation of behaviour as motivated by rational self-interest in which subjective factors are mere secondary rationalizations, or on the search for 'cultural survivals' which might appear in disguised form as 'reinterpretations.' This is clear in the case of religion where practically no attention is paid to meaning, while great emphasis is laid on class, political motives or on African and Indian survivals. An example from Asia will help to make clear the kind of incremental gain in understanding which comes from paying careful attention to ideas.

7. A comparative example: Bengali kinship

Inden and Nicholas have shown how misleading it has been to interpret Bengali behaviour in European terms, even when those terms are dressed up as social science concepts (Inden and Nicholas 1977). European culture assumes the individual to be the basic unit of society; an autonomous, rational entity made up of two distinct elements – body and mind, soul or spirit. Kinship is also believed to have two distinct aspects. It is a natural relationship of common blood (blood being the symbol for substance, sometimes rendered as flesh and blood), but kinship also implies a specific

---

[1] There are exceptions to this generalization, notably the work of Professor George W. Roberts of the University of the West Indies whose work is touched upon at the end of this chapter, and will be discussed more fully in a subsequent work reviewing developments in kinship studies in the Caribbean.

'code for conduct' which says that you should support and, if possible, love, your relatives regardless of circumstances. Bengali culture can easily appear to make the same distinctions but a careful examination shows that it does not. A few examples of the differences will have to suffice. Bengali culture asserts that certain kinsmen are indeed of the same 'flesh and blood' but it does so in a much more literal way than does European culture; they are believed actually to constitute one body, the substance of which is constantly being augmented: it can even be exchanged by the giving and receiving of gifts. The most important gift is that of a virgin bride.

European culture divides the kinship universe into two sections; blood relatives and in-laws; consanguines and affines. Europeans and Americans have some difficulty in characterizing the relationship of husband and wife in kinship terms. Informants know that they are not blood relatives but they find it difficult to categorize a spouse as an 'in law.' There is a feeling that somehow they are united – both physically and spiritually. In Bengali culture the wife is believed to share the actual substance of her husband; she becomes, literally, his 'half-body' (Inden and Nicholas 1977, pp. 39-55). These beliefs about shared substance are linked to beliefs about the daily strengthening and fortifying of shared substance by virtue of eating, worship, the mingling of substance in the act of sexual intercourse and so on. No sharp line is drawn between body and mind comparable to that in European culture.

Perhaps their most important contribution has been to show how misleading it is to classify Indian families into 'nuclear,' 'joint' and 'extended' as is the usual practice, and to show how one can be misled by assuming that households are the basic units of the kinship system. The most important unit in Bengali kinship is the *parivara*, a unit which takes a living male as its reference point and consists of all the persons who share the bodily substance of this *svami*, or master: 'his wife, his sons, his sons' wives and sons, and perhaps even their wives and sons' (Inden and Nicholas 1977, p. 5). Although it may appear that a man, his wife and their unmarried children constitute a unit identical to that of the European 'nuclear family,' especially since Bengalis often live in households that appear to consist of just such a group, there is no such cultural unit in Bengali kinship. In particular, such a unit is not distinguishable from those that include more than one married couple, usually termed 'joint' or 'extended' families.

The difficulty with respect to the Bengali Hindu family is that such a 'nuclear' unit is not a culturally closed set. . . . [The] process of including additional dependants may go on indefinitely: the wives of a man's sons become dependants of their masters (husbands), and so do the children. However, these added sets of masters and dependants do not form distinct families, since their respective masters are themselves dependants of their father and master so long as he remains alive. (Inden and Nicholas 1977, p. 6)

Contrary to the usual European notion that the head of a household or a kinship unit is the person who is the economic provider or the political leader or the status giver, here the master of the *parivara* has the crucial function of performing acts of worship or sacrifice on behalf of his bodily dependants. When members of a family of this kind go off to constitute separate households, sometimes far away, they do not thereby set up a separate family unit. They continue to be a part of the family, and the body, of their *svami*.

Bengali kinship may appear to be remote from the concerns of West Indians – even those of East Indian descent – but the analytic principles are most relevant and we can profit by following Inden and Nicholas in paying the strictest attention to our informants' statements and the structure of concepts that is embedded in them. The analysis of that structure is the beginning, not the end, of understanding kinship practices.

8. Conclusion

The need for a break with past traditions of quantitative analysis based upon preconceived ideas of the naturalness of certain patterns of kinship and family behaviour is becoming widely recognized. Professor George W. Roberts of the University of the West Indies is the leading demographer of the Caribbean and he has laboured for some forty years to document in precise detail the frequency of different forms of West Indian family, kinship and mating patterns. No person knows more than he about the minutiae of these matters, nor commands a greater understanding of the strengths and weaknesses of demographic and census data. In 1975 he carried out, in collaboration with Sonja A. Sinclair, a study that makes a decisive break with past tradition in that it makes use of extensive case material collected by interviewers who tape recorded respondents' comments (Roberts and Sinclair 1978). The study was specifically designed to capture respondents' own phrasing and understanding in order to throw light on mating and reproductive behaviour. This major advance in West Indian sociological research is only a beginning; the theoretical framework remains positivistic and the technique of extending a standard questionnaire to capture 'qualitative' data is only a small step in the right direction. What is required is a combination of the methods of anthropological and demographic analysis to steer between the twin perils of uncomplicated cultural analysis and unthinking enumeration.

3

What is kinship in the West Indies?

In discussing the social structure of the West Indies the obvious starting-place is the family, for it is, even when quite ephemeral, the outstandingly important social institution of the West Indies.

The prevailing type of West Indian family which is encountered over and over again in all the colonies is very loose in organization.

T.S. Simey 1946

Even the most superficial observer would not make the mistake of thinking that kinship is unimportant to West Indians. Much has been written about the 'looseness' of family relations, about sexual promiscuity and about the inadequacies of child rearing, but it is generally acknowledged that family ties are both strong and extensive. Before we try to resolve the seeming paradox of coexistent strength and looseness it is necessary to get a clearer idea of the way in which our informants think and talk about kinship. What is a relative? How do kinship ties arise? What are the obligations of kinship and how do they vary? It is commonly assumed that there are differences in family structure as between classes and races, but there has been no attempt to discover whether the concepts of kinship and family are uniform throughout these societies, and whether the same terms mean the same thing to different sections of the population.

1. Spontaneous kin lists

If 'kinship' is not a universal human institution, or should not be assumed to occur everywhere in the same form, then it is important not to bias an investigation at the outset by asking questions that structure the answers in a particular way. This is as true of 'open ended' questions as it is of more highly structured questionnaire categories. A technique was devised by Dr. Millicent Ayube that limits the eliciting stimulus to one simple question: 'Please give me a list of all your relatives.' The term 'relatives' is, of course, culturally particular, and interviewers did not always use it in the precise form set out here. They tried to find a phrase, such as 'Tell me all your family – relatives then,' that would convey the idea of a comprehensive account without providing categories. The technique can be effective if the interviewer refuses to provide guidance beyond that involved in the initial stimulus question, thus throwing the responsibility for deciding what to include or not include, and the order of presentation, back on the respondent.[1] The initial spontaneous listing of relatives was only a starting point for the subsequent exploration of the respondent's kin universe; it has to be regarded, in spite of a degree of cultural presupposition, as a point of entry into the conceptual world of the respondents and not as a listing of a predefined category of relatives or kin.

A: Could you list for me all the people you consider to be related to you?
I: You mean all the people related to me? That would take me till next week and a day because of all the people. What a lot; what a lot. There's my husband . . . you want names too? What a lot. My husband and seven children, mother, father – you mean those alive?
A: However you want to do it.
I: Those who are near to me or what? Relatives or friends or what? Sisters and brothers? There are so many . . . it's a very big family.

Similar expressions of hopelessness at the enormity of the task were common. Some people pleaded that they could never remember all the names; others doubted that we had enough paper to write them all down; one woman began by saying 'Lord, mi ent have none, is only me, all ah them nearly dead and gone,' but she then proceeded to list exactly 100 individuals before running out of steam on her spontaneous list. She started by making a clear distinction between the nebulous concept of 'all' relatives stretching off into the dim distance, and the more easily handled 'close' ones who really mattered. Only a couple of informants pointed out that if you go back far enough everybody in the world is related, though it was interesting that the observation should be made at all. Many more commented on the complexity of ties in their own country, neighbourhood, or in the West Indies generally. 'I have plenty of relatives I could tell you about, all across the island. You know Jamaica is like one family.' Another informant made the point that white Jamaicans no longer exist; they are 'all mixed up' by now. The same idea of mixing occurs in the eastern Caribbean where kinship ties stretch between the islands and down into the Guyanas, drawing individuals together even as nationalism drives them apart.

Alexander has made a detailed analysis of the spontaneous kin lists of middle class Jamaican informants; he shows that in spite of variations in

---

[1] See Wolf 1964 and Alexander 1973 for a full discussion of the use of this technique.

the order in which categories of kin are presented, certain underlying principles or structures seem to be constant. Two of the most important constants are the bifurcation of the relatives into 'mother's side' and 'father's side,' and the tendency to present kin as nuclear family units, of which this bifurcation is one aspect. At least that is how Alexander expresses it (Alexander 1976, pp. 21-6). His informants share an abstract image of what should be included in a list of 'relatives' and they try to fill out this image with the names of real individuals – if they exist. It is obvious that this image, or structure, is prior to the particular experience of individuals, for informants often remark that they do not have anyone to fill a particular place in the schema. Remarks such as 'I have no aunts on my mother's side' show this clearly. The spontaneous kin lists of lower class informants, whether from Jamaica or Guyana, do not differ fundamentally from those of the middle class. However, they cannot be characterized in the way that Alexander suggests. He says, 'Fundamentally, informants seems to see the domain of kinship as consisting of an interlocking set of nuclear families with the families organized relative to each other by genealogical distance and bifurcation, and secondarily by age, sex, and a "subjective" principle' (Alexander 1976, p. 23). The use of the term 'nuclear family' in this passage, and throughout the analysis, can be misleading. He uses it to refer to the abstract image of man and woman as the parents of children. Thus any individual must have a father and a mother by virtue of the shared belief in the transmission of 'blood' or substance, in the act of generation. Should this be called 'the nuclear family'? The question could just as well be asked of Schneider in his analysis of American kinship. Both Schneider and Alexander are dealing with middle class informants to whom the idea of a coresident, nuclear family of husband, wife, and children is both statistically and ideally normal. Middle class West Indian genealogies can be read easily as a series of interlocking nuclear families, just as Alexander says, but not lower class genealogies. Multiple unions are more common than among the middle class, and residential arrangements less orderly. Even so, the principles for structuring the spontaneous kin list are the same, with the addition of a few auxiliary influences. To avoid any confusion about residence or marriage it would be better to refer to 'interlocking sets of parents and children,' instead of 'nuclear families.'

No extensive analysis of lower class kin lists will be made here, but a few examples will illustrate the general principles. Elva Lawrence (case number 405) listed 123 relatives in her first interview, a listing interspersed with a great deal of fascinating commentary. She started with her mother who was about to celebrate her one hundredth birthday, and proceeded systematically to her father, and then her brothers and sisters, distinguishing them by birth order, sex and whether they were alive or dead.

Sometimes if an individual was married she would mention that fact, recalling the name if possible, and she would also mention where they were living at the time. This turned out to be an important principle, as we shall see. She next moved 'down,' as it were, to her own children; she had mentioned her husband immediately after the name of one of her father's sister's husbands, as if it had reminded her to get her own husband's name on the list. In listing her children, which she did systematically from the oldest to youngest, she neglected to mention that her first two daughters were born as the result of two youthful visiting unions before she entered a more stable relationship with the man who eventually became her husband. These early unions were discussed in subsequent interviews. It is unlikely that she suppressed this information deliberately, but its omission from the initial kin list does raise some interesting issues. In listing her own children and their spouses and offspring she would refer to her 'married husband,' and, where appropriate, say such things as 'that child is not for her married husband.' In other words, she generally distinguished between children of different fathers. This was also true when she listed her parents' siblings and their children, her grandparents' siblings and their children and her husband's relatives.

The principle of bilateral inheritance of 'blood' was clearly operative in Mrs. Lawrence's manner of moving through the kin list, but whether this means that 'The linkage of parents and children represents the fundamental importance of the nuclear family' or not, is a matter of definition (Alexander 1976, pp. 23-4).

For informants like Mrs. Lawrence the 'nuclear family' group is often split between households, and not just as a result of the maturation of children and their subsequent marriages. Her own household included her eldest daughter's son, now twenty-two years old, who had built most of her house; a younger daughter and her child by a visiting union; her son, his non-legal wife and their child.

In another case, Mrs. Jewel Green (case number 601), started by listing her mother, grandfather, and her mother's brothers and sisters. She then gave her father's name, saying 'Me have grandparents by the father now; Esther and Joshua Williams,' and then listing 'uncle by my father' and several aunts. Things began to get more complicated as it turned out that Mrs. Green's mother had children by four different men and was married to none of them. Mrs. Green and her six brothers and sisters had four fathers between them, with a corresponding array of paternal grandparents. Mrs. Green knew something about each of them, and often a great deal. In addition, she had at least one brother by her father, listed in the initial interview. The same pattern is repeated throughout the genealogy as grandparents, aunts, uncles and cousins each have multiple unions and sets

34

of children by each one. Little wonder then that it was Mrs. Green who said 'You know Jamaica is like one family.'

On such a genealogy it is impossible to circle off coresident nuclear families, even though the generative principle creating 'blood' ties is the union of male and female. Does an informant such as Mrs. Green use any other principle to organize her spontaneous kin list? She uses several. The first is the *principle of locality*.

We have some more family up by the McReady's there. Joan McReady – she married now. All the same, still a relative. Iris McReady, she's 'mistress,' married now; Mrs. Jordan. Now all these now is from my grandmother's side. The same Taylor is from the same family. The one that drove the car this morning, they're all the same family.

When she said 'up by the McReady's there' she was referring to a specific location in the rural community where she lived, a location where the McReadys congregate, many of them on 'family land.' The McReadys are Mrs. Green's mother's mother's family. Her mother's mother, Rebecca Sloane, was the outside child of Arthur McReady who subsequently married and had children by his wife. Rebecca Sloane's mother also married and had children by her husband, James Munroe. Interestingly enough there were two marriages between the Munroe and McReady offspring in the next generation, and Mrs. Green was careful to explain that while these people were the brothers and sisters of Rebecca Sloane they were not related to each other and thus were able to marry. The Munroes live in another part of the same community. Mrs. Green's father was from a neighbouring town and she thinks of his family as being in that locality. In speaking of her own children she said

This one, Mrs. Smith, she marry and live in Coco Hill. Mrs. Astor, she marry and live in Coco Hill. Ronald Green, he marry and live in Coco Hill. So those are the four of them who live in Coco Hill [she included an unmarried son living with her]. The other ones live in town, they live together in one home rented. But here is their real home, you see. They rent one house so they don't live scattered. You have Elsie and Ernest and Ilsa and Iris. Those four rented one home in town.

We shall see later that many informants think of kin being either in a particular location or being 'scattered,' but for the present the point is that locality is a way of organizing thought about blocs of kin.

Alexander, in the passage quoted above (page 33), refers to a 'subjective principle' as a constituent of the informant's view of the kinship domain, but this principle was noted for only two middle class informants. One referred to 'those who live in the house' when listing his kin, and the other spoke of 'those who have made an impression on me.' Alexander suggests that a subjective principle is always present as a factor in thinking about kinship but it only becomes obtrusive when there is some disjunction between a 'normal' pattern of kinship relations and the one experienced by the informant. In both these cases 'Their parents, of their own free choice, did not continue to raise their children jointly' (Alexander 1976, p. 25). For lower class informants, being raised by someone other than both parents – or even one – is common. It need not arouse emotions that influence the way in which a kin list is presented but it does affect the conception of who should, or should not, be counted as a relative, and it causes informants to explain over and over again why they feel themselves to be closer to one person than to another. For example, Mrs. Green was asked whether she was closer to some relatives than to others. She answered:

The children now. My children are the nearest, grandchildren, aunts and uncles. All the children just move in one unit. Sometime you have family where there are children who are special, you understand? Where one or two, they are special above the others. We just move as one. Anything hurt it affect the other, that's how we are. They are just one unit . . . My affection was mostly for my grandmother because it's she I grow with. I love my mother of course but it's my grandmother I feel close affection for.

Megan Bayley of Georgetown, Guyana (case number 151), had barely got started on the listing of her kin when she said:

Could you include anyone else who is not related by blood but who is so close – the relationship is such that you include them as related to you? (Interviewer nods). Sister Merle – I regard her as an aunt, and her sister too – we call her Sister Liz. Sister Merle was very kind to my mother and me – both of us. She has a daughter, Hilda, well I regard her as a cousin, I would say – and the other sister too, Sister Liz, she has four children – I regard them as cousins though we are not actually related by blood – blood connections.

After a pause she continued:

Well, I should mention my father – by adoption so to speak. It is rather interesting; when I was young I called him 'father-daddy,' but when I got older I realized it did not make sense – you know as a teenager – I changed off and called him 'daddy' . . . I was adopted by an adopted father and this father was my mother's godfather – my grandfather's good friend. So I never knew my father; he and his wife adopted me. She [adopted mother] died when I was very small but when she was alive I called her Aunt Bee – she died when I was about three.

Megan Bayley was not legally adopted – few West Indian children are – and she certainly did not sever relationships with her own mother. In fact her mother now lives with her and she still addresses her, as she has since childhood, as 'Sister Edna.' Given the complexity of the proliferating ties resulting from multiple unions and the frequent practice of moving children from one household to another, it is not surprising that close emotional ties develop between children and the person raising them. There is frequent reference to the one 'who grow me,' often the maternal

36

grandmother. It is understood that 'blood' is the 'real' basis of kinship but informants are insistent that surrogate parents are real relatives.

Finally, how do informants deal with affines? In a spontaneous kin list affines usually appear because they are spouses of consanguines, either legal or non-legal, visiting or coresident, and that usually means they are the parent of a consanguine. However, the relatives of such spouses are often listed extensively, as though the informant felt obliged to go through them. A distinction is made between blood relatives and relatives 'by law,' but these terms are not used as they are in Europe and north America (see page 39 below).

So much for spontaneous kin listings. Our data confirm Alexander's analysis; there is a shared image of what should be included on a list of kin. All informants, regardless of class or race have the same general theory of conception. 'Blood' is passed from both mother and father at the moment of conception. They make the same distinction between 'father's side' and 'mother's side.' They distinguish between blood relatives and relatives in law. And they distinguish relatives by sex and by generation. Differences arise when these general principles are used in building actual relationships, and the actual relationships react back on the informants' conception of what kinship is all about. Thus it is argued that people who are more 'really' relatives than real relatives (because of their actions) should be included on a kin list. This is only the beginning of the complications; I now examine the way they develop as the interviews proceed.

2. Mother blood and father blood: bilaterality in West Indian kinship

Almost all kinship terms used by West Indians are English; therefore the kinship system appears to be bilateral in form. How accurate is this appearance?

The literature on Caribbean kinship contains many reports that people believe 'blood' to be transmitted through only one parent. Edith Clarke, writing about land tenure in Jamaica, says that rights to land may be inherited 'through the blood' or 'by the name,' a distinction that suggests Jamaicans think of 'blood' passing through females and 'the name' through males (Clarke 1957, pp. 44,48). She footnotes an extensive quotation from Rattray on the Ashanti distinction between blood, inherited matrilineally, and spirit or semen, inherited patrilineally (Clarke 1957, p. 71, note 27). Without saying so directly, the placing of the quotation suggests that Jamaicans are continuing a West African tradition. To what extent can this be verified?

There is nothing in our interview material similar to the statement reported by Clarke, but some informants distinguished between male and female transmission of inheritable characteristics. For example, a Guyanese questioned the use of the term 'half brothers' for children of the same woman, saying that children 'from the same belly' cannot be 'half.' Jamaicans often say that 'mother blood is stronger than father blood.' An East Indian argued that mother's relatives have blood that is different from that of the father's kin, with whom one shares common substance. Discussing blood transfusion, he said that blood donated by a relative on the mother's side would be useless, whereas any of the father's relatives could give blood.

To set against these statements is material showing that 'blood' is believed to be transmitted from both parents, and that conception is the result of a single act of sexual intercourse during which the male seed is implanted in the female womb to fertilize an egg which grows into a baby. There is much confusion about the anatomical and physiological details of the process, as there is in the United States and Britain, but this does not create social problems (see Roberts and Sinclair 1978). Though it is said that children inherit gestures, speech patterns, temperament or manner of walking from one or other parent, it is not necessary for 'blood' to show itself in this way. As one Jamaican said, 'relatives come by birth.' Sexual intercourse, leading to conception, determines the child's blood connections – whether they show or not. Another informant, discussing the way in which blood is carried said, 'I'll say it go by nature – ah mean the blood spread by nature in sexual form. How can me put it? By having sex. Ah don't know if that is the right answer?' This last appeal was interesting in that most informants assumed that the interviewer should know better than they how babies are formed since there must be a correct 'scientific' explanation.

How are we to interpret these variations in belief about conception, the transmission of kinship substance, and even the nature of kinship itself? Let us examine more closely the statements of the Afro-Guyanese who argued that same mother siblings with different fathers could not be 'half' because they are from the same belly, and the Indo-Guyanese who argued that blood of the mother and her relatives is different from that of her child. Without reliable guides or procedures for interpreting statements of this kind, anthropologists use the interpretation that best fits their argument. Generally they assume that any given statement should fit logically and consistently into a 'cultural system.' It would be easy to assume that Afro-Guyanese and Indo-Guyanese have different cultural systems, as evidenced by these statements, and – by extension – that they have different theories of conception and different kinship systems. That assumption would be wrong. When the statement about blood and blood transfusions was discussed with another East Indian he laughed knowingly and said, 'Certainly; it is so we Indians believe.' The implication was that certain beliefs held by Indians, this being one, contrast with the beliefs of other Guyanese. Or to put it more generally, certain beliefs are 'Indian' and they differ from 'Guyanese' beliefs. Indo-Guyanese are also Guyanese, and are becoming less 'Indian' (in one sense) as time goes by, so that 'Guyanese beliefs' are theirs as well. The informant who made the original statement passed easily, even in the same interview, to discuss kinship as equal descent from both sides of the family. His remark merely challenged the rigid application of the rule.

One could deal with these variations by supposing that the 'survival' of different cultural traditions in different segments of the population produces a differential stress on patri- or matrifiliation. But 'segments of the population' are not easy to define and there is no clear boundary between 'races' and 'classes.' Different concepts are used in different contexts by the same people; the meaning of a given usage has to be interpreted in its context of use. The situation has been likened to the 'post-creole speech continuum' (DeCamp 1971) where a particular speaker commands a certain range of the continuum of linguistic variation, deploying speech abilities in different ways depending on the context (Drummond 1980). This leads to the question of whether the contexts themselves fall into any kind of pattern, bringing us back to class and racial group variation by another, though perhaps more rewarding, route.

A final example reinforces this point and leads into the next stage of the discussion – on affines. A Jamaican informant was asked what makes a person a relative. Her answer was 'they come from birth.' She was then asked, 'If your father had children with a woman who was not your mother, would those children be relatives?' She answered, 'Well if she not my mother . . . I shouldn't think so. They come along with him: they would be relatives by law, but not by blood. Am I right? It's like my husband's children would be my children in law; if I divorce they would not be my children again. With my father would be the same. Right?' Both father and husband are treated as affines, distinct from the closer blood ties of matrilateral kin, though the informant's constant appeals for confirmation suggest that she could be persuaded otherwise. On other occasions she traced blood ties through her father.

3. Intended husbands and aunts-in-law: affinal relationships

Judged by British and north American ideas about affinity, West Indians' statements about relatives 'in law' seem garbled. West Indians are more consistent and logical in applying the modifier 'in law' to all (or many more) non-consanguineal relationships. Thus one finds reference to 'aunt-in-law,' 'cousin-in-law,' and the term 'son-in-law' is applied to a spouse's child. Another aspect is more complicated. In English and north American usage the in-law relationship is created by legal marriage; increasing numbers of non-legal coresidential unions in the United States now causes terminological difficulty. In 1980 the United States census used a new category: Person of Opposite Sex Sharing Living Quarters (POSSLQ). Informally, West Indians often solve this problem by using the terms 'husband,' 'wife,' and the modifier 'in-law' where no legally sanctioned relationship exists.

This is not a new phenomenon. In 1836 a Barbados Magistrate noted that 'the kept mistress of a colonel in the militia of the colony; . . . [who] at his death, . . . was left, besides other property, the services of eight or ten slaves, now apprentices, referred to herself in court as, "Mrs Colonel — ," using the name of her deceased keeper' (Marshall 1977, p. 123). She was not the Colonel's wife of course.

Ladies living in non-legal unions today do not generally refer to themselves as 'Mrs.' but they do refer to their mate as 'my husband,' or sometimes as 'my husband to be' or 'my intended husband.' This does not erase the distinction between legal and non-legal unions, nor do people insist that it is correct usage, but it is practical. The primary distinction is between 'relatives by blood' and 'relatives by law.' In making that distinction legality is often ignored. Relatives by law are those who have 'come into the family' through the establishment of a conjugal union of some kind; legal or non-legal, coresidential or even visiting. Those who have 'come into the family' may also be called 'bye family,' a term derived, apparently, from the old English meaning of 'bye' as secondary or subsidiary.

Schneider says that the distinction between blood relatives and in-laws is part of a broader distinction within American culture between an order of nature and an order of law; between that which is created and that which is given; between what is voluntary and what is obligatory (Schneider 1980 [1968]). It would be difficult to derive this distinction from West Indian materials. Informants generally reduce the difference between blood kin and in-laws by stressing the assimilation of some affines to the family.

As we shall see in Chapter 5, the concept of marriage as alliance is found in West Indian society, but (except for East Indian marriage) the partners should be 'in love.' Informants had difficulty defining the marital relationship; although the spouse is not a consanguineal, it disturbed them to regard him or her as an 'in-law.' Alexander's middle class informants transform the conjugal relation from a matter of choice to one of discovery; 'we found that we were in love' (Alexander 1978, pp. 12-13). By the same token, if the love no longer exists the marriage is effectively dead, and should be terminated, though that is not the way things generally work out in practice. The lower class also believes love to be the proper basis for conjugal relations, but is more likely to put other aspects in the foreground. The mutual responsibilities of support, domestic services and child rearing often are established before the couple marry. East Indians again contrast the 'traditional' arranged marriage with 'modern' ways of doing things, in which children expect to make their own choice. In all these cases, a conjugal relationship brings people into 'the family.' Just what that means depends to a large extent on the meaning of 'the family' and on the genealogical range of the included affines. This is taken up more fully in Chapter 4.

4. What is the family?

The word 'family' as used by West Indians has a number of meanings. Failure to discriminate these meanings has caused confusion. By 1970 the West Indian Census had abandoned incautious references to 'the family,' concentrating instead on the analysis of household composition. Even the law has begun to move away from its assumption that the normal family consists of a legally married couple and their legitimate offspring sharing a common home. However, this image of the family continues to be widely disseminated, especially by the churches. Some informants have it in mind when they speak of 'my family,' but spontaneous kin lists show more complex meanings attaching to the word family.

A: Now, I want first just the plain list of your relatives, all your relatives.
I: Jesus, I have a big family. But I'll tell you those that I know. Living at the moment, my mother – my father died just three months ago. I have one brother, and he is married, without any children. I have one sister, and she is married with two children. I have one son; I'm related to him or him to me. That's the immediate family. (Case number 205)

He went on to discuss mother's side and father's side relatives. This middle class Jamaican, B. Johnson, comes from the rural middle class. He is married but when asked specifically if he included his wife in 'the circle of relatives' to which he made frequent reference, his answer was 'I'm not related to my wife . . . I am dealing purely with family.' He explained later that his mother and his wife's mother were classmates at teacher training college, so that 'when I married into that family it was like marrying a sister.' Again, when the interviewer asked if Johnson's son would have a different experience of family because he had grown up in town, Johnson immediately replied

Yes, I think his experience would be entirely limited to the immediate family, that is to say, his grandmother, who lives there [in the old rural house], his uncle and aunt who live just outside, that is my brother and my sister and then his relations on his mother's side now, his maternal grandparents are still alive there and all their children, who are scattered incidentally.

Johnson was not peculiar among the middle class informants in his treatment of 'family.' Perhaps because they were trying to provide a complete list of all their relatives, informants tended to begin with their parents or grandparents, but they used 'family' in a more general sense than is conveyed by the term 'nuclear family,' though many said subsequently that husband (or wife) and children are 'closest.'

Bertha Small (case number 304) has lived with her common law husband for almost ten years. They live in one half of a small, deteriorated wooden house in Kingston, Jamaica, with their four children. Both grew up in the country and both are working, she as a waitress and he as porter at a hospital. After listing several members of what she described as her 'large family,' mostly related through her mother, she said, 'Well, my closest family is gone. Both my parents are dead. I have some godparents but they come in like good friends, but not family.' A little later she added, unexpectedly, 'Well, Agatha Chase. She is my husband's mother and she lives at August Town. I visit her regularly, but I don't know any other from his family. But his mother is different; she come in like "sort of family".' Though Bertha Small found it difficult to keep in touch with her relatives, even those living in town, the word 'family' did not conjure up in her mind an image of herself, her common law husband and their four children.

Cybelline Brooks started her kin list with her children, her husband (he was sandwiched between two of the children), and her husband's father, because she started by listing 'those in the house here,' previously mentioned in the locating survey (case number 403).

In its most general sense 'family' means the same thing as 'relatives.'

A: Is there a difference in Jamaica between people you call relatives and people you call family?
I: Family and relatives are alike. I would say I and you is relatives; that's one way I use it; and I can go back and say that me and you is family; it's the same. Yes, it's the same. (Case number 504)

However, a distinction is always made between family as consanguineals and those who are related by law. Some of the latter will be included as family because they 'have come into the family.' Cybelline Brooks, when asked who she considered to be her close relatives, said 'Mi mother, yuh wouldn't say so? Because without she I wouldn't be here. Some people will say "mi husband," but him only a bye-family; him come in a the family.' It can be stressed either way. One can say that a person is only bye-family, or really one of the family. Informants generally know many blood relatives of those married to their own consanguineals. This is discussed further in Chapter 4, where genealogies are analysed. Few of these individuals were considered to be 'family;' it depended almost entirely on the nature of the interaction among them.

What is kinship in the West Indies?

The term 'family' can also be used to designate a subset within the broader range of family as a whole. For example, 'my father's family,' 'my mother's side family,' 'there's a whole set up there in Canada,' 'my grandfather's clan,' and similar geographical and genealogical delimitations of bodies of kin. B. Johnson (case number 205), was explicit in his discussion of the difficulty of drawing boundaries between various sets within the larger entity of 'family.'

I: There comes a time when one draws the line around the limit of family.
A: So you would say that these are the people that are within that line . . . and other people are out?
I: Yes, though occasionally somebody turns up and you hear, 'Don't you know so-and-so are related?' And then it depends on subsequent relationship that they get drawn into the family circle.

He then gave several examples. By the same token, others drop out.

I told you that my grandfather was one of ten. Now ten people originating in a small area tend to send branches out – and as the branches, some of them remain within the line and some outside the line and occasionally you hear oh such and such person is related. Ahm Chris Crocker, Deputy Prime Minister, I hear that he is related. The Crearies, I know that they are related, now this is my paternal grandmother, there is a whole lot of those, who were at one time within the family circle, now I hardly see them. When I see them they come in the family circle. It is a difficult thing this; where do you draw the line? . . . I don't think the line is a fixed line. I think it, it varies ahm sort of with circumstances.

Some East Indian informants showed a tendency to stress paternal relations in constructing the meaning of 'family.' A middle class Guyanese, Reginald Singh (case number 101), said the blood tie makes a person family rather than a friend, and 'it is from the union of husband and wife that the family start – it is that union makes the blood tie. Every one that springs from that is a blood tie.' He also insisted that when children and grandchildren marry there is a dilution of the blood. Initially this came up in a discussion of the marriages of two of his daughters to non-Indians, one a Chinese and one a European, but he raised it again specifically when only Indians were being discussed.

A: What of your wife, is she family?
I: Yes, because it is from the union of husband and wife that the family start – it is that union makes the blood tie. Every one that springs from that is a blood tie – the couple are at the top and when you move down other strains come in. The basis is the parents – that's how I look at it.

After grandchildren, he said, 'the strain run out.' This theory rests squarely on the recognition of bilateral kinship ties.

Another Indian, Sukdeo, listed his kin starting with his father's parents,

43

his own parents, his paternal uncles and aunts, his own siblings, his wife and children; he then asked whether the interviewer wanted his mother's family and listed them. He went on, 'they are family yes, but they don't come so close like my father's brother's children them. . . I consider my brother's children very closely related – I can depend on them very much you know, for any assistance or anything. The blood runs through their veins and mine come right down from my grandfather them – that's how Indians consider it you know. Brothers are more close than sisters.' Having said that he changed tack and began to discuss closeness in terms of being able to depend on people for assistance, and here his wife's brother scored high.

5. 'Fe we': some kinship terms and their uses

In the West Indies a relative is a person related by blood or by marriage, and informants often include among their relatives people to whom they cannot trace a kinship tie, but who they say should be included. Sometimes the word 'relative' is used in a more restricted sense to mean only blood relatives. Similarly 'family' is used sometimes to mean only blood relatives in which case the term 'relative' may be contrasted with it; 'he is not family, only a relative.' Rules of use for these terms do not seem to be clear cut. Cassidy points out that in Jamaica the expression 'fe we' can mean 'our family or kin' (Cassidy 1961, p. 221). The expression 'generations' turns up in our interviews – meaning the same as 'relatives' – as in the phrase 'all his generations.' All these terms are used to draw the distinction between blood kin and in-laws, and between kin and non-kin.

Most West Indian kinship terms are identical with those reported by Goodenough, Schneider and others for north America, and with those used in England. They also can be divided into two groups. The basic terms are 'father,' 'mother,' 'son,' 'daughter,' 'brother,' 'sister,' 'uncle,' 'aunt,' 'nephew,' 'niece,' 'cousin,' 'husband' and 'wife.' These basic terms are combined with a modifier to constitute derivative terms, the modifiers being 'in-law,' 'step,' 'foster,' 'great,' 'grand,' 'first,' 'second,' 'third,' 'half' and 'ex.' The modifiers 'once removed' or 'twice removed' are not in common use in the West Indies. Apart from some Hindi words widely used among Indo-Guyanese, remarkably few kinship terms are not English in origin. The peculiarities arise from the way in which the terms are used rather than from the existence of completely different words. The more extensive use of the modifier 'in-law' has been mentioned (pages 39-40 above), and the reluctance to use the modifier 'half' for siblings, instead of expressions such as 'by father.' Other novel usages arise out of non-legal conjugal unions and the complexities arising from multiple unions.

In Jamaica 'intended' and 'to be' are frequently found with 'husband'

and 'wife.' Some informants commented on the use of 'husband' and 'wife' for common law partners; one informant said 'that's stupid to call it that. It don't come to that.' She thought that 'sweetheart' was more appropriate, and indeed the expression 'living sweetheart life' has a pleasing sound. On the other hand this woman regarded her brother's common law wife as a relative. 'Yes, in my own little way I consider her a relative, for she has children for my brother and she may become his wife some day.' The terms 'keeper' and 'kep' miss' have been used for centuries in the West Indies, the former almost certainly an abbreviation of 'housekeeper.' 'Living home' is a precise Guyanese expression used when a couple are actually living together in the same house, whereas 'friending' need involve no coresidence.

When an unmarried couple have a child, a consanguineal tie is created between the child and each 'side' of his family. Even if the couple have never lived together and break off sexual involvement immediately, a relationship usually develops between the partners and their relatives. The partners may now refer to each other as 'the baby father,' 'my child's mother' and so forth. No matter how fleeting the relationship between the parents, the tie between parent and child is permanent and indestructible; a child is almost always taken to meet the kin of the 'missing' parent and it is usual for the mother of the child to develop friendly relations with the mother of the baby's father.

Other special uses of terms will be noted throughout the following chapters; they are all special adaptations of basic terms to meet special circumstances. A few terms are used to designate so-called 'fictive' kin, an inappropriate expression since there is nothing fictional about the relationship, or people's view of it. Esther Goody has used the term 'proparenthood' to cover a variety of forms of created kinship, and 'prokin' would be a better term than those now in use in Caribbean and Latin American studies (Goody, E. N. 1971, pp. 331-45). 'Shipmate,' used between individuals who travelled together on the same ship as slaves or indentured servants, denoted a real kinship tie, precluding marriage of the descendants of shipmates. I have not come across prokin relations being treated as a burden as reported by Gutman for Maryland in 1863 where a free black referred derisively to 'swap-dog kin' (Gutman 1976, p. 224). Age grading is a common way of referring to people, but not a prokin practice. An informant's reference to his mother's classmate was noted above (page 41); referring to two people as 'grow match' is common. Godparenthood and cogodparenthood are important ways of establishing ties of generalized solidarity, though not nearly so well developed as in Latin America. Nor do these ties seem to be purely spiritual bonds (see Gudeman 1972, 1976). In Guyana the terms *Macmay* and *Compay* are used to refer to the godmother and godfather respectively of one's child.

Finally, Hindi kinship terms are used extensively among Indians, particularly *Chacha* (father's brother), extended as a term of respect to all older men in one's father's village; *Bauji* (elder brother's wife), often generalized to women with whom one has (or would like to have) an easy and friendly relationship; and the terms *beta* (m) and *beti* (f) used to address all relatives younger than the speaker. Other Hindi kinship terms may be alternated with English terms depending on the circumstances.

6. Conclusion

This chapter started by asking 'What is kinship in the West Indies?' and showed the underlying logic of its structure to be similar to that of English kinship. It is bilateral, genealogies are shallow but have wide lateral extension, and a distinction is made between blood kin and in-laws. On that basic structure many variations are developed, their range extending far beyond the West Indies to the north American continent and Latin America. A systematic comparison within this wider field must be deferred (see R.T. Smith 1984b for a preliminary discussion of such comparison); here I am concerned with variations particular to the Caribbean and its historically developed circumstances. The range of that variation, and the contexts in which variants are found, is the most interesting part of West Indian kinship, and I turn to a more detailed examination of it in the next chapter.

4

The structure of genealogies

The genealogical method makes it possible to investigate abstract problems on a purely concrete basis. It is even possible by its means to formulate laws regulating the lives of people which they have probably never formulated themselves, certainly not with the clearness and definiteness which they have in the mind trained by a more complex civilization.

W.H.R. Rivers 1914

Writers on the Caribbean are preoccupied with disorganization, the destructive effects of slavery, plantation agriculture, poverty, or with the supposed moral degeneration among peoples who have been cut off from their 'homelands' and ancestral cultures. These themes are part of the fabric of West Indian life; firmly lodged in the minds of poets, novelists, academics, and ordinary men and women. At the same time, the texture of everyday life in the Caribbean is neither individualistic nor anomic. Individuals are enmeshed in complex and ramifying networks of kinsmen, friends and neighbours. When West Indians migrate to Britain or the United States or Canada they settle in enclaves which are not West Indian, but more specifically Jamaican, Barbadian, Guyanese, Puerto Rican, Cuban, or Haitian. Letters, money, numerous gifts and visits flow back and forth along the lines of previous connection. In the West Indies, rituals marking the individual's passage through life – baptism or its equivalent, marriage and funerals – are impressively elaborate and well attended compared to the almost furtive ceremonies of urban dwellers in the more developed societies.

The contrast between supposed disorganization or fragmentation, and the reality of dense and supportive social relationships, is clearly seen in family and kinship relations. While the academic conference circuits are kept busy with meetings devoted to the 'problems' of West Indian family life, and the literature bristles with such terms as 'broken,' 'denuded,' and 'incomplete,' study of the complexity of kinship ties reveals the extraordinary extension and solidity of social relations. This is not to deny the existence of, or minimize the importance of, social problems in West

Indian life, including family life. Nor is it to deny that in the very fabric of kinship and family life, structural features have been incorporated that derive from the historical experience of hierarchical relations and exploitation. It is to suggest that kinship relations are highly structured, and indeed if they were really 'disorganized' it would be somewhat easier to envisage their change to that state often referred to as 'normality.'

In this chapter I concentrate on the gross characteristics of the genealogies collected from informants in Jamaica and Guyana; even a superficial analysis of these materials calls into question the accepted wisdom about West Indian kinship. Some of the genealogical materials are presented at appropriate points in other chapters; for example, it has been more convenient to discuss marriage and mating in Chapters 5 and 6. Here I present a general overview of the informants' kin ties; the size of genealogies, the relative proportion of consanguineal and affinal kin that appear on them, the proportion of mother's to father's relatives, and so on. I also ask whether legal marriage gives rise to more recognized kin ties than either common law unions or visiting relationships. But first, how were categories chosen for constructing the tables?

Chapter 1 described the separation of cases into rural, urban and class based categories (see page 15). Urban and rural cases were dealt with separately for *a priori* reasons; it is generally assumed that urban living induces changes in family life. West Indians share this idea of a contrast between the quiet and innocence of the countryside and the bright lights signifying a more rapid pace of living in the city. It seemed natural to divide our cases along this axis, but it is not as significant a division as believed. West Indians have always been mobile in search of work, whether they were labourers or civil servants, and the ties between rural and urban families are both strong and complex.

'Class' divisions in the tabulations are there because of a decision to select 'middle class' and 'lower class' informants. The uncritical use of these labels can cause confusion. They are not used uniformly by Jamaicans and Guyanese. I mean this in two senses; not all Jamaicans and Guyanese use the terms 'middle class' and 'lower class,' nor do they use them as badges of identification for themselves and others. When these, or other terms, are used to indicate status, they are varied and modified in different situations. This has been discussed already and is repeated here to stress that the tabulations must be read with caution. The primary division of cases into lower and middle class, and the secondary divisions into upper and lower, old and new, are based on my judgement after a careful reading of the cases, or on my personal knowledge of the families. Occupation is the most important criterion for category assignment.

Because the number of genealogies in each 'class' category is small, I have combined them for some purposes into broad categories that ignore country distinctions and concentrate on differences between old, or established, middle class, the new middle class, and the lower class. This is not to ignore significant differences between Guyana and Jamaica, or between urban and rural areas, but to experiment with the data and establish a method of analysis for application to larger samples in the future. With all these qualifications in mind I now examine the data.

1. Size and variability of genealogies

Table 3 presents an overview of the numbers and size of the analysed genealogies, their distribution into the class and urban-rural categories, and the sexual composition of the genealogical universe within each category.[1] The proportion of living to dead kinsmen is shown in Table 4.

Variations in the size of individual genealogies (see page 59) do not coincide with the informant's class, age or sex, and the range of that variation must be kept in mind when considering the mean size of genealogies in Table 3. The overall mean size of genealogies for all 51 cases tabulated is 284; this compares with an overall mean size of 136.5 obtained by Schneider in a study of 84 genealogies of urban middle-class white Americans (Schneider 1980 [1968]), and a mean size of 207 for 21 lower class urban black Americans studied by Schneider and Smith (1978 [1972]). The genealogies range in size from 41 to 1,106 in the West Indian cases; for the middle class white Chicagoans in Schneider's study the range is from 23 to 584, and for the lower class black Chicagoans it is from 30 to 625. In a study of middle class families in London the size of the kin universe was even smaller than that found among middle class Chicagoans (Firth, Hubert and Forge 1970). However, the authors of the London study excluded certain categories of kin from their totals, including children and grandchildren of the informant, and the consanguines of affines. The exclusion of these latter makes a considerable difference; in the West Indies they are an important component of the genealogical universe.[2] Here I include all categories of kin, but indicate wherever possible whether the kin are related through parents, siblings, children or spouses – if that information is relevant.

[1] The term 'genealogical universe' is used here to refer to all the individuals recorded on a genealogy. Many of them will not be regarded as kinsmen by the informant, even though a 'kinship' link of some kind – or a chain of links – joins every individual to Ego. Adoption or 'fictive' kinship ties are treated as valid links.

[2] Firth and his co-authors give no reason for the exclusion of consanguines of affines, merely asserting that 'consanguines of affines, who presented a special problem of interpretation' were excluded from the kin universe (Firth *et al.* 1970, p. 158). Schneider and Cottrell (1975) exclude the informant's children and all persons related through the children from most of their discussions of the size and structure of the genealogies because, they say, the numbers of such kin are a function of whether the children are married or not. One could exclude siblings on the same grounds.

49

TABLE 3 SEX AND AGE OF INFORMANTS AND SIZE OF GENEALOGIES

	Old Middle Class		New Middle Class		Lower Class		ALL CASES		
	Male	Female	Male	Female	Male	Female	Male	Female	Both
Number of Cases	7	3	6	7	7	21	20	31	51
Mean age of informants	42	44	44	41	45	46	44	44	44
Mean size of genealogy	246	599	225	222	258	299	243	311	284
Size range of genealogies	80 to 427	335 to 733	125 to 465	41 to 475	52 to 661	79 to 1106	52 to 661	41 to 1106	41 to 1106

TABLE 4 KIN LIVING AND DEAD BY SEX

		Living				Dead				Both		
		Male	Female	Unknown	Total	Male	Female	Unknown	Total	Living	Dead	Total
Old Middle Class	Number	1220	1276	112	2608	340	450	122	912	2608	912	3520
	Percent	47	49	4	100	37	49	13	100	74	26	100
New Middle Class	Number	976	928	380	2284	189	264	135	588	2284	588	2872
	Percent	43	41	17	100	32	45	23	100	80	20	100
Lower Class	Number	2913	2874	910	6697	567	723	85	1375	6697	1375	8072
	Percent	43	43	14	100	41	53	6	100	83	17	100
ALL CASES	Number	5109	5078	1402	11589	1096	1437	342	2875	11589	2875	14464
	Percent	44	44	12	100	38	50	12	100	80	20	100

2. Who should be included on a genealogy?

In this study every individual known to be connected in any way by an intervening relationship of consanguinity, marriage (broadly interpreted), adoption or any other tie defined by the informant as being equivalent, was included. The informant considers many of them to be unrelated, often saying 'He is nothing to me' when asked for a kin term. Nonetheless it was considered important to obtain the largest universe possible so that we could then distinguish various degrees of interaction, closeness and distance within it.

The following example shows how important it is to document this widest universe. It shows that individuals within a kinship universe who are not considered 'relatives' may become such at any time if social interaction changes to make recognition meaningful.

Rohan Ragbir lives in a large Guyana coastal village with his wife and four children. His wife is from another community, as is customary, and in his natal village Ragbir is surrounded by a large body of patrilateral kin. In exploring the limits of this man's kinship universe many individuals were accumulated onto his genealogy who were known to him primarily as fellow villagers, but about whose family he happened to know a great deal. Thus, if his father's brother's wife's sister's daughter, actually from another village, marries a man in this village known to Ragbir because of his prominence in local religious and political affairs, that individual will appear on the genealogy along with all his relatives. It now becomes difficult to decide whether these individuals are 'kin' or just well-known fellow villagers. One could ask him directly, but the answer would be conditioned by what he thinks the anthropologist wants to know. It is better to observe interactions, which show considerable variation.

For example, a person may have a friendly, neighbourly relationship with a particular fellow villager. They meet at a wedding in another village and discover that each is related by kinship to the bride, a circumstance that has brought them together on this occasion. Henceforth they may begin to think of themselves as distant family, or do so only on occasions when that relationship seems appropriate. A further complication arises because of the common assumption in both Afro- and Indo-Guyanese villages that the village is 'all one family.' Thus, in Indian villages it is customary to address, and refer to, older village men as *chacha*, (father's brother), especially on ritual occasions. To decide whether this term is being applied because of a kinship or village tie is difficult and pointless.

The kinship universe is, then, that body of persons known by Ego to be linked to him in some way by a tie of kinship, but not necessarily the body of persons considered by him to be relatives, family or 'close family.' These latter will be contained within the kin universe but do not exhaust it. It should also be clear that the kin universe is not capable of rigid boundary definition because the informants do not apply rigid principles of inclusion and exclusion.

3. Proportion of living to dead kinsmen

Table 4 provides preliminary information on a subject that will become more important as the discussion progresses. The proportion of dead males is consistently higher than dead females in every status category. Since New World black family structure is often assumed to be matriarchal, or at least to have a female bias, this is of particular interest. Our research shows that males are important as kinsmen, and this evidence confirms it. The numbers of dead kinsmen do not seem to result from demographic factors; on genealogies the proportion of living males to living females is approximately equal. To be absolutely accurate age specific mortality rates should be taken into account but those complex calculations have not been made; these limited data are presented for what they are worth, they are suggestive rather than definitive.

4. Occupations of kinsmen

Informants did not always know the occupation of every kinsman on their genealogy and so these tables are limited. Sometimes the informant is wrong in his identification of a kinsman's specific occupation, but unlikely to be wrong on the general occupational category. Where the occupation is unknown, or the individual has no occupation (as in the case of children), the case is not included in these tables. Few adults are reported as having no occupation; informants generally reported an individual's normal occupation, so that most of the unemployed are included in the tabulations.

i. Occupation and class

Tables 5 and 6 show the close relationship between class status of the informant and the occupations of his kinsmen. Those born into middle class families who are themselves of middle class status, have 40.3 percent of their male kinsmen in the two highest occupational categories – managerial and professional – while another 44.7 percent are Own Account workers, Supervisory or Clerical and Technical workers; only 14.9 percent are Manual and Casual workers. Those upwardly mobile from lower class origins have a much higher proportion of manual workers on their genealogies. Only 14.6 percent of male kinsmen, for whom informa-

TABLE 5   OCCUPATIONS OF INFORMANTS' MALE KIN

Occupation	Old Middle Class		New Middle Class		Lower Class		All Cases	
	Number	Percent	Number	Percent	Number	Percent	Number	Percent
Professional & High Managerial	163	20.7	25	5.1	32	2.1	220	7.8
Para Professional & Low Managerial	154	19.6	47	9.6	65	4.2	266	9.5
Own Account Workers	139	17.7	89	18.1	100	6.5	328	11.7
Supervisory	69	8.8	23	4.7	62	4.0	154	5.5
Lower Grade Clerical & Technical	143	18.2	109	22.2	209	13.6	461	16.4
Manual - Skilled	53	6.7	70	14.2	314	20.4	437	15.5
Manual - Unskilled	64	8.1	126	25.6	722	47.0	912	32.4
Casual Worker	1	0.1	3	0.6	32	2.1	36	1.3
TOTALS	786	100.0	492	100.0	1536	100.0	2814	100.0

TABLE 6   OCCUPATIONS OF INFORMANTS' FEMALE KIN

Occupation	Old Middle Class		New Middle Class		Lower Class		All Cases	
	Number	Percent	Number	Percent	Number	Percent	Number	Percent
Professional & High Managerial	8	1.9	3	1.4	3	0.4	14	1.1
Para Professional & Low Managerial	27	6.4	10	4.6	12	1.8	49	3.7
Own Account Workers	41	9.8	20	9.3	23	3.4	84	6.4
Supervisory	62	14.8	18	8.3	18	2.6	98	7.5
Lower Grade Clerical & Technical	221	52.7	107	49.5	143	21.0	471	35.8
Manual - Skilled	33	7.9	16	7.4	110	16.2	159	12.1
Manual - Unskilled	26	6.2	29	13.4	288	42.4	343	26.1
Casual Worker	1	0.2	13	6.0	83	12.2	97	7.4
TOTALS	419	100.0	216	100.0	680	100.0	1315	100.0

tion is available, are in the two highest occupational categories, while 40.4 percent are Manual and Casual workers. For the lower class the position is the reverse of the established middle class; fully 69.5 percent of male kinsmen are manual or casual workers and only 6.3 percent are in the two top categories.

Jamaican informants judged to be of upper middle class status and born into upper middle class families have about half of their employed male kinsmen in professional, paraprofessional or managerial positions of some kind. Another quarter are self-employed. In Guyana the situation is slightly different. While a third of the male kinsmen of established upper middle class informants are in professional, paraprofessional and managerial types of employment, almost another third are in lower grade technical or clerical jobs. Guyana is a less populous country than Jamaica – despite its larger size – with a less clearly defined class structure. Since 1970 there has been little private economic enterprise, but even before then the economy was dominated by large companies leaving little room for the self-employed middle class, except in shop keeping and rice milling. Indians, Chinese and Portuguese dominated these occupations. Interestingly, the informants who comprise the new upper middle class in the Guyana tabulations are East Indians, hence the high proportion of self employed among their kinsmen.

In the established upper middle class of both countries the majority of kinsmen have white collar jobs. Less than 10 percent in Jamaica, and only 14 percent in Guyana, have manual occupations. The new upper middle class shows more spread, especially in Jamaica which has a more differentiated and volatile economy.

The employment pattern of male kinsmen of Jamaican lower middle class informants is similar to that of the upper middle class except that the occupational status levels are shifted downwards slightly. Male kinsmen of established lower middle class informants are predominantly white collar workers, with a high proportion (28.4 percent) of professionals and managers, but with a higher proportion of manual workers. For the new, or upwardly mobile, lower middle class, the proportion of manual workers is much higher, reaching 56.6 percent in Jamaica and 53.2 percent in Guyana. The pattern is the same for the rural middle class.

ii. Occupation and gender

There are sharp differences between the occupations of male and female kin. On the genealogies of upper middle class individuals, females generally have lower status jobs than men; on the genealogies of lower middle class and lower class individuals, female kin have occupations of equal, or higher, status than men. These differences are discussed further in Chapter 7 where sex role differentiation is examined.

iii. Summary: limitations of the data on occupation

To summarize: informants who are 'established upper middle class' and 'lower class,' the two extremes of the status scale, have genealogies on which the occupations of males are relatively homogeneous. This should not be exaggerated. Some may find the spread of occupations significant; we are not dealing with closed groups. The deviation of actual distributions from a model of total homogeneity, or a model of random distributions, would show the true nature of the patterns. These tables tell us nothing about contact between the informant and kinsmen of varying occupational status, nor do they tell us which of the individuals are recognized kin, effective kin, close kin, and the like. In some cases, especially with the consanguineal kin of affines, the actual relationship may be tenuous.

In the middle range of the class categories there is occupational spread, consonant with the increase in social mobility since World War II. The differences between Jamaica and Guyana reflect the lesser degree of class differentiation in Guyana and its different pattern of economic development (or stagnation). However, the tables are limited and cannot show such things as the patterns of difference between racial groups (see Graham and Gordon 1977 and R.T. Smith 1977 for a fuller discussion).

5. Overview of categories of kin on genealogies

i. General

Each individual recorded on a genealogy is related to Ego in a specific way through a series of intermediate ties. Therefore the relationship may be specified precisely. A given individual may be related as Ego's mother's brother's wife's father's sister's husband's brother's daughter's son's wife, for example. In transferring this information from the genealogies the relationships were coded in full, as well as in categorical form. Table 7 shows the categories in extended form, useful for comparative purposes, but too unwieldy. In the above example the person would be placed in Category 18, 'Relative of a spouse of Ego's matrilateral consanguine.' Owing to an error in data collection, a few married couples had genealogies recorded separately and exclusively, resulting in a serious loss of 'spouse's kin' in a few class categories. For calculations involving affinal relationships these cases have been excluded where appropriate, but they are included in Table 7 so that this limitation should be borne in mind. The same applies to Tables 8 and 9 where the kin categories have been compressed to make them easier to understand.

ii. Patrilateral and matrilateral consanguineal kin

Consanguineal relatives through the father appear to be more numerous than those through the mother. This reinforces the impression, gained

TABLE 7   GENERAL KIN CATEGORIES (RELATIONSHIP TO EGO)

CATEGORY OF KIN	URBAN										RURAL			C.
	Old Upper Middle		New Upper Middle		Old Lower Middle		New Lower Middle		Lower Class		Middle Class	Lower Class		
	Jam.	Guy.	Jam.	Guy.	Jam.	Guy.	Jam.	Guy.	Jam.	Guy.	Jam.	Jam.	Guy.	
EGO	4	2	5	2	3	1	1	3	13	5	2	9	1	
1. Patrilateral Consanguine	226	108	126	142	175	10	1	119	621	128	66	396	494	2
2. Matrilateral Consanguine	182	46	203	90	69	14	101	106	294	118	45	309	114	1
3. Sibling	24	14	25	9	20	7	4	23	76	33	21	80	17	
4. Direct Descendant	9	3	14	21	2	5	7	8	102	15	11	115	-	
5. Descendant of Sibling	35	9	42	68	23	10	14	4	130	100	29	261	47	
6. Spouse	4	2	6	3	2	1	2	2	22	10	5	14	-	
7. Consanguine of Current Legal Spouse	46	56	-	98	46	5	69	24	381	159	24	211	-	1
8. Cons. of Ex-Legal Spouse	1	-	-	-	-	-	-	-	-	-	-	13	-	
9. Consanguine of Current Common Law Spouse	-	-	-	-	-	-	-	4	46	-	-	52	-	
10. Cons. Ex-Comm. Law Spouse	-	-	-	-	-	-	-	-	-	13	-	3	-	
11. Consanguine of Current Visiting Spouse	-	-	-	-	-	-	-	-	7	-	-	-	-	
12. Cons. Ex-Visit. Spouse	-	-	-	2	-	-	-	-	34	2	2	3	-	
13. Legal Spouse of Ego's Consanguineal Kin	171	56	121	99	102	23	27	62	278	92	40	262	173	1
14. Comm. Law Spouse Ego's Cons. Kin	1	5	13	11	1	-	13	10	93	37	6	97	63	
15. Visiting Spouse of Ego's Consanguineal Kin	4	6	7	3	14	-	10	6	101	12	6	82	49	
16. Spouse of Ego's Spouse's Consanguineal Kin	19	17	-	37	10	4	20	17	151	30	13	93	-	4
17. Relative of Spouse of Ego's Patrilateral Consanguines	348	94	9	12	124	-	-	13	195	4	43	379	137	1
18. Relative of Spouse of Ego's Matrilateral Consanguines	233	38	20	3	115	-	186	7	138	10	78	291	7	1
19. Rel. of Spouse of Ego's Siblings' Consang. Kin	32	-	9	2	-	-	-	-	1	1	-	8	3	
20. Rel. of Spouse of Ego's Spouse's Consang. Kin	280	127	-	32	13	-	2	-	60	63	8	119	-	
21. Adopted Kin	4	-	1	-	1	-	-	4	3	-	-	-	-	
22. Rel. of Spouse of Sibling	354	14	61	25	79	-	-	-	15	10	44	85	-	
23. Relative of Adopted Kin	-	-	-	-	-	-	-	142	-	-	-	-	-	
24. Adopted Kin of Spouse	1	-	-	-	-	-	-	-	1	22	-	-	-	
25. Spouse's Spouse	-	-	-	2	-	-	1	-	10	5	-	4	-	
26. Relative of Spouse of Direct Descendant	-	-	-	9	-	-	15	-	203	-	-	147	-	
27. Rel. of Spouse of a Spouse	-	-	-	-	-	-	2	-	2	-	-	9	-	
28. Spouse of Ego's Consanguine (Union Type Unknown)	1	-	3	-	2	-	-	3	8	4	2	7	-	
29. Type Unknown	27	-	28	1	36	-	-	29	50	-	2	9	1	
TOTALS	2006	597	693	671	837	80	475	586	3035	873	447	3058	1106	14

TABLE 8   KIN CATEGORIES (ABBREVIATED)

CATEGORY OF KIN	URBAN										RURAL			ALL CASES
	Old Upper Middle		New Upper Middle		Old Lower Middle		New Lower Middle		Lower Class		Middle Class	Lower Class		
	Jam.	Guy.	Jam.	Guy.	Jam.	Guy.	Jam.	Guy.	Jam.	Guy.	Jam.	Jam.	Guy.	
Patrilateral Consanguines	226	108	126	142	175	10	1	119	621	128	66	396	494	2612
Matrilateral Consanguines	182	46	203	90	69	14	101	106	294	118	45	309	114	1691
Siblings & Direct Descendants of Self & Siblings	68	26	81	98	45	22	25	35	308	148	61	456	64	1437
TOTAL CONSANGUINES	**476**	**180**	**410**	**330**	**289**	**46**	**127**	**260**	**1223**	**394**	**172**	**1161**	**672**	**5740**
Spouses of Ego's Consanguines	177	67	144	113	119	23	50	81	480	145	54	448	285	2186
Relative of Spouse of Ego's Consanguines	967	146	99	51	318	-	201	20	552	25	165	910	147	3601
TOTAL AFFINES THROUGH CONSANGUINES	**1144**	**213**	**243**	**164**	**437**	**23**	**251**	**101**	**1032**	**170**	**219**	**1358**	**432**	**5787**
Spouse & His/Her Consanguines	51	58	6	103	48	6	71	30	490	184	31	296	-	1374
Spouse of Spouses Consanginues	19	17	-	37	10	4	20	17	151	30	13	93	-	411
Relative of Spouse of Spouse's Consanguines	280	127	-	34	13	-	5	-	72	68	8	132	-	739
TOTAL AFFINES THROUGH SPOUSE	**350**	**202**	**6**	**174**	**71**	**10**	**96**	**47**	**713**	**282**	**52**	**521**		**2524**
ADOPTED KIN	5	-	1	-	1	-	-	146	4	22	-	-	-	179
EGOS	4	2	5	2	3	1	1	3	13	5	2	9	1	51
UNKNOWN	27	-	28	1	36	-	-	29	50	-	2	9	1	183
GRAND TOTALS	**2006**	**597**	**693**	**671**	**837**	**80**	**475**	**586**	**3035**	**873**	**447**	**3058**	**1106**	**14464**

TABLE 9   KIN CATEGORIES (ABBREVIATED)

Category of Kin	Old Middle Class	New Middle Class	Lower Class	All Cases
Patrilateral Consanguines	519	454	1639	2612
Matrilateral Consanguines	311	545	835	1691
Siblings & Direct Descendants of Self & Siblings	161	300	976	1437
TOTAL CONSANGUINES	**991**	**1299**	**3450**	**5740**
Spouses of Ego's Consanguines	386	442	1358	2186
Relative of Spouse of Ego's Consanguines	1431	536	1634	3601
TOTAL AFFINES THROUGH CONSANGUINES	**1817**	**978**	**2992**	**5787**
Spouse & His/Her Consanguines	163	241	970	1374
Spouse of Spouse's Consanguines	50	87	274	411
Relative of Spouse of Spouse's Consanguines	420	47	272	739
TOTAL AFFINES THROUGH SPOUSE	**633**	**375**	**1516**	**2524**
ADOPTED KIN	6	147	26	179
EGOS	10	13	28	51
UNKNOWN	63	60	60	183
GRAND TOTALS	**3520**	**2872**	**8072**	**14464**

from the examination of numbers of dead males and females (see pages 51-2 above) that whatever the maternal bias in close kinship relations, it does not mean that men are unimportant as kinsmen. The relative numbers of patrilateral and matrilateral consanguines can be seen in Tables 7, 8 and 9, where, for all cases, there are 2,612 patrilateral consanguines as opposed to only 1,691 matrilateral consanguines. This seems to be reversed for the upwardly mobile middle class. However, these consolidated figures are misleading.

Table 10 lists individual cases within the class categories and shows no consistent pattern of predominance of one type of kin. There is marked variation, with one individual knowing almost none of his or her father's relatives and another knowing few if any of his or her mother's. These differences are produced by the exigencies of the individual's early life and upbringing.

Ronald Bayley (case number 111) is a good example; his parents were never married, nor did they ever live together, but his father took an interest in his welfare and paid the fees for his high school education. At the age of about seven he was sent to live with his father's sister for a couple of years. The result is that Ronald Bayley recognizes more patrilateral than matrilateral kin, although he has closer relations with his mother's family, and with his mother's children by other men. These half siblings by his mother are treated as full brothers and sisters, whereas half siblings by his father are much less close and rarely seen.

The question of which kinsmen should be included in the categories 'patrilateral' and 'matrilateral' is an important one, altering the totals if half siblings are included. Technically, one could classify a paternal half sibling as 'patrilateral' kin, and for some purposes half siblings were classified this way. To make meaningful comparisons between classes, and with other studies, kin related through half siblings have been excluded from the laterality tables, or designated separately. Where early unions are common and unstable, the number of kin generated through half siblings will be larger than where unions are stable and entered at a later age.

iii. Half siblings and parenthood

Half siblings pose another problem. As reported in Chapter 2, informants sometimes deny that children of the same mother are 'half.' Although West Indians sometimes say that a group of children are 'all one father,' in contrast to a woman's 'sets' of children by different men, the category 'half sibling' is rarely used.

Although children are generally made known to their immediate relatives, knowledge of the kin of a 'missing' parent is not inevitable. Mr. A. Benton was the illegitimate child of a poor woman and a lawyer. His father

TABLE 10 CONSANGUINEAL KIN BY LATERALITY: INDIVIDUAL CASES

Case Number	Patrilateral Consanguines		Matrilateral Consanguines		Totals	
	Number	Percent	Number	Percent	Number	Percent
pper Middle Class: Jamaica						
	69	71.9	27	28.1	96	100.0
	34	29.3	82	70.7	116	100.0
	102	70.3	43	29.7	145	100.0
	21	41.2	30	58.8	51	100.0
Total	226	55.4	182	44.6	408	100.0
pper Middle Class: Guyana						
	24	88.9	3	11.1	27	100.0
	84	66.1	43	33.9	127	100.0
Total	108	70.1	46	29.9	154	100.0
ower Middle: Jamaica						
	26	83.9	5	16.1	31	100.0
	99	81.1	23	18.9	122	100.0
	50	54.9	41	45.1	91	100.0
Total	175	71.7	69	28.3	244	100.0
ower Middle: Guyana						
	10	41.7	14	58.3	24	100.0
Total	10	41.7	14	58.3	24	100.0
pper Middle: Jamaica						
	1	1.3	79	98.8	80	100.0
	34	34.7	64	65.3	98	100.0
	16	35.6	29	64.4	45	100.0
	71	71.0	29	29.0	100	100.0
	4	66.7	2	33.3	6	100.0
Total	126	38.3	203	61.7	329	100.0
pper Middle: Guyana						
	1	50.0	1	50.0	2	100.0
	141	61.3	89	38.7	230	100.0
Total	142	61.2	90	38.8	232	100.0
ower Middle: Jamaica						
	1	1.0	101	99.0	102	100.0
Total	1	1.0	101	99.0	102	100.0
ower Middle: Guyana						
	68	58.1	49	41.9	117	100.0
	48	64.9	26	35.1	74	100.0
	3	8.8	31	91.2	34	100.0
Total	119	52.9	106	47.1	225	100.0
Middle Class: Jamaica						
	7	24.1	22	75.9	29	100.0
	59	72.0	23	28.0	82	100.0
Total	66	59.5	45	40.5	111	100.0
Class: Jamaica						
	1	6.3	15	93.8	16	100.0
	184	96.3	7	3.7	191	100.0
	8	17.4	38	82.6	46	100.0
	1	12.5	7	87.5	8	100.0
	43	39.4	66	60.6	109	100.0
	103	73.6	37	26.4	140	100.0
	27	96.4	1	3.6	28	100.0
	133	70.0	57	30.0	190	100.0
	11	30.6	25	69.4	36	100.0
	22	95.7	1	4.3	23	100.0
	19	51.4	18	48.6	37	100.0
	57	83.8	11	16.2	68	100.0
	12	52.2	11	47.8	23	100.0
Total	621	67.9	294	32.1	915	100.0
Class: Guyana						
	30	50.0	30	50.0	60	100.0
	30	54.5	25	45.5	55	100.0
	47	72.3	18	27.7	65	100.0
	6	14.3	36	85.7	42	100.0
	15	62.5	9	37.5	24	100.0
Total	128	52.0	118	48.0	246	100.0
Lower Class: Jamaica						
	24	40.7	35	59.3	59	100.0
	43	66.2	22	33.8	65	100.0
	42	58.3	30	41.7	72	100.0
	15	62.5	9	37.5	24	100.0
	47	66.2	24	33.8	71	100.0
	55	32.9	112	67.1	167	100.0
	108	79.4	28	20.6	136	100.0
	9	22.0	32	78.0	41	100.0
	53	75.7	17	24.3	70	100.0
Total	396	56.2	309	43.8	705	100.0
Lower Class: Guyana						
	494	81.3	114	18.8	608	100.0
Total	494	81.3	114	18.8	608	100.0
OVERALL TOTALS	2612	60.7	1691	39.3	4303	100.0

refused to recognize him, he did not take his father's name, and was brought up by his mother's mother. As an adult he discovered his father's identity, but even then he never met him, knows nothing of his father's family, nor has any contact with them. If he does know anything, he was not willing to include that knowledge on his genealogy, and we have no record of it.

Sometimes when a woman has children by several different men, and eventually settles into a stable relationship with one of them, the children of the earlier unions grow up treating the mother's spouse as a father, which he is, and neglect to establish contact with the genitor. There are several cases of this kind. Victoria Cramer (case number 303) is one of four children by at least two different fathers. She grew up with her mother and her mother's maternal aunt, knowing nothing of her father's family, as he was from a different Jamaican parish. None of the children took their fathers' surnames. There was nothing secret about the identity of the father, as there might have been had he been married, or of superior social status. Even in those cases the identity of the father is generally established by the time the child is of school age. Victoria Cramer knows her father's name but nothing else about him, or his family.

Close contact with the mother and her kin is not inevitable, as is shown by the case of Alice Smith (case number 302) who continued to live with her father when her parents separated. After a short time she was sent to live with her mother's father and his wife. Her father entered a new common law union and, after about a year, sent for Alice, placing her under the care of her stepmother. Friction soon developed and Alice was sent to live with relatives of her father, on a piece of family land in which he had rights. Because of these various moves she knows many more relatives on her father's 'side' than on her mother's, and has had little contact with her mother.

iv. Factors affecting laterality

Situational factors do much to explain the particular distributions in a given case – as do the exigencies of birth and death, sterility, spinsterhood and the like. However, the importance of patrilateral kin remains; in only two cases does the number of matrilateral consanguines exactly equal that of patrilateral consanguines. In 31 cases (63.3 percent) there is a preponderance of patrilateral consanguines, while in the other 18 cases (36.7 percent) the situation is reversed. This preponderance is often considerable. A variation one way or the other of about 10 percent would be normal, but in 15 cases the patrilateral consanguines constitute over 70 percent of all consanguines, while in only 10 cases do matrilateral consanguines predominate to that extent.

The question of laterality is an important one and more complex than at first appears; we shall come back to it.

v. Relatives of spouses of consanguineal kin

Genealogies are large because most informants can list many relatives of affinal kin; that is, the relatives of those married to (or in non-legal unions with) their own consanguineal kin. Including these people is stretching the definition of 'kinsman' but West Indians take considerable interest in these connections even when they are not counted as 'relatives.'

Table 10 shows how and where patrilateral consanguines predominate on genealogies. Tables 11 and 12 show how this is extended to the relatives of the spouses of the consanguines enumerated in Table 10 (or, more accurately, the spouses of some of them). There is nothing surprising about this; for an informant to have 'relatives of spouses of consanguines' on his genealogy he must first have consanguines. Where consanguines of a particular kind predominate, this new category of kin will also predominate. Thus, the relative proportions of matrilateral to patrilateral kin in Tables 11 and 12 follow closely those in the preceding Tables. This is not uniformly the case.

The proportion of more distant relatives increases slightly on the maternal side if all cases are taken together. The proportion of matrilateral consanguines is only 39.3 percent of all cases taken together, but relatives of spouses of these consanguines constitute 44.4 percent of the total. These proportions differ widely among the middle class cases; less so among the lower class. In eight of the twelve subgroups for which we have information, the proportion of more distant kin declines slightly on the maternal side but increases sufficiently in the other four to more than offset this loss.

The extent to which informants know and relate to these more genealogically distant persons is a complex matter and we now turn to a more detailed analysis of the kin categories.

6. Kin-type chains and their composition

Each individual on a genealogy can be characterized by the series of specific relationships which link him or her to Ego, and the full chain of links was coded for this study. The relationships were also coded in category terms (see page 56). A third code was also used for classifying these relationships – the 'kin-type chain.'

This mode of designation was developed by Schneider for the American kinship study and used to some extent by Firth and his associates in

TABLE 11 RELATIVES OF SPOUSES OF CONSANGUINES: BY LATERALITY

CATEGORY OF KIN		URBAN									RURAL			ALL CASES
		Old Upper Middle		New Middle		Old Lower Middle		New Lower Middle		Lower Class		Middle Class	Lower Class		
		Jam.	Guy.	Jam.	Guy.	Jam.	Guy.	Jam.	Guy.	Jam.	Guy.	Jam.	Jam.	Guy.	
Relatives of Spouses of Patrilateral Consanguines	No.	317	88	12	9	115	-	-	13	166	4	20	307	96	1147
	Percent	58	71	48	82	51	-	-	65	61	57	24	64	97	56
Relatives of Spouse of Ego's Matrilateral Consanguines	No.	229	36	13	2	110	-	172	7	106	3	62	174	3	917
	Percent	42	29	52	18	49	-	100	35	39	43	76	36	3	44
Total Relatives of Spouses of Consanguines	No.	546	124	25	11	225	-	172	20	272	7	82	481	99	2064
	Percent	100	100	100	100	100	-	100	100	100	100	100	100	100	100

Note: This table does not include relatives through half-siblings, siblings or children

TABLE 12 RELATIVES OF SPOUSES OF CONSANGUINES: BY LATERALITY

Category of Kin		Old Middle Class	New Middle Class	Lower Class	All Cases
Relatives of Spouses of Patrilateral Consanguines	No	520	54	573	1147
	%	58.1	17.4	66.7	55.6
Relatives of Spouses of Matrilateral Consanguines	No	375	256	286	917
	%	41.9	82.6	33.3	44.4
Total Relatives of Spouses of Consanguines	No	895	310	859	2064
	%	100.0	100.0	100.0	100.0

Note: This table does not include relatives through half-siblings, siblings or children

London. It summarizes the chain of relationships between Ego and each individual on the genealogy by describing each link as being either consanguineal or affinal. Starting from Ego and moving toward the relative being coded, the first relationship is described by the appropriate letter; C for consanguineal and A for affinal. When a different type of link is encountered the letter designation is changed appropriately. In the example given earlier (Ego's mother's brother's wife's father's sister's husband's brother's daughter's son's wife, or MBWFZHBDSW), the 'kin-type chain' is as follows. From Ego to mother's brother is a consanguineal line (C); an affinal link now intervenes in the form of the mother's brother's wife (A); another consanguineal line (C) proceeds from mother's brother's wife to her father's sister; at this point we have another affinal link (A); followed by yet another consanguineal line (C) from mother's brother's wife's sister's husband to his brother's daughter's son; and finally an affinal link (A) occurs. Thus the whole chain would be coded as CACACA, representing the kin-type chain between Ego and the person in question.

We may think of these as circles of relatives, or potential relatives, spreading out around Ego. Immediately surrounding him are his consanguineals (varying in social and genealogical 'distance' of course); then come the spouses of these consanguineals followed by the consanguineals of these spouses, followed by *their* spouses, and so on. The term 'spouse' is used here, as throughout this book, to mean not only husband and wife, but also common law and visiting 'spouses.' The distinction between types of unions is discussed more fully in Chapters 5 and 6.

If the kin-type chain begins with an A we know immediately that we are dealing with Ego's affines through his or her spouse.[3]

Tables 13 and 14 show the simple distribution figures for kin-type chains running through Ego's consanguineals (Table 13) and through his or her spouse (Table 14). Simple distribution figures are not very informative, except to show in a preliminary way the importance of the more distant consanguines of affinals as a component of the kin universe. To make them more useful an 'index of accumulation' has been calculated.

The meaning of 'index of accumulation' may be illustrated by Table 15. The first line lists the number of Egos in each simplified class category. The second line lists the total number of their consanguineal kin. The index of accumulation is the average number of consanguines per informant in that class category. Lower class informants have more consanguineals per Ego than the new middle class, and they in turn have slightly more than the established middle class, on average. Lower class genealogies are no

[3] This usage differs from that of Schneider and Cottrell (1975). They start all kin-type chains with C – meaning Ego. This designation obscures the distinction between the kin of Ego's spouse and the kin of his consanguines' spouses.

TABLE 13   KIN-TYPE CHAINS THROUGH CONSANGUINEALS

| CHAIN TYPE | URBAN | | | | | | | | | | RURAL | | | | ALL CASES |
| | Old Upper Middle | | New Upper Middle | | Old Lower Middle | | New Lower Middle | | Lower Middle | | Middle Class | | Lower Class | | |
	Jam.	Guy.	Jam.	Guy.	Jam.	Guy.	Jam.	Guy.	Jam.	Guy.	Jam.	Guy.	Jam.	Guy.	
EGOS	4	2	5	2	3	1	1	3	13	5	2		9	1	51
Consanguines of Ego (C)	478	180	411	331	289	46	127	279	1222	394	173		1168	672	5770
Spouses of Consanguines of Ego (CA)	177	65	145	112	122	23	50	91	484	144	55		452	286	2206
Consanguine of Spouses of Ego's Consang.	447	94	74	35	203	83	–	144	390	13	126		558	68	2235
Relatives of Spouses of Consang. of Ego (CACA+)	400	49	14	9	101		47	23	94		35		270	33	1075

TABLE 14   KIN-TYPE CHAIN THROUGH SPOUSE

| CHAIN TYPE | URBAN | | | | | | | | | | RURAL | | | | ALL CASES |
| | Old Upper Middle | | New Upper Middle | | Old Lower Middle | | New Lower Middle | | Lower Middle | | Middle Class | | Lower Class | | |
	Jam.	Guy.	Jam.	Guy.	Jam.	Guy.	Jam.	Guy.	Jam.	Guy.	Jam.	Guy.	Jam.	Guy.	
SPOUSES (A)	1	2	–	3	2	2	1		22	10	5		14		62
Consanguines of Spouse (AC)	49	58	–	101	46	5	69		467	195	26		280		1296
Spouses of Consang. of Spouse (ACA)	19	17	–	39	12	4	20		154	32	13		102		412
Relatives of Spouses of Consang. of Spouse (ACAC+)	267	126	–	26	11		2		43	63	8		116		662
Total Relatives of Spouse	335	201	–	166	69	9	91		664	290	47		498		2370

*Note: Certain cases have been excluded from this table because the genealogies were collected in such a way as to make the spouse's kin unavailable for analysis.

bigger, on average, than those of the middle class (see Table 10). How then do the middle class genealogies become so large if not through the recognition of consanguineals? The answer is clear from the rest of the table, and from Table 16.

There are 387 spouses of the 993 consanguineal kin of the ten informants belonging to the established middle class. Each of these spouses 'brings in' to the genealogy 1.92 consanguineal kinsmen of their own, and 1.42 spouses and/or relatives of spouses of these consanguineal kinsmen. (The chain has been stopped at CACA by aggregating all relatives beyond this point, indicated by a + sign.) This adds a considerable number of individuals to the genealogies. For the new middle class and the lower class, these figures are much smaller. For each spouse of a consanguineal only 1.3 individuals are added to the average new middle class genealogy, and only 1.04 for the lower class, compared to 3.34 individuals added per spouse of a consanguine of the established middle class.

The differences are even more dramatic when the accumulation of affines through Ego's spouse is examined. (Certain cases had to be excluded from this calculation because of the way in which data had been collected, and this is noted in Table 16.) In Table 16 the number of spouses is greater than the number of Egos because some Egos have, or had, more than one spouse. On line 2, the average number of consanguineal kin of each spouse falls from 26.3 for the established middle class to 19.6 for the new middle class, to 20.48 for the lower class.

Class differences are more marked in the farther reaches of the spouses' kin-type chains. For the established middle class the average number of spouses' relatives actually increases with genealogical distance, instead of diminishing as it does in the other class groups.[4] This can be seen by comparing the actual numbers in the various columns of Table 16 instead of looking at the Index of Accumulation (calculated here from the number of spouses of consanguineals of the spouse, rather than from the spouse himself). Moving outward along the kin-type chain of the established middle class, the number of individuals increases from 52 to 182 to 222; for the lower class, with over seven times as many spouses involved, the figure drops from 288 to 170 to 52. The Index of Accumulation in this table shows little difference in the average number of consanguines per Ego's spouse between class categories, but considerable difference in the numbers of extra individuals 'brought in' to the genealogy by their spouses. The Index of Accumulation for the established middle class increases from 3.50 to 4.27, but for the lower class falls from 0.59 to 0.18.

What significance attaches to these data? Do they say something about class differences in kinship in Jamaica and Guyana? The sample of

---

[4] 'Genealogical distance' means distance along these chains of affinal links and not distance within a genealogical cluster.

TABLE 15 KIN-TYPE CHAIN WITH INDEX OF ACCUMULATION: THROUGH CONSANGUINES CLASS ABBREVIATED

CHAIN TYPE	Old Middle Class Number	Index Acc	New Middle Class Number	Index Acc	Lower Class Number	Index Acc	ALL CASES Number	Index Acc
EGOS	10		13		28		51	
Consanguines (C)	993	*99.30	1321	101.62	3456	123.43	5770	113.14
Spouse of Consang. (CA)	387	*38.70	453	34.85	1366	48.79	2206	43.25
Consanguine of Spouse of Consanguine (CAC)	744	**1.92	462	1.02	1029	0.75	2235	1.01
Relative of Spouse of Consang. of Spouse of Consanguine (CACA+)	550	**1.42	128	0.28	397	0.29	1075	0.49
Total Relatives through Spouses of Consanguines	1681	*4.34	1043	2.30	2792	2.04	5516	2.50

Note: Index of Accumulation is used here to mean - * number of individuals per Ego, and ** number of persons on genealogy who are 'produced' by an average spouse of Ego's spouse's consanguineal kin.

TABLE 16 KIN-TYPE CHAIN WITH INDEX OF ACCUMULATION: THROUGH AFFINES CLASS ABBREVIATED

CHAIN TYPE	Old Middle Class Number	Index Acc	New Middle Class Number	Index Acc	Lower Class Number	Index Acc	ALL CASES Number	Index Acc
SPOUSES (A)	6		10		46		62	
Consanguines of Spouse (AC)	158	*26.33	196	19.60	942	20.48	1296	20.90
Spouses of Consang. of Spouse (ACA)	52	*8.67	72	7.20	288	6.26	412	6.65
Consang. of Spouse of Spouse (ACAC)	182	**3.50	29	0.40	170	0.59	381	0.92
Relative of Spouse of Consang. of Spouse of Consang. (ACACA+)	222	**4.27	7	0.10	52	0.18	281	0.68
Total Relatives through Spouse	614	*102.33	304	30.40	1452	31.57	2370	38.23

Note: Index of Accumulation is used here to mean - * number of individuals per Ego, and ** number of persons on genealogy 'produced' by an average spouse of Ego's spouse's consanguineal kin.

genealogies is too small, and the variability within the sample too great, to permit definitive statements based on these data alone. The questions they raise need to be answered by other research. For example, it appears that middle class informants have greater knowledge of persons connected to them through more distant affinal ties. Is this because marriage for a middle class person involves important status factors, requiring more extensive knowledge of the families of individuals linked through marriage?

i. Kin-type chains: union types

So far all unions have been treated alike, but the data allow distinctions between legal, non-legal coresidential and visiting unions. Do the different types of union produce varying numbers of affines? This question raises the more general issue of marriage and marital instability.

Unions between Ego's consanguineal kin and their spouses will be dealt with first; the numbers are large enough to make the conclusions more significant. Table 18 shows types of union among consanguineal kin of informants.

The distribution of union types reflects the class composition of the genealogies, with common law and visiting unions being rare, but not absent from, established middle class genealogies.

Conventional wisdom holds that legal marriage is more stable than other forms of union and, by extension, relationships generated by non-legal unions will be few and fragile. Table 19 shows how many individuals known to the informant are in unions with the informant's consanguineal kin, and how many relatives of those individuals are known to the informant. It would be interesting to know whether these individuals are in unions with Ego's female consanguines, rather than males; whether most of them are connected through close consanguines such as aunts, uncles or first cousins; and whether there is much difference according to the age of the informant or the age of the consanguine involved; and so on. Those data are not contained in Table 19.

Most CA relatives (individuals in conjugal unions with consanguines) of established middle class informants are legally married; the few non-legal unions bring onto the genealogy only a small number of spouses' relatives. Every legally married CA relative brings onto the genealogy an average of 3.57 individuals, whereas the common law spouse of a consanguine produces only 1.57 individuals who are known to, or significant for, Ego. Visiting spouses produce only 1.26.

Lower class informants show different results. For some reason both common law and visiting unions result in the recognition of more relatives than legal marriage (Table 19). Whereas the legal marriage of a consan-

TABLE 17 TYPES OF UNION BY CLASS: EGOS

TYPE OF UNION	Old Middle Class		New Middle Class		Lower Class		ALL CASES	
	Number	Percent	Number	Percent	Number	Percent	Number	Percent
Legal Marriage	8	100.0	12	66.7	19	41.3	39	54.2
Common Law Marriage	-	-	-	-	11	23.9	11	15.3
Visiting Union	-	-	6	33.3	16	34.8	22	30.6
TOTALS	8	100.0	18	100.0	46	100.0	72	100.0

TABLE 18 TYPES OF UNION BY CLASS: EGO'S CONSANGUINES

TYPE OF UNION	Old Middle Class		New Middle Class		Lower Class		ALL CASES	
	Number	Percent	Number	Percent	Number	Percent	Number	Percent
Legal Marriage	353	91.9	359	80.7	811	60.2	1523	70.0
Common Law Marriage	7	1.8	52	11.7	293	21.8	352	16.2
Visiting Union	24	6.3	34	7.6	243	18.0	301	13.8
TOTALS	384	100.0	445	100.0	1347	100.0	2176	100.0

guine brings in only 0.82 spouses' relatives, a common law union produces 1.62 and a visiting union 1.16. This is even more marked if the Guyana cases are excluded leaving only the Jamaican lower class, bearing out that Jamaican informant who said 'We don't have many weddings in our family.'

These data do not show the relative importance of different types of union, but they cast doubt on the idea that non-legal unions are anomic, producing few significant kinship ties. More careful and searching analysis may reveal reasons for the low number of affinal kin of consanguines connected through legal marriage. For example, if marriage occurs later in life among lower class individuals, it is possible that the informants may be less aware of older kinsmen than they are of those younger individuals who are still in non-legal unions. Whatever modifications result from more refined analysis, non-legal unions are of demonstrated importance in producing recognized kinship ties.

Table 20 produces somewhat different results. Here we are dealing with the informants' own spouses' relatives. None of our middle class informants were themselves in a common law union, and few of them had been in visiting unions. The proportion of visiting unions experienced by middle class informants was unrepresentatively low, judging by case materials and general knowledge of the society.

Most noticeable is the large number of distant kin recognized by the established middle class informants. Each consanguineal kinsman of the informant's legal spouse produced an average of 2.90 more distant relatives, as compared to 0.56 for the new middle class and 0.57 for the lower class (Table 20). Lower class informants recognize slightly more relatives of legal spouses than of common law spouses, and slightly more relatives of common law than of visiting spouses. The differences are small and could well be accounted for by the difference in age at which various types of union are contracted.

7. Genealogical distribution of the kin universe

The data on kin-type chains linking Ego to each person on the genealogy is informative, but not easy to follow. The distribution of informants' kin into positions on a genealogical grid, where each individual's position is defined by generation and degree of collateral removal from Ego, is much easier to visualize.

Table 21 gives an overview of the English relationship terms used to refer to positions on a genealogical grid. Only the most often used cells have been labelled. Our informants do not necessarily use these terms to describe individuals on their genealogies (for example, some referred to the children of a cousin as 'second cousin'). Table 21 gives the reader a

TABLE 19 KIN-TYPE CHAIN BY TYPE OF UNION OF EGO'S CONSANGUINEALS CLASS ABBREVIATED

UNION TYPE	CHAIN TYPE	Old Middle Class		New Middle Class		Lower Class		ALL CASES	
		Number	Index Acc	Number	Index Acc	Number	Index Acc	Number	Index Acc
Legal Marriage	CA	353	2.02	359	1.04	811	0.62	1523	1.04
	CAC	712	1.53	372	0.31	503	0.20	1587	0.54
	CAC+	541		111		166		818	
Common Law	CA	7	0.71	52	0.65	293	1.06	352	0.99
	CAC	5	0.86	34	0.13	311	0.56	350	0.50
	CACA+	6		7		163		176	
Visiting	CA	24	1.13	34	1.62	243	0.88	301	0.99
	CAC	27	0.13	55	0.26	215	0.28	297	0.27
	CACA+	3		9		68		80	

Note: Index of Accumulation in this table means the number of additional individuals per spouse of a consanguine of Ego

TABLE 20 KIN-TYPE CHAINS BY TYPE OF UNION OF EGO CLASS ABBREVIATED

UNION TYPE	CHAIN TYPE	Old Middle Class		New Middle Class		Lower Class		ALL CASES	
		Number	Index Acc	Number	Index Acc	Number	Index Acc	Number	Index Acc
Legal Marriage	AC	158	0.33	220	0.40	773	0.30	1151	0.33
	ACA	52	2.56	89	0.16	234	0.27	375	0.56
	ACAC+	404		36		206		646	
Common Law	AC	-		-		125	0.30	125	0.30
	ACA	-		-		38	0.13	38	0.13
	ACAC+	-		-		16		16	
Visiting	AC	-		4		44	0.36	48	0.33
	ACA	-		-		16		16	
	ACAC+	-		-		-		-	

Note: Index of Accumulation here means number of individuals per consanguine of Ego's spouse preliminary orientation to the genealogical grid. Genealogical cells are not necessarily filled by persons whose position is physiologically determined. Adopted, step and half relationships are included where they are recognized, and many relationships assumed to be 'blood' ties are socially defined. All kinship relations are socially defined. 'Consanguineal' kin are linked by relationships *culturally defined* as blood ties; they are not biological pedigrees.

i. Consanguineal kin

a. Distribution

Table 22 presents the genealogical distribution of consanguines of Ego for each of the class groups and for the overall sample of 51 cases. This table includes all the consanguines of the informants including those related to Ego through children, parents and siblings, but here the exact distribution of consanguines can be seen in a way not possible in previous tables.

The most noticeable class difference is in the mean number of individuals in the genealogical cells close to, and below, Ego. Whereas the established middle class informants have an average of 1.6 children (cell G-1/R0), 7.4 nieces and nephews (cell G-1/R1), and 11.5 first cousins' children (cell G-1/R2), the lower class informants have 4.6, 13.6 and 23.2 in those respective categories. The same is true of the next descending generation with the lower class having a much greater average number of kin in each of the genealogical cells. The greater numbers of children born to people in the lower class means that more individuals are available for recognition. The differences are not likely to be due to differences in the ages of the informants since the mean age difference across class categories is not great (see Table 1, page 19).

The other principal class difference is in the numbers of persons in the ascending generations. Here the position is reversed and the middle class informants recognize greater numbers of genealogical ascendants, on average, than do lower class informants.

The distribution of consanguines is roughly similar in all classes, with the greatest numbers clustering immediately around Ego in genealogical space, filling relationships such as aunt, uncle, nephew, niece, and cousin. The most distantly related consanguineals tend to be in the same generation as, or in the first descending generation from, Ego, though a few informants know of ancestors in direct, or close, collateral lines as far as five generations back. This is more common among informants from the old middle class; the lower class know few ancestors above the grandparental generation.

TABLE 21   KEY TO GENEALOGICAL GRID

DEGREES OF COLLATERAL REMOVAL

		R0	R1	R2	R3	R4
	G+6	Great-Great Great-Great Grandparent				
	G+5	Great-Great Great-Grand Parent				
	G+4	Great-Great Grandparent	Great-Great Grandparent Sibling			
G	G+3	Great-Grand Parent	Great-Grand Parent's Sibling	Great-Grand Parent's 1st Cousin	Great-Grand Parent's 2nd Cousin	
E						
N	G+2	Grandparent	Great-Aunt or Uncle	Grandparent's 1st Cousin	Grandparent's 2nd Cousin	
E						
R	G+1	Parents	Aunts and Uncles	Parent's 1st Cousin	Parent's 2nd Cousin	
A						
T	G0	EGO	Siblings	1st Cousin	2nd Cousin	3rd Cousin
I						
O	G-1	Children	Nephews and Nieces	1st Cousin's Children	2nd Cousin's Children	3rd Cousin's Children
N						
	G-2	Grand- children	Sibling's Grand- children	1st Cousin's Grand- children	2nd Cousin's Grand- children	
	G-3	Great-Grand children	Sibling's Great-Grand children	1st Cousin's Great-Grand children		

NOTE: Only those cells have been designated for which we
have data. Therefore this table represents the
maximum range of recognition of consanguineals by
the informants.

ii. Spread

The range of genealogical spread is greater for West Indians than that
reported by Schneider for middle class Americans, or the middle class
Londoners studied by Firth and his associates (Schneider and Cottrell
1975; Firth *et al*. 1970). However, the *pattern* of recognition is not very
different; the major difference is in the greater mean numbers in each cell
in the West Indian cases, a circumstance due mainly to the higher

TABLE 22 GENEALOGICAL DISTRIBUTION OF EGO'S CONSANGUINEAL KIN

Old Middle Class

Number

	R0	R1	R2	R3	R4
G+5	2				
G+4	10	3			
G+3	19	6			
G+2	38	61	7		
G+1	20	79	97	12	
G0	10	66	139	110	15
G-1	16	74	115	39	11
G-2	3	3	10	1	
G-3					
Total 966

Percent

	R0	R1	R2	R3	R4
G+5	0.2				
G+4	1.0	0.3			
G+3	2.0	0.6			
G+2	3.9	6.3	0.7		
G+1	2.1	8.2	10.0	1.2	
G0	1.0	6.8	14.4	11.4	1.6
G-1	1.7	7.7	11.9	4.0	1.1
G-2	0.3	0.3	1.0	0.1	
G-3					
Total 100

Mean Number Per Ego

	R0	R1	R2	R3	R4
G+5	0.2				
G+4	1.0	0.3			
G+3	1.9	0.6			
G+2	3.8	6.1	0.7		
G+1	2.0	7.9	9.7	1.2	
G0	1.0	6.6	13.9	11.0	1.5
G-1	1.6	7.4	11.5	3.9	1.1
G-2	0.3	0.3	1.0	0.1	
G-3					
Total 96.6

New Middle Class

Number

	R0	R1	R2	R3	R4
G+5					
G+4	4				
G+3	16	12			
G+2	43	42			
G+1	28	119	90		
G0	13	83	317	69	
G-1	54	113	226	21	
G-2	7	45	22		
G-3					
Total 1324

Percent

	R0	R1	R2	R3	R4
G+5					
G+4	0.3				
G+3	1.2	0.9			
G+2	3.2	3.2			
G+1	2.1	9.0	6.8		
G0	1.0	6.3	23.9	5.2	
G-1	4.1	8.5	17.1	1.6	
G-2	0.5	3.4	1.7		
G-3					
Total 100

Mean Number Per Ego

	R0	R1	R2	R3	R4
G+5					
G+4	0.3				
G+3	1.2	0.9			
G+2	3.3	3.2			
G+1	2.2	9.2	6.9		
G0	1.0	6.4	24.4	5.3	
G-1	4.2	8.7	17.4	1.6	
G-2	0.5	3.5	1.7		
G-3					
Total 101.8

Lower Class

Number

	R0	R1	R2	R3	R4
G+5					
G+4	2				
G+3	17	1			
G+2	95	75	2		
G+1	56	226	148	10	
G0	28	210	577	207	11
G-1	129	381	649	85	
G-2	103	153	272	12	
G-3	1	18	22		
Total 3490

Percent

	R0	R1	R2	R3	R4
G+5					
G+4	0.1				
G+3	0.5	0.0			
G+2	2.7	2.1	0.1		
G+1	1.6	6.5	4.2	0.3	
G0	0.8	6.0	16.5	5.9	0.3
G-1	3.7	10.9	18.6	2.4	
G-2	3.0	4.4	7.8	0.3	
G-3	0.0	0.5	0.6		
Total 100

Mean Number Per Ego

	R0	R1	R2	R3	R4
G+5					
G+4	0.1				
G+3	0.6	0.0			
G+2	3.4	2.7	0.1		
G+1	2.0	8.1	5.3	0.4	
G0	1.0	7.5	20.6	7.4	0.4
G-1	4.6	13.6	23.2	3.0	
G-2	3.7	5.5	9.7	0.4	
G-3	0.0	0.6	0.8		
Total 124.6

All Cases

Number

	R0	R1	R2	R3	R4
G+5	2				
G+4	16	3			
G+3	52	19			
G+2	176	178	9		
G+1	104	424	335	22	
G0	51	359	1033	386	26
G-1	199	568	990	145	11
G-2	113	201	304	13	
G-3	1	18	22		
Total 5780

Percent

	R0	R1	R2	R3	R4
G+5	0.0				
G+4	0.3	0.1			
G+3	0.9	0.3			
G+2	3.0	3.1	0.2		
G+1	1.8	7.3	5.8	0.4	
G0	0.9	6.2	17.9	6.7	0.4
G-1	3.4	9.8	17.1	2.5	0.2
G-2	2.0	3.5	5.3	0.2	
G-3	0.0	0.3	0.4		
Total 100

Mean Number Per Ego

	R0	R1	R2	R3	R4
G+5	0.0				
G+4	0.3	0.1			
G+3	1.0	0.4			
G+2	3.5	3.5	0.2		
G+1	2.0	8.3	6.6	0.4	
G0	1.0	7.0	20.3	7.6	0.5
G-1	3.9	11.1	19.4	2.8	0.2
G-2	2.2	3.9	6.0	0.3	
G-3	0.0	0.4	0.4		
Total 113.3

reproduction rates. The distribution figures for the American sample are shown in Table 23.

TABLE 23 DISTRIBUTION OF CONSANGUINEAL KIN:
NORTH AMERICAN MIDDLE CLASS SAMPLE

		Number					Percent		
	R0	R1	R2	R3		R0	R1	R2	R3
G+2	292	312	24	1	G+2	5.0	5.3	0.4	0.0
G+1	160	647	410	20	G+1	2.7	11.1	7.0	0.3
G0	80	222	1040	348	G0	1.4	3.8	17.8	6.0
G-1	118	445	1154	165	G-1	2.0	7.6	19.8	2.8
G-2	30	137	216	15	G-2	0.5	2.3	3.7	0.3
	Total	5836				Total	100		

Source: adapted from Schneider and Cottrell (1975), p. 44

Schneider and Cottrell discuss the relationship between the number of recognized kin within each category and the number that would be present if kin of this type were in fact physiologically related 'blood kin.' They demonstrate that the correspondence between the number of hypothetically possible consanguines, and the number actually recognized is close in those genealogical positions near to Ego, but diminishes rapidly as one moves away in genealogical space. The same is true for our cases. It is not necessary to repeat that demonstration here; suffice it to say that our informants appear to know *something* about the majority of people available as siblings, cousins, aunts, uncles, nephews, nieces, parents and grandparents, but beyond those relationships the number recognized is much smaller than the number possible.

iii. Vital status

Roughly a fifth of all individuals on genealogies are dead. How does this compare with the proportion of deceased consanguines, and where are these dead kin located in genealogical space? Tables 24 and 25 compare the proportion of dead consanguines with the proportion of all persons on the genealogy who are dead. The established middle class recognize slightly more dead consanguines, and more dead relatives generally, than do informants from the other two class groups. This could result from the lower class having a higher proportion of young relatives who are likely to be alive.

Table 25 shows the distribution of the dead consanguines; again the highest proportion of dead consanguines are in the genealogical cells nearest to Ego. The implication is that distant relatives are known only

TABLE 24 KIN LIVING AND DEAD BY CLASS GROUP

VITAL STATUS	Old Middle Class No	%	New Middle Class No	%	Lower Class No	%	All Cases No	%
Living	2608	74.1	2284	79.5	6697	83.0	11589	80.1
Dead	912	25.9	588	20.5	1375	17.0	2875	19.9
TOTAL	3520	100.0	2872	100.0	8072	100.0	14464	100.0

TABLE 25 PERCENTAGE OF CONSANGUINEALS WHO ARE DEAD IN EACH GENEALOGICAL POSITION: BY CLASS

Old Middle Class

	R0	R1	R2	R3	R4
G+5	100				
G+4	100	100			
G+3	100	83			
G+2	84	85	29		
G+1	55	35	31	17	
G0	10	14	11	11	13
G-1	0	7	6	21	46
G-2	0	0	20	0	
G-3	0				

Total number dead = 257
Total Percent dead = 26.9

New Middle Class

	R0	R1	R2	R3	R4
G+5	100				
G+4	100	100			
G+3	93	100			
G+2	85	78			
G+1	50	45	27		
G0	13	23	5	12	
G-1	2	1	9	0	
G-2	0	5	0		
G-3	0				

Total number dead = 248
Total Percent dead = 19.4

Lower Class

	R0	R1	R2	R3	R4
G+5	100				
G+4	100				
G+3	94	0			
G+2	93	67	50		
G+1	70	51	20	20	
G0	28	42	10	4	9
G-1	14	4	2	12	
G-2	1	1	3	0	
G-3	0	0	5		

Total number dead = 556
Total Percent dead = 16.2

All Cases

	R0	R1	R2	R3	R4
G+5	100				
G+4	100	100			
G+3	96	90			
G+2	89	75	33		
G+1	62	46	25	18	
G0	51	32	8	8	12
G-1	10	4	4	13	46
G-2	1	2	4	0	
G-3	0	0	5		

Total number dead = 1061
Total Percent dead = 18.7

because they are alive, or recently deceased, whereas closer kinsmen are remembered longer after they die. The apparent exception is children of second and third cousins among the established middle class, but the numbers are so small that they could be accounted for in other ways.

iv. Contact and name knowledge

While recording genealogies each informant was asked to describe the nature and frequency of contact with each person recorded, and the individual's name, so far as it was known by the informant, was recorded. This material provides a picture of the extent of contact and name knowledge according to genealogical position. The same kind of analysis could be made for non-consanguineals.

Unfortunately, the contact information for many genealogies was not consistent enough for easy and rapid coding; many cases were coded as 'unknown' even though it would have been possible, given time and money, to recover the information for data processing. The lost information occurs more frequently in the more distant relationships and these should be treated with caution.

Residence, name knowledge and frequency of contact with consanguines are presented in Tables 26 and 27.

The established middle class and the lower class have a higher proportion of consanguines living in the same, or an adjacent, community than do new middle class informants. This reflects the geographical mobility of the upwardly mobile, as does the fact that 20.6 percent of their consanguineals live in a distant community. The other two groups have less than 1 percent of kin scattered in that way. All three groups have a sizeable proportion of consanguineal kin living in a foreign country. This is due to the heavy migration of West Indians during the twentieth century.

The most interesting aspect of Table 26 is the general similarity in the patterns of contact and name knowledge of the different class groups. A person's knowledge of the name of a relative is some index to their more general knowledge and contact. Differences are probably due to the more constricted, homogeneous community life of the rural lower class, but the overall proportion of consanguines with whom the informants have no contact whatsoever is between a quarter and a fifth for all class groups. The upwardly mobile middle class seems to have frequent contact with a smaller range of kin, but this is compensated for by the higher incidence of infrequent visiting (Table 26).

8. Conclusion

The overview of genealogical structure in this chapter is no more than an

TABLE 26 RESIDENCE IN RELATION TO EGO, CONTACT AND NAME KNOWLEDGE: CONSANGUINES OF EGO

	Old Middle Class No	%	New Middle Class No	%	Lower Class No	%	All Cases No	%
RESIDENCE IN RELATION TO EGO								
Same or adjacent community	312	38.5	303	34.2	1208	49.7	1823	44.2
Medium Distant	236	29.1	251	28.4	730	30.1	1217	29.5
Far distant	2	0.2	182	20.6	17	0.7	201	4.9
Different country	260	32.1	149	16.8	474	19.5	883	21.4
TOTAL	810	100.0	885	100.0	2429	100.0	4124	100.0
FREQUENCY OF CONTACT WITH EGO								
Frequent visits	205	24.1	190	19.8	601	33.9	996	27.8
Infrequent visits	116	13.6	296	30.9	399	22.5	811	22.6
Meet occasionally	326	38.3	228	23.8	397	22.4	951	26.5
No contact	205	24.1	244	25.5	376	21.2	825	23.0
TOTAL	852	100.0	958	100.0	1773	100.0	3583	100.0
EGO'S KNOWLEDGE OF NAMES								
Knows full name	669	69.9	685	53.6	1835	53.5	3189	56.3
Knows partial name	238	24.9	355	27.8	1217	35.5	1810	32.0
Knows no names	50	5.2	237	18.6	378	11.0	665	11.7
TOTAL	957	100.0	1277	100.0	3430	100.0	5664	100.0

Note: Cases where the information was not obtained, or was not coded, are excluded from this table and from Table 27.

TABLE 27   RESIDENCE, CONTACT AND NAME KNOWLEDGE OF EGO'S CONSANGUINEAL KIN BY GENEALOGICAL POSITION

1. Percent residing in same community as Ego or adjacent community

Old Middle Class (Total Cases 810)

	R0	R1	R2	R3	R4
G+5					
G+4					
G+3	17				
G+2	31	17	17		
G+1	60	45	28	42	
G0		48	42	34	40
G-1	73	41	37	42	100
G-2	100	0	38		
G-3					

New Middle Class (Total Cases 885)

	R0	R1	R2	R3	R4
G+5					
G+4	0				
G+3	0	0			
G+2	19	29			
G+1	26	32	34		
G0		33	37	25	26
G-1	86	31	25	0	
G-2	43	21	41		
G-3					

Lower Class (Total Cases 2429)

	R0	R1	R2	R3	R4
G+5					
G+4					
G+3	100				
G+2	55	43	100		
G+1	67	42	51	100	
G0		47	44	49	
G-1	65	47	42	66	
G-2	42	46	60	100	
G-3	0	17	58		

All Cases (Total Cases 4124)

	R0	R1	R2	R3	R4
G+5	0	0			
G+4	0	0			
G+3	36	0			
G+2	41	32	29		
G+1	56	47	37	46	
G0		43	42	40	33
G-1	71	43	38	53	100
G-2	44	39	57	100	
G-3	0	17	58		

2. Percent who visit or are visited frequently (more than once per month)

Old Middle Class (Total Cases 852)

	R0	R1	R2	R3	R4
G+5					
G+4	0				
G+3	6				
G+2	42	9	17		
G+1	65	29	15	27	
G0		62	15	11	0
G-1	81	27	22	0	0
G-2	100	0			
G-3					

New Middle Class (Total Cases 958)

	R0	R1	R2	R3	R4
G+5					
G+4	0				
G+3	17	0			
G+2	11	6			
G+1	58	13	5		
G0		50	9		
G-1	96	18	5	0	
G-2	71	0			
G-3					

Lower Class (Total Cases 1773)

	R0	R1	R2	R3	R4
G+5					
G+4	0				
G+3	0				
G+2	23	29	100		
G+1	76	26	11		
G0		49	21	13	
G-1	90	31	22	36	
G-2	32	34	43		
G-3	0				

All Cases (Total Cases 3583)

	R0	R1	R2	R3	R4
G+5	0				
G+4	0	0			
G+3	8	0			
G+2	25	14	29		
G+1	68	23	12		
G0		52	16	10	0
G-1	91	27	17	10	0
G-2	37	20	31		
G-3	0				

3. Percentage of consanguineals for whom Ego knows full name (including married name if applicable)

Old Middle Class

	R0	R1	R2	R3	R4
G+5					
G+4	0	67			
G+3	16	17			
G+2	66	58	43		
G+1	100	90	82	75	
G0		95	76	64	67
G-1	100	81	60	33	9
G-2	100	67	50	0	
G-3					

New Middle Class

	R0	R1	R2	R3	R4
G+5					
G+4	0				
G+3	0	0			
G+2	54	39			
G+1	86	71	57		
G0		96	59	39	
G-1	100	60	28	5	
G-2	71	21	5		
G-3					

Lower Class

	R0	R1	R2	R3	R4
G+5					
G+4	50				
G+3	29	0			
G+2	59	65	50		
G+1	100	92	53	80	
G0		79	64	36	55
G-1	93	59	36	20	
G-2	72	31	14	0	
G-3					

All Cases

	R0	R1	R2	R3	R4
G+5	0				
G+4	6	33			
G+3	16	5			
G+2	59	57	44		
G+1	96	86	63	77	
G0		86	64	45	62
G-1	95	62	37	22	9
G-2	73	29	15	0	
G-3					

introduction to the possibilities of such analysis. Some more detailed tabulations will be found in other chapters, and some are reserved for separate publication. The focus here on differences between classes has shown them to be few. Where differences do occur they are often produced by the way in which classes are defined. Thus, variation in the occupational status of informants and their kin arises because occupation was taken as the most significant index to the class of the informant. The most significant finding is that non-legal unions generate extensive and enduring kinship ties; the tables do not tell anything about the content of relationships, but they indicate the frequency of contact and Ego's knowledge of names is a clue to the degree of recognition. Equally important is the finding that men are important links in the chain of kinship in all groups, contradicting the idea that unstable conjugal unions expunge males from kinship networks and genealogies.

i. Half siblingship

A final piece of evidence on class differences (or their absence) is material on half siblingship. Half siblings posed a problem for this study. Nothing complicates a genealogy more than multiple unions and 'sets' of half siblings. Some lower class informants were reluctant to categorize children of the same mother as 'half' no matter how many different fathers were involved. At the same time, women are proud if their children are 'all one father.' The half sibling problem appears to be a by-product of non-legal and multiple unions, but the appearance is false. Half siblings are produced just as readily by legal marriage followed by divorce or death. Setting aside the nature of the unions producing half siblings gives a better view of class differences, or similarities.

Tables 28 and 29 contain this information. The indeterminacy in these tables comes from the individuals coded as 'unknown' or 'possible' because of the lack of definitive information. The informants simply did not know. From the data available it appears as if there are few differences between classes, even though women of the established middle class have fewer multiple unions than lower class, or upwardly mobile women. No less than 12.7 percent of individuals on established middle class genealogies have half siblings, while 22.9 percent of those on lower class genealogies have half siblings. The experience of members of different classes is closely intertwined, and the reason that this is so will be seen more clearly in the next two chapters.

TABLE 29   NUMBER OF PERSONS WITH HALF SIBLINGS
(Broad Class Categories)

Type of Half-sibling	Old Middle Class		New Middle Class		Lower Class		All Cases	
	No	%	No	%	No	%	No	%
Definitely by Father	341	9.7	299	10.4	884	11.0	1524	10.5
Definitely by Mother	17	0.5	81	2.8	396	4.9	494	3.4
Definitely by Both	89	2.5	158	5.5	567	7.0	814	5.6
Total with Half sibs	447	12.7	538	18.7	1847	22.9	2832	19.6
None	1483	42.1	1239	43.1	3295	40.8	6017	41.6
Unknown and Possible	1590	45.2	1095	38.1	2930	36.3	5615	38.8
TOTALS	3520	100.0	2872	100.0	8072	100.0	14464	100.0

TABLE 28   NUMBER OF PERSONS WITH HALF SIBLINGS

U R B A N

TYPE OF HALF-SIBLING	Old Upper Middle				New Upper Middle				Old Lower Middle				New Lower Middle				Lower Class			
	Jamaica		Guyana		Jamaica		Guyana		Jamaica		Guyana		Jamaica		Guyana		Jamaica		Guyana	
	No	%	No	%	No	%	No	%	No	%	No	%	No	%	No	%	No	%	No	%
Definitely by Father	210	10.5	53	8.9	30	4.3	92	13.7	78	9.3	0	0.0	98	20.6	45	7.7	416	13.7	64	7.3
Definitely by Mother	3	0.1	5	0.8	9	1.3	4	0.6	9	1.1	0	0.0	48	10.1	12	2.0	171	5.6	26	3.0
Definitely by Both	40	2.0	15	2.5	34	4.9	14	2.1	31	3.7	3	3.8	26	5.5	32	5.5	182	6.0	43	4.9
Total with Half sibs	253	12.6	73	12.2	73	10.5	110	16.4	118	14.1	3	3.8	172	36.2	89	15.2	769	25.3	133	15.2
No half siblings	790	39.4	305	51.1	369	53.2	313	46.6	345	41.2	43	53.8	54	11.4	302	51.5	1151	37.9	423	48.5
Unknown and Possible	963	48.0	219	36.7	251	36.2	248	37.0	374	44.7	34	42.5	249	52.4	195	33.3	1115	36.7	317	36.3
TOTALS	2006	100.0	597	100.0	693	100.0	671	100.0	837	100.0	80	100.0	475	100.0	586	100.0	3035	100.0	873	100.0

R U R A L

TYPE OF HALF SIBLING	Middle Class				Lower Class			
	Jamaica		Guyana		Jamaica		Guyana	
	No	%	No	%	No	%	No	%
Definitely by Father	34	7.6			266	8.7	138	12.5
Definitely by Mother	8	1.8			168	5.5	31	2.8
Definitely by Both	52	11.6			195	6.4	147	13.3
Total with Half siblings	94	21.0			629	20.6	316	28.6
No half siblings	201	45.0			1298	42.4	423	38.2
Unknown and Possible	152	34.0			1131	37.0	367	33.2
TOTALS	447	100.0			3058	100.0	1106	100.0

ALL CASES

	No	%
Definitely by Father	1524	10.5
Definitely by Mother	494	3.4
Definitely by Both	814	5.6
Total with Half siblings	2832	19.6
No half siblings	6017	41.6
Unknown and Possible	5615	38.8
TOTALS	14464	100.0

5

Marriage in the formation of West Indian society

To the average normal person, in whatever type of society we find him, attraction by the other sex and the passionate and sentimental episodes which follow are the most significant events in his existence, those most deeply associated with his intimate happiness and with the zest and meaning of life.

Malinowski 1929

Few married English women, of rank and character, are at any time induced to make their appearance in these distant edges of the world, to exhibit the fashions of domestic elegance, and teach the graces of moral dignity.

Henry Bolingbroke, 1809

It is difficult to know just when marriage became a focus of social concern in the West Indies; probably not until after the abolition of slavery, although some eighteenth-century writers commented on widespread immorality. Preliminary research shows that formal campaigns to stamp out illegitimacy were not begun until the 1880s, and met with little success even then (see pp. 104-6 below and Braithwaite 1953, p. 91). The non-legal union is one of the institutional foundations on which creole society was erected, and as such it reflects accurately the modes of integration, categorization and differentiation within the social order. Marriage was for status equals, concubinage for unequals, and as for those at the bottom of the hierarchy, their familial arrangements were of interest only as they affected the 'breeding' of new labourers. Modern West Indian society did not spring full grown out of slavery, but the meaning of marriage has a long and particular history which we must consider.

1. Creating the system

i. The English background

The European men and women who first settled in the West Indies came from all ranks of society, a society in which there was no uniform pattern of marriage. The marriage alliances of wealthy English families, in which the couple had little or no personal choice, differed considerably from the marriages of the lower orders, effected by betrothal and subsequent cohabitation. Stone describes the arrangements made in 1665 for the marriage of the daughter of the Earl of Sandwich to the son of Sir George Carteret, a fellow official at the Admiralty. The young couple were presented with a *fait accompli* in that a contract had been signed, the details of the settlement agreed and the approval of the king obtained before the couple met. Samuel Pepys, who acted as go-between, described the wedding dinner as being stiff and joyless (Stone 1977, pp. 298-9). Among the lower classes premarital sexual behaviour was freer and marriage a less formal institution. There were many different types of marriage, including spousals *de praesenti* creating a legally binding union without the intervention of either church or state (see Powell 1917 for a full discussion).

ii. West Indian marriage

The families who made fortunes through sugar planting in the West Indies often used marriages as a means of cementing alliances to increase the size and diversity of holdings, secure political influence, or enhance status through marriage into noble or influential families. The history of Worthy Park Estate in Jamaica demonstrates this. According to Craton and Walvin, 'The early histories of the successful founding families of the Jamaican plantocracy were characterized by fruitful business connections and dynastic bonds' (Craton and Walvin 1970, p. 37). The Prices, who established and developed Worthy Park, were allied by marriage to the Roses, through the marriage of the founder's daughter, Elizabeth, to Francis Rose. He owned extensive lands that reverted to the Prices upon the extinction of the Roses' male line in Jamaica (Craton and Walvin 1970, pp. 40-1, 50). A great deal of manoeuvring took place in England, where the wealthiest West India planters lived in the eighteenth century. For example, the Beckfords used the income from their Jamaican holdings to create an influential political dynasty in Britain (see Knight 1978 for a discussion of the Beckford marital alliances). The same general pattern established itself among the lesser landowners in the islands. Even though the West Indies were lands of opportunity for penniless adventurers, and the high death rates coupled with the shortage of white women resulted in opportunities for them to make good marriages, alliances were based on careful consideration of both property and status. The same is true today, especially among those who possess land, businesses or status based on colour, and this in spite of the spread of what Lawrence Stone calls 'affective individualism' (Stone 1977).

By the end of the eighteenth century creole society was mature; part of that maturity was the increasing importance of the People of Colour – racially mixed descendants of Africans and Europeans. Descriptions of the categories into which persons of mixed racial origin were placed are to be found in such contemporary authorities as Bryan Edwards (1794 Vol II, pp. 16-18). The diagram provided by Higman (1976, p. 139) simplifies the picture.

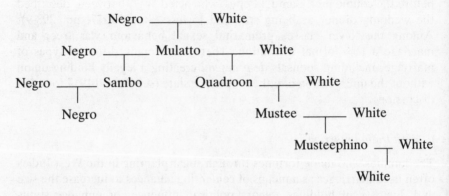

Diagram 1.

Bryan Edwards states that the offspring of a Mustee (Mestize) by a white man were white by law (ibid., p. 16n[h]); repeated descent from whites did result in offspring becoming legally white, unlike the north American colonies or Barbados (Handler 1974, p. 192). Such whites were termed 'Jamaica White' (see Craton 1978, p. 236). The circumstances of the initial contacts between whites and blacks are not known in any detail; accounts of Port Royal, Jamaica, during the latter half of the seventeenth century show a growing slave population living in intimate daily contact with whites in the crowded yards and dwellings of the town (Pawson and Buisseret 1975, pp. 98-119). In towns like Port Royal, and on the larger plantations, concubinage was most extensive, resulting in a growing racially mixed population. Rape and sexual coercion, though real, was rarely as crude as it is often portrayed. Higman has shown that by the end of the eighteenth century, slave women in Jamaica who bore coloured children generally did so consistently throughout their reproductive career.[1] Rarely were they wrested away from African husbands by force (Higman 1976, pp. 139-56). On smaller properties where the owner had a

---

[1] For a case that does not follow this pattern see Craton 1978, p. 239.

wife present, fewer coloured offspring were found. The men most likely to develop unions with slave women were the 'lesser whites' on the large plantations.

In 1801 Maria Nugent and her husband George, Lieutenant-Governor and Commander-in-Chief of Jamaica, only two months in the island, visited Hope Estate near to where the University of the West Indies now stands. While her husband toured the distillery she went to the Overseer's house and there talked to the black women:

who told me all their histories. The overseer's *chère amie*, and no man here is without one, is a tall black woman, well made, with a very flat nose, thick lips, and a skin of ebony, highly polished and shining. She shewed me her three yellow children, and said, with some ostentation, she should soon have another. The marked attention of the other women, plainly proved her to be the favourite Sultana of this vulgar, ugly, Scotch Sultan, who is about fifty, clumsy, ill made, and dirty. (Wright 1966a, p. 29)

The more prosperous whites had access to the free coloured women. Maria Nugent makes passing reference to the private life of General Nugent's predecessor as Governor, Lord Balcarres, who did not have his wife in Jamaica. She comments on Balcarres' filthy appearance, his dirty hands that he uses to take food from the serving dishes, and the terrible state of his country property, or Penn, which the Nugents later occupied. She was even more upset when she learned of his domestic life, but did not confide the details to her diary, beyond saying that it was 'profligate and disgusting' (Wright 1966a, p. 38). A later governor, the Duke of Manchester (1808 to 1811 and 1813 to 1821), was, according to Lord Olivier, 'a begetter of numerous brown-skinned illegitimate progeny' and 'five of his bastards were at school in Kingston' in 1836 (quoted in Brathwaite 1971, p. 110). It is not surprising that governors should follow the custom of the country, for custom it certainly was, though the Duke may have had extra cause since his marriage was unhappy; the Duchess, daughter of the Duke of Gordon, ran away with one of her footmen (Cokayne 1932, Vol. VIII, p. 376).

In 1794 Bryan Edwards described the marriage system in careful detail.

The accusation generally brought against the free people of Colour, is the incontinency of their women; of whom, such as are young, and have tolerable persons, are universally maintained by White men of all ranks and conditions as kept mistresses. (Edwards 1794, Vol. II, pp. 21-2)

Note that 'men of all ranks and conditions' are involved. Today the term 'kep' miss' is used almost exclusively by the lower class, but the origin of the system is clear. Edwards continues,

The unhappy females here spoken of, are much less deserving reproach and reprehension than their keepers . . . unhappily, the young men of their own complexion, are in too low a state of degradation, to think of matrimony. On the other hand, no White man of decent appearance, unless urged by the temptation of a considerable fortune, will condescend to give his hand in marriage to a Mulatto! (Edwards 1794, Vol. II, p. 22)

He points out that these women are not prostitutes; indeed the unions are much like marriage, with the women 'giving themselves up to the husband (for so he is called) with faith plighted, with sentiment, and with affection' (Edwards 1794, Vol. II, p. 23).

Exactly the same system prevailed, and was commented on, in other parts of the West Indies (see R.T. Smith 1987), though we have fewer data easily available for Guyana in the seventeenth and eighteenth centuries. Henry Bolingbroke, who arrived in Demerara (Guyana) in 1799, pointed out that all Europeans in the West Indies – and he surely included Guyana – find it necessary to provide themselves with a 'housekeeper, or mistress.'

The choice he has an opportunity of making is various, a black, a tawney, a mulatto, or a mestee; one of which can be purchased for 100 pounds or 150 pounds sterling, fully competent to fulfill all the duties of her station . . . They embrace all the duties of a wife, except presiding at table; so far decorum is maintained and a distinction made . . . If a young progeny of coloured children is brought forth, these are emancipated, and mostly sent by those whose fathers can afford it, at the age of three or four years, to be educated in England. (Bolingbroke 1809, pp. 26-7)

iii. Concubinage among European colonists

The Europeans who settled Jamaica, and the West Indies generally, were part of a much larger contingent of overseas settlers, almost all of whom entered into sexual or conjugal relations with the strangers among whom they lived. The history of these relations and their social consequences remains to be written, but partial glimpses of activities at the frontier of the 'conjuncture' are available. The enthusiasm with which the Hawaiian women demanded sexual relations with Captain Cook's seamen was unusual (Sahlins 1981, p. 40), but there are many other examples of willing hospitality. The Hudson's Bay Company kept extensive records of its operations in Canada between 1670 and 1867, including the wills of individual employees. From this material it has been possible to reconstruct the history of Indian-white contact, and to study 'fur-trade marriages.' The social enclaves that developed in fur-trading posts constituted coherent and continuing systems of social relations into which new generations of persons of mixed descent were born (Brown 1980). non-legal unions with Indian or 'mixed blood' women were not considered improper until the 1820s when increased numbers of white women and clergymen arrived. The trading relationship between Indians and Europeans in Canada had been regarded as analogous to slavery, and missionary opposition to Caribbean slavery was extended to the fur trade in the 1840s (Hickerson 1966, p. 823).

Before India became the brightest jewel in the British crown Englishmen were entering into non-legal unions with Indian women as frequently as they were in the West Indies. However, India was an established and complex society, unlike the West Indies, and there was a good deal of variation from time to time and place to place. In the eighteenth century open concubinage was common and the children of high ranking officials or wealthy merchants were often sent to England to be educated, as were the coloured offspring of West India planters. Also like the West Indian coloured population they suffered social disabilities when they returned. The men had to accept employment as clerks unless they were supported by their fathers. William Hickey's memoirs of India in the late eighteenth century provide a glimpse of the social life of the wealthy. Hickey took an Indian concubine following his wife's death, and lived openly with her. When she died giving birth to his child he arranged for some close friends, Europeans, to care for it, but it died at the age of two years. In spite of Hickey's attachment to 'Fatty,' as he called her, he never considered marrying her and would probably have left her in India with an allowance when he returned to England (Spencer 1918).

Most marriages between Europeans and Indians were contracted by lower ranking, or 'vagabond,' whites, who generally lived outside the social circles of the higher status Europeans (see Kincaid 1973 and Spear 1932). With the extension of British control in India in the nineteenth century more European women went there and irregular unions became less open and frequent. The Eurasians were pushed into a marginal position quite unlike that of the coloured in the West Indies. The British (and the French and Portuguese) in India were small minorities establishing themselves in complex and hierarchical societies. Their settlements were set apart with only tenuous ties to the main society, and they had their own internal stratification. European trading settlements were often divided into a White Town and a Black Town, with the lower ranking whites, the Eurasians and the Indian servants all living in the Black Town. Eurasians were not defined in racial terms alone. In India the main contrasts were between European Christian culture and the culture of Muslim and Hindu caste society. Thus an Indian who became culturally European, by conversion to Christianity or the adoption of European clothing, also became Eurasian (Spear 1932, p. 62).

iv. Marriage, concubinage and the ideology of race

The West Indies differs from most other colonial situations in that the mixed population, produced mainly by the unions of European men and coloured women, attained a position of prominence and eventual near dominance, so that the experience of this group has become the basis of an ideological system used to oppose white domination in the name of the whole society. The key concept in that ideology is that West Indian societies are 'mixed,' and progressing towards a common culture and a common nationhood. This is not the place to examine the political implications of the ideology; the point is that an important segment of the population continued to see itself as originating in the archetypical union of a slave woman and a white master (see pages 96-8 below).

The slave population of eighteenth-century West Indies was made up of Africans, creoles of African descent and some slaves of mixed racial origin who had not been manumitted. The masters' ideas about the slaves were generally stable and coherent, an inherent part of creole culture. Bryan Edwards is a good source; he was trying to be objective, and was genuinely concerned about the evils of the slave regime, though he could not escape generally accepted ideas about Africans.

After discussing the temperament and characteristics of the various African tribes making up the slave population, and offering some generalizations about the slaves' cowardice, their propensity to lie, their loyalty toward each other, their affection for those who came in the same ship, their tyranny when invested with even a modicum of power, and their cruelty to animals, he takes up the question of whether they are highly susceptible to the passion of love.

If by love is meant that tender attachment to one individual object, which, in civilised life, is desire heightened by sentiment, and refined by delicacy, I doubt if it ever found a place in an African bosom. – The Negroes in the West Indies, both men and women, would consider it as the greatest exertion of tyranny, and the most cruel of all hardships, to be compelled to confine themselves to a single connection with the other sex; I am persuaded that any attempt to restrain their present licentious and dissolute manners, by introducing the marriage ceremony among them, as is strenuously recommended by many persons in Great Britain, would be utterly impracticable to any good purpose. (Edwards 1794, Vol. II, p. 82)

The slaves enter and leave unions entirely at their own pleasure, without any control by the slave owners.[2] The motive is not 'love' but 'mere animal desire,' and their temporary unions are entered without 'ceremony, and dissolve without reluctance.' Edwards stops short of characterizing the sexual life of the slaves as promiscuity, and he notes – as others have done since – that they settle into stable unions as they grow older. 'When age indeed begins to mitigate the ardour, and lessen the fickleness of youth,

---

[2] This passage from Edwards appears to be taken almost word for word from a deposition made before the Assembly in 1788 by Dr. John Quier, a well-known physician and surgeon who specialized in the care of slaves and who had extensive first hand experience of their customs and preferences (see Craton 1978, pp. 396-7 and p. 84 above).

many of them form attachments, which, strengthened by habit, and endeared by the consciousness of mutual imbecility, produce a union for life' (Edwards 1794, Vol. II, p. 83). Legal, Christian marriage had no place among slaves and even if it had been available to them they may not have accepted it. Edwards refers to an old woman who died in 1792 at the age of 120 years. Consistently she had refused to be baptized because she wanted 'a grand Negro dance at her funeral, according to the custom of Africa; a ceremony never allowed in Jamaica at the burial of such as have been christened' (Edwards 1794, Vol. II, p. 84, fn[e]).

Only when Christianity became intimately tied to the abolition movement did slaves begin to show a more marked interest in conversion, but even then the tide did not flow as strongly as is sometimes suggested. Or, if it did flow strongly for a while, it soon began to ebb. The meaning of marriage for the slave came to be closely related to status within the church and within the local community; for most the question of legitimate rights to inheritance was a minor issue. Marriage was only loosely related to the kinship system, or perhaps it would be better to say that marriage was related to the kinship system in ways that were not envisaged in the official Christian doctrine; in ways that were essentially creole.

To summarize, one can say that the eighteenth-century origin of the present day system of marriage was rooted in the structure of creole society, with its hierarchical system of status groups. At the beginning of the nineteenth century the cultural assumptions about marriage were:

1. Whites marry only whites, and marriage should be between status equals.
2. White men engage in keeper unions with coloured or black women of lower status than themselves.
3. Coloured men engage in keeper unions with coloured or black women of lower status than themselves.
4. Blacks are promiscuous, guided essentially by animal instinct, though they may settle into stable unions late in life.

This is a view from the top of the hierarchy of course, and one can only guess how it looked from the bottom. One unanswered question is how the marriage system of the lowest status groups articulated with the family system, consideration of which will be deferred for the moment. We must first understand how marriage has come to be of such concern to the group that is politically, and ideologically, dominant – the so-called 'middle class.'

2. Marriage and middle class ideology

Alexander has made an interesting analysis of what he calls the 'origin myth' of the Jamaican middle class, abstracted from the statements of informants interviewed as part of the project reported here (Alexander 1977). The myth is, he says, 'the charter of the middle class, and perhaps of the society' (Alexander 1977, p. 431). In what does it consist? Those of his informants who were born into the middle class all root their genealogies in an original ancestral pair; a 'white male master, black female slave, and mulatto or brown offspring' (p. 431). The pair is not known specifically but is merely tacked on to a shallow genealogy, but the pattern is so stereotyped that it becomes a myth of origin of the whole of the middle class. 'Informants believe that the middle class originated in the non-legal union of a white male master and a black female slave that produced an illegitimate brown offspring midway in status between slave and master' (Alexander 1977, p. 431). At this point in mythical time there is perfect concordance between race, economic class position and social status, and it is against this primordial state that all variations, and the progress of social change, can be measured.

Every time a person experiences inconsistency among race, physical appearance, status, and class, he is referring the present to a past in which there were two original groups – one English, white, civilized, master, and solidary, the other African, black, uncivilized, slave, and solidary – that mixed without amalgamating. (Alexander 1977, p. 432)

It is interesting that the origin myth, extracted from the statements of modern informants, does not say that the child takes the slave status of the mother, though historically that was the legal position. It discusses status in two separate ways related to two separate cultural domains. The father decides, according to the myth, to educate his children and arrange for their manumission, and he does this out of sentiment and affection. They become the Free People of Colour. In the kinship domain the diffuse enduring solidarity appropriate to those sharing common blood impels the father to act in this way. However, class separates the father from his mistress and her children, decrees that the union is non-legal, and the children illegitimate. Racially, the children are in the middle in terms of both substance and status. Structurally, non-legal unions between higher status men and lower status women are not negative; they result in a positive status increment for the offspring. Ideologically, the existence of the middle class depends on these unions. The statements of Alexander's informants about their own genealogical origins and physical make-up are more interesting than self-conscious general statements about class, race and the structure of Jamaican society, since they embody the fundamental assumptions which inform social and political institutions.

The West Indian middle class has been maligned in recent years, its revolutionary role in the development of West Indian society underestimated. One reason is the contradiction embodied in its position, and in the ideology used to legitimate its struggle, contradictions that were apparent from the beginning.

We saw that by the eighteenth century there was a complex classification system for persons of mixed origin; the women were in demand as the kept mistresses of white men while the men occupied an anomalous and degraded position (pages 84-6 above). The first quarter of the nineteenth century saw a marked increase in the number of people of mixed racial origin, in Jamaica in particular but also in other colonies. Abolition of the slave trade in 1807 halted the input of Africans, while the coloured population continued to mate with whites, blacks and each other. Contrary to the myth of origin of the middle class, the offspring of white men and slave women were not always freed. Higman estimates that 10 percent of the slave population of Jamaica in 1832 was coloured; even slaves with white fathers had less than a 50 percent chance of being manumitted (Higman 1976, p. 141). White men showed a definite preference for young, light-coloured women as mistresses. Such women did not usually mate with men of their own colour, or darker, unless they were growing older, had several children and were thus less attractive to whites. Whether slave or free, coloured men rarely were able to father children lighter in colour than themselves, while light-coloured women were likely to have children even fairer than themselves (Higman 1976, pp. 139-53). Divergence of colour status of the children of various unions became an integral part of the dynamics of the marriage system, as we shall see. If the system had proceeded unchecked it would, in theory, eventually have polarized the offspring into black and white. It did not proceed unchecked.

3. Political and economic aspects of class

In the eighteenth century some free coloured persons had been accorded the privileges of whites by the passage of special bills. Brathwaite reports that between 1772 and 1796 'at least sixty-seven petitions involving 512 free coloured (and only one free black) had passed before the Assembly. Of those involved, 176 were mulattoes, 245 quadroons, and 90 mustees' (Brathwaite 1971, p. 172). Even if the petition was granted, some restrictions remained. Between 1802 and 1823 the hearing of these special petitions was suspended (Hall 1972, p. 201). The majority continued to suffer severe disabilities; they could not vote, hold political office or commissions in the militia, give evidence against whites or inherit property above a certain value.

The first stirrings of political consciousness seem to have been produced by the revolutions in north America, France and Haiti. As early as 1792 a petition complained that people of colour were denied the protection of

British law even though they paid taxes (Heuman 1981, p. 24). The whites were forced increasingly to rely on coloured men for manning the militia and filling other positions previously occupied by whites, but they did not trust the coloured, fearing they may form an alliance with the slaves. By 1813 there were 174 coloured and black sergeants in the militia, compared to 238 whites; in the rank and file 2,705 free coloured and blacks almost matched the 3,132 whites (Heuman 1981, p. 27). The free coloured did not, initially, challenge the slave system, nor did they wish to antagonize the whites. They wanted to join them, arguing that they constituted an important and loyal part of the free population with many educated men fully capable of exercising the rights of freedom. No matter how prejudiced the coloured may have been against the black slaves, struggle for their own rights was expressed in universalistic terms; all free men, no matter what their race or colour should be treated equally under the law. They were a classic example of the process of class struggle described by Marx, in that they embodied the interests of their class in an ideology that expressed the suffering of all, and articulated a general opposition to the oppressors (Marx and Engels 1965, pp. 61-2).

H. P. Jacobs has described the changing composition of the dominant political class in Jamaica during the early nineteenth century. From being a body of planters closely linked to the British aristocracy it became a collection of attorneys and managers. Slavery was under increasing attack from powerful forces in Britain, resistance and rebellion quickened among the slaves, and the plantation system became less profitable (Jacobs 1973). This was the period of the making of the coloured middle class. By 1823 there was an island-wide organization in Jamaica dedicated to furthering of the interests of the people of colour – by petitioning, representing their case in Britain and by seeking alliance with the anti-slavery forces.

The contradiction between alliance with anti-slavery forces and protestations of loyalty to the existing system persisted in one form or another into the present, but between them the free blacks and coloured formulated, between 1820 and 1866, the principles of modern Jamaican nationalism. In 1830 free blacks and coloured finally were accorded all the privileges of whites. Two coloured men, Price Watkis and John Manderson, were elected to the Assembly – Watkis a barrister-at-law and Manderson a merchant (see Heuman 1981 for a detailed discussion of coloured and black members of the Assembly). In spite of changes in the law, whites continued to discriminate against brown men (and blacks of course). Coloured people complained of this, in their own press, in the Assembly, and in public speeches, and those complaints continued for the next 100 years. A major grievance was the importation of whites to fill positions for which local people of equal, if not superior, ability were available (Heuman 1981,p. 72; R.T. Smith 1980 [1962], pp. 54-7).

Marriage in the formation of West Indian society

The abolition of slavery in 1838 swept away all legal distinctions based on race. However, classes now seemed to be defined in terms of race and the ex-slaves had become a black lower class. The 'coloured middle class' contained some blacks and some Jews as well as people of mixed racial origin, but such minor inconsistencies were ignored. The creation of a nominally free market in labour, and a more extensive money economy, provided new opportunities for production and internal trade, and even for new export markets. New crops were developed, many of them grown by ex-slaves on small holdings, or on small plantations owned by coloured, creole white and Jewish landowners. There was increasing opportunity for educated people to find employment in the professions and in teaching as well as in government service. New secondary schools were founded and old ones opened up to coloured people. The solid material base which the coloured population developed for themselves justified their being defined as the core of the new middle class.

That material base was not sufficiently independent of white domination to enable this class to effect a radical transformation of the society even if they had wanted to, as some surely did. In Jamaica the impetus to radical change could not prevail and by 1866, following the Morant Bay rebellion, a counter movement was dominant (see Curtin 1955; Jacobs 1973; Heuman 1981; Hart n.d.). The middle class became firmly established, totally respectable, deeply resentful of white prejudice and discrimination (not to mention political exclusion), but also fearful of losing its privileged position. Certain elements struggled against the planter class and its patrons in the Colonial Government, a struggle rooted in economic interests, allying them with the working class against the sugar planters. However, they could not rid themselves of the idea that the legitimacy of their leadership of the black masses lay in their education, refinement and essentially English characteristics. The contradiction was painful and apparent. It appeared in all the colonies. In British Guiana there were constitutional crises in the late nineteenth century and again in 1928 when the old constitution was suspended and direct Crown Colony Government imposed. The intelligentsia (as it styled itself), composed here of Portuguese, Chinese, and East Indians as well as coloured and black people, claimed political legitimacy on the basis of culture, refinement, civilization and the ability to replace the British (R.T. Smith 1980 [1962], pp. 51-7). A persistent strain of African (and in Guyana, East Indian) 'cultural nationalism,' or what Post (1978) calls 'Ethiopianism,' was found among black leaders of the upper lower and lower middle class, but this was not taken up as an explicit legitimating ideology until the 1960s when the middle class began to fragment into warring factions as it fought over the spoils of independence.

In this social and political context middle class ideas about marriage were created. Before we revisit the myth of origin of the middle class, this is an appropriate point to consider briefly whether there is a West Indian upper class and where it fits in this discussion.

4. Whatever happened to the upper class?

No very wealthy families were included in this research, but a study is now in progress that will make good this omission. Detailed studies of the family life and marital patterns of the wealthy segments of Caribbean society have been curiously neglected. For Jamaica, information about the Clarke family is linked to the study of Worthy Park plantation records and is secondary to the history of the founding family, the Prices (Craton and Walvin 1970; Craton 1978). Perhaps that is as it should be. There is much archival material on the prominent British families with West Indian connections, but they were neither active nor present after about 1850. The place of these landed families has never been filled. Corporate ownership of a smaller number of consolidated plantations was achieved by means different from marriage alliance, though some of the descendants of the old families – Beckfords, Draxes, Pinnocks, Haynes, Parkers, Davsons, Campbells, Lascelles, Dawkins, Mannings, Codringtons, Hailshams, Homes and Gladstones – may still be active in the City of London or in the big corporations. During the second half of the nineteenth century and the first half of the twentieth, the colonial upper class consisted of the British bureaucratic elite, with only a nostalgic memory of the great planting families. The plantations were mechanized and enlarged, and production was rationalized. Some creole whites occupied managerial positions, but the plantation elite was generally recruited abroad. Even the top managers were salaried employees and, no matter what their pretensions, they were not an upper class in the way that planters had been in the eighteenth and early nineteenth centuries. Planting sugar was no longer the only road to economic success.

Many local people, creole whites, Portuguese, Jewish, Chinese, coloured, Syrian, Lebanese, East Indian (local in the sense that they settled and made their way as part of West Indian society), were economically successful and amassed substantial family fortunes. For Jamaica, Stanley Reid has described the complex ties of marriage linking a small number of Jewish families prominent in land ownership, legal practice and industrial enterprise, the members of which occupy interlocking and controlling positions in the modern corporate economy (Reid 1977). But control of the Jamaican economy is vested mainly in companies outside Jamaica. Although Reid focusses on Jewish families for the purpose of genealogical illustration, there are close intermarriages with other circles of prominent creole whites, Syrians, and Chinese (see Holzberg 1977). George Cumper has also shown how close marriages between prominent merchant families in Barbados has effected property consolidation (Cumper 1962; see also Barrow 1983). All the same, there is no detailed study of wealthy families comparable to recent work on a wealthy Mexican family (Lomnitz and Pérez Lizaur 1978, 1984). Wealth alone does not create an upper class. The new entrepreneurial families are closely tied to foreign capital and international companies, or they are dependent upon the political elites with whom they have close relations.

In the early 1950s Raymond Scheele studied the prominent families of Puerto Rico as part of a project directed by Julian Steward (Scheele 1956). He reported that men were expected to have sexual relations with lower status women at an early age while relations with girls of their own class were carefully controlled. Although it was proper to express romantic love during courtship, in choosing a marital partner primary consideration must be given to property and status. Members of this class were generally educated abroad, at American universities, and when they returned to the island they moved within closed social circles. The same is now true for children of wealthy families elsewhere in the Caribbean, but more careful study is needed. In the meantime we can assume that the orientation of the members of this elite is as much towards the United States as was the orientation of the eighteenth-century upper class towards Britain.

5. The middle class: its myth of origin revisited

We saw that informants born into the middle class had a stereotyped idea that their family history began somewhere back in the days of slavery with the union of a white master and a black slave, but none was able to trace a genealogy through known links to such a union. Established middle class families have names that were already coming into prominence in the middle of the nineteenth century. In Jamaica they include Gordon, Jordon, Manderson, Sherlock, Lake, Burke, Nunes, Mais, Gibb, Nathan, Johnson, Osborne, DeLeon, Taylor, and Hill. Few attempts have been made to link present day families with these forebears. There is little evidence of interest in family histories, in spite of the availability of wills and registers of births, marriages and deaths. Some of our genealogies could be extended back in time through archival research, but that was not the aim of these studies. At least one historian has worked forwards to the present from the period of the formation of the middle class – say 1790 to 1850 – showing what can be done with existing materials and revealing the importance of marriage in structuring class relations (Craton 1978).

It was noted that some coloured children remained slaves, that women of mixed racial origin tended to bear children lighter in colour than themselves, and that it worked the other way for men (pages 84-5 above).

Craton's case histories flesh out these generalizations and show how much variation they conceal (Craton 1978, pp. 235-43, 331-54). Some preliminary research on nineteenth and twentieth century Jamaican wills, and on material referring to Antigua contained in the Codrington Papers, supplement Craton's analysis (see R.T. Smith 1987).

Mulatto Kitty, daughter of Robert Ellis, white bookkeeper and overseer, and Amy, black creole field slave, was born in 1795. Because of her colour she was put to work as a house slave in the overseer's quarters. The rapid turnover of white employees on Jamaican estates during the slavery period is well documented and explains the childbearing history of this woman. She had six quadroon children by three different white men – bookkeepers and overseers – and two sambo children by two black men whose names are unknown. As Craton suggests, it is likely that Kitty became housekeeper of the overseer's house, a position of some authority, and she was probably the most permanent and stable member of that household in which she brought up her eight children. What happened to her, or her children, after emancipation is not known but her life seems to have been the very archetype of what is now regarded as the unstable domestic life of the lower class, and the very archetype of the 'matrifocal' household (R.T. Smith 1956).

Other interesting cases abound, not least of which is the household of Dr. John Quier, the Lluidas Vale physician who made a comfortable living attending the slaves, and whites, of the nearby plantations. Quier lived in Jamaica from 1767 until his death in 1822 without ever returning to Europe, and 'As he became an old man his house at Shady Grove became an easygoing menage of several generations of his lovers and children.' (Craton 1978, p. 262). He had at least four children by four different women; all who survived him were provided for in his will. Perhaps the most interesting case is that of Rose Price, great-great-grandson of Francis Price, the founder of Worthy Park estate in Lluidas Vale, Jamaica (see Craton and Walvin 1970, p. 50 for the Price genealogy). In 1791 Rose Price, then 23 years old, sailed for Jamaica accompanied by his old Oxford tutor, the Reverend John Vinicombe. The family's Worthy Park estate had been allowed to deteriorate under many years of administration by attornies; he intended to salvage the family fortunes by making the estate profitable again. This he accomplished in three years of intense effort, being rewarded with an income of at least £6,000 a year thereafter. This permitted him to return to Cornwall, purchase Trengwainton House, and use that as his title when he was made a baronet in 1815. In 1797, shortly after his return from Jamaica, he married Elizabeth Lambart, a woman with aristocratic connections but no fortune (Craton and Walvin 1970, p. 185). He grew to love this woman, for he wrote in his will:

I . . . desire to be buried with the Locket of hair of my beloved wife around my neck and that the fine hair that was taken from her head at her death may be placed beside me in my coffin as testimonies of the love I bore her. (Will dated 28 November 1834, JIRO)[3]

She bore him fourteen children, all born and brought up at Trengwainton House. The daughters 'married new capital or old titles' and the sons 'served the Empire during its Victorian heyday and afterglow' (Craton 1978, p. 332). The family history is well documented and easily available.

During his three years in Jamaica Rose Price had a mistress who was born a slave.[4] Lizette Nash was thirteen or fourteen years old when she bore the first of two children fathered by Rose Price. Lizette's mother, Eleanor Price, was a mulatto slave probably fathered by a white book-keeper named Nash, so Lizette was a quadroon. Eleanor Price subsequently lived with Peter Douglas, the English owner of Point Hill estate, for whom she bore ten children. Douglas had freed Eleanor Price in 1789, but Lizette, not being his child, was not manumitted until 1794 when Rose Price made that arrangement. Lizette's first child, Elizabeth Price Nash, was soon followed by a son, John Price Nash, born in 1796. Both these children were mustees, sometimes referred to as octoroons, and therefore quite European in appearance.

Rose Price left Jamaica before his son was born and Lizette went to live with her mother (who else?) in the house of Peter Douglas who took responsibility for the care of Lizette's children. Rose Price provided for the two children and kept in touch with Peter Douglas about their progress. In 1810 he decided that they should travel to England to be educated. The eldest, Elizabeth, was sent to a finishing school and, in 1815, became a governess in the household of James Dennistoun of Colgraine in Scotland. There she met her future husband, Alexander Lochore, a tutor in the same household who subsequently became a clergyman. She bore him four sons and four daughters whose descendants, when Michael Craton completed his research, were white (Craton 1978, pp. 331-9). Some New Zealand descendants had no idea of any slave connection.

John Price Nash studied engineering and returned to Jamaica in 1823. He went to live with his mother, aunts, uncles, and cousins in Lluidas Vale, assuming management of the family properties. Craton gives the full story of this man's life and the details will not be recounted here. Bequests from the Price family, from Douglas and from Dr. Quier, were consolidated by the interrelated coloured families of the district, who tried to operate their property as a plantation under the direction of John Price Nash. Emancipa-

---

[3] All references to wills refer to copies deposited in the Jamaica Island Record Office at Spanish Town.

[4] I am indebted to Michael Craton's account of this case, which is supplemented by my reading of the Price and Quier wills in the Jamaica Island Record Office.

tion, coupled with economic depression, made this impossible and he was forced to work as a millwright on Worthy Park and other plantations. Although John Price Nash attained a certain prominence in the parish as an officer in the militia, churchwarden, poundkeeper and collector of petty debts, he could not maintain the standard of living of a planter. The properties gradually ran down and the rest of the family seem to have moved to Spanish Town and Kingston. Some of the living descendants of John Price Nash, traced by Craton, had grown up on his property in Lluidas Vale, but only one of them had a vague idea that Rose Price was an ancestor.

This case is a classic, embodying the structural principles of the system in a particularly vivid way. The divergence between the legitimate lines and the illegitimate is most significant, as is that between those who moved out of Jamaica and those who remained, or returned. Elizabeth Price Nash and her descendants disappeared into the Scottish population; John Price Nash and his descendants became part of the Jamaican middle class, and their descendants became progressively darker as they were absorbed into the Jamaican population. A part of the family struggled to maintain as much occupational and colour status as possible in a difficult situation, but like other members of the West Indian middle class (often pictured as 'marrying light'), they increasingly married, or formed unions with, people of darker colour. Elizabeth maintained a correspondence with her brother and in 1840 sent gifts by a friend who was travelling to Jamaica – a custom that survives in this day of jet travel. Rose Price's slave mistress, Lizette, lived to a ripe old age surrounded by relatives and becoming the centre of affectionate ties, but contact between the European and Jamaican branches of the family ceased sometime in the mid-nineteenth century.

Comparable material for other parts of the West Indies has not been analysed as fully as this Jamaican case, but the system seems to have been the same. Similar customs were found in Demerara and Berbice at the end of the eighteenth century and described by such travellers as Bolingbroke and Dr. Pinckard. Bolingbroke says that all white men found it necessary to have a coloured housekeeper, or mistress, and he even gives the price – 100 to 150 pounds sterling – and the source – Barbados, Martinique and Grenada – from which specialists in this trade imported women (Bolingbroke 1809, pp. 26-7; see also Pinckard 1816). The best known and most romanticized account is that of Captain John Stedman, who published in 1796 in London an account of a visit to Suriname and Berbice, from 1772 to 1777.[5] Stedman recounted in detail his passionate affair with a mulatto slave girl, Joanna, who nursed him back to health after a bout of fever.

---

[5] Stedman's book has appeared in many editions and was one of the best known works dealing with slavery. The edition used here is a reproduction of the original 1796 edition,

Joanna was one of five children born to a black slave woman named Cery, fathered by 'a respectable gentleman named Kruythoff' who, unfortunately, was denied the opportunity to purchase the freedom of either mother or children (Stedman 1971, Vol. I, p. 53). Joanna was about fifteen at the time she became Stedman's keeper. Although he refers to 'A decent wedding, at which many of our friends made their appearance, and at which I was as happy as any bridegroom ever was' it is clear that Joanna remained a slave, since he could not afford to purchase her freedom, and slaves could not be legally married (Stedman 1971, Vol. I, p. 62).

Their son, Johnny, was born at the end of 1774; before he left Suriname on 1 April 1778, Stedman secured Johnny's manumission. He writes at length of his wish to take both Joanna and Johnny back to Europe, and of Joanna's stubborn refusal to go. In February 1782 Stedman married Adriana Wiertz van Coehoorn, a Dutch lady who bore him two daughters and three sons. He did not learn of Joanna's death, on 5 November 1782, until the following year, whereupon he arranged for Johnny to be sent to England to be raised as a part of Stedman's family at their home in Devon (see van Lier 1971). Entering the British navy as a midshipman, Johnny was drowned off Jamaica in 1791. Stedman himself died on 5 March 1797, just a year after his book was published.

Less romantic but more detailed accounts of the working of the marriage system in Berbice and Demerara, from about 1800 to 1890, are to be found in a government report published in Georgetown, British Guiana in 1892 (Titles to Land Commissioners 1892).[6] The report was written by a small commission appointed to settle claims to land titles in the riverain areas of the colony. Among the first to be brought under cultivation, these riverain lands ceased to be profitable after the abolition of slavery. While many had well-authenticated titles up to about 1840, subsequently they were subject to conflicting claims. In hearing claims and settling titles the commissioners compiled a valuable body of evidence which, wisely, they published almost verbatim. The report on Berbice is particularly full, containing evidence from wills, narrative accounts of land transfers, and the comments of the commissioners.

---

[6] The existence of this report was brought to my attention by the Guyana Government Archivist, Mr. T. Payne, but the Guyana Government Archives are, or were, in such bad condition that serious work on it had to be delayed until I went to London, where at least one copy exists in the old Colonial Office Library, now a part of the Commonwealth Library.

---

but it should be noted that Stedman himself was dissatisfied with the treatment given to his work by the original publishers. They toned down some of his more forthright passages and added colour to what they thought would appeal to the public. The original manuscript is now at the University of Minnesota in Minneapolis; a definitive version edited by Richard Price from the original manuscript is in preparation.

Most of these riverain lands were allotted in the eighteenth century in parcels of about 500 acres, each with a narrow river frontage. The men and women acquiring these lands were of various nationalities: Dutch, English, Scots, Welsh, Irish, German, French and other Europeans. The area of land that could be put under coffee, cotton or sugar depended on the number of slaves available, and these slaves and free servants bore children for the owners, as in Jamaica. The case material has to be read with care as some claims to land were probably based on fabricated evidence. Even so, a clear picture emerges of the marriage system during the first half of the nineteenth century.

A crisis developed when slavery was abolished. The properties were useless without adequate labour and from the early 1830s land changed hands at ever decreasing prices. Only large plantations, owned by corporations and able to import indentured labour, could survive in the new economic climate. Many whites left after fighting a losing battle; those who stayed on were gradually absorbed into the coloured population.

Plantation Cruysburg on the West Bank of the Berbice River is an example of this. The plantation consisted of some 500 acres of riverain land granted to Cornelius Cruys in 1769. From 1830 it began to pass through the hands of a series of owners until it was bought by an Englishman, Thomas Williams, in 1838, the year of the final abolition of slavery. Later the land was transferred to Junor and McKay, but reverted to Williams in 1850 by Letters of Decree. At this time some 20 acres were detached and sold to a group of labourers, presumably ex-slaves. Thomas Williams subsequently left Berbice, returning to England where he died in 1875. His wife, Matilda Williams, residing at 37 Grove-end Road, St. John's Wood, Marylebone, London, was his sole heir. It would take only a little more research to find out more about Thomas Williams; all we know from the report is that in 1891 the principal claimants to this plantation were Robert Coventry Williams and Charles Milton Williams, illegitimate sons of Thomas Williams. The background to the claim was complex, and most of it will be omitted here.

In 1885 the taxes had fallen into arrears and the land was seized by the Administrator General, whereupon a lengthy correspondence took place between his office and Mrs. Williams's solicitors in London – Norton, Rose Norton and Company. Mrs. Williams made clear her intention of leaving the land for 'Mr. Robert Coventry Williams and his two (if not more) brothers.' The Administrator General replied saying that this generous action would enable Mr. R. C. Williams, 'who is in very humble circumstances, to make a small income by renting.' However, Mrs. Williams's solicitors also refused to incur further expense; if disputes arose the Administrator was at liberty to sell, and divide the proceeds among 'the family.'

The two brothers, Robert and Charles, made depositions before the Commission. Both say their father had five illegitimate children, four brothers and a sister, but Charles adds two others who died young. Robert says that one brother is in America and the other a missionary in Africa, while the sister is a nun in Curaçao. According to Charles, brother Christopher died in London, at William Thompson's boarding house, 19 Queen Street, Shadwell Lane, in 1857, while Andrew died in a lunatic asylum, also in London, in 1859. The sister Jane, according to Charles, died in a convent in Curaçao in 1861. These outside children of Thomas Williams may not all have had the same mother. Charles says that his mother was Jane Milton, from whom he took his middle name. Robert Coventry Williams probably had a different mother; he says that he came to Guyana in 1837, but does not say from where.

The commissioners were intrigued by the fact that under Roman Dutch law, which remained in effect in British Guiana, 'a mother makes no bastard.' That is, all of a woman's children, irrespective of paternity, are entitled to equal shares of her property. The claimant to Land Anna Clementia, Inkerman section, was a natural daughter of Lambert McKenzie, who held the land by title dated 27 September 1856. Lambert McKenzie had four children by the mother of the claimant, three of whom died as infants. Of Lambert McKenzie's two sisters, both dead and neither of them married, one had two children, Kitty Davson and Annie Rose. The Commissioners observe:

Lambert McKenzie apparently died intestate. To whom does his property go? His own natural children are excluded; but the children of his sister? They would seem to come in, for the mother makes no bastard. Thus it comes about that a man's own illegitimate children cannot succeed to his property as heirs *ab intestato*, while those of another man may. (Titles to Land Commissioners 1892, p. 18)

6. Transition to the modern period

When did marriage, or its absence, become a preoccupation of the West Indian middle class? It would be reasonable to assume that missionary activity combined with changes in plantation organization to bring about a transformation in ideas and behaviour between, say, 1820 and 1860. Careful examination suggests that this was not the case.

New elements began to enter the colonies after 1840; new kinds of magistrates and government officials, new kinds of clergymen and teachers, and new kinds of plantation employees. However, the customs of creole society did not disappear. Writing in the 1860s Duff showed that the average life expectancy of members of the clergy in British Guiana could be measured in months rather than years, alcoholism and venereal disease contributing to this state of affairs (Duff 1866, pp. 359-61). In Jamaica there was a good deal of social ferment, culminating in the rebellion of 1865 (Robotham 1982), but social practice changed slowly. Genealogical study suggests that the upwardly mobile coloured population met the downwardly mobile remnants of the white planter class, combining with them to constitute the recent ancestors of the modern West Indian 'middle class.' Preliminary historical research strengthens this impression. The amnesia of Alexander's Jamaican middle class informants obscures some interesting developments in the second half of the nineteenth century.

Abolition suddenly erased all legal distinctions based upon race, colour or servile status. On 21 September 1834 the secretary to the Lord Bishop of Jamaica sent an order to all parishes instructing that as the whole population was now free, the same registers of births, marriages and deaths should be used for all. The *London Gazette* of Tuesday 8 September 1838 set out procedures for marriage in the colonies and it was pointed out that as there may be some doubt as to the validity of the marriages of slaves, or even of free coloured people, solemnized prior to emancipation, 'This Order-in-Council declares such marriages to be valid.' Furthermore, if people had married *de facto*, provision was now made for them to solemnize the union simply by signing a declaration (*London Gazette*, Number 19656, pp. 2004-5). There was no rush to legalize unions.[7]

Wills filed in the Jamaica Island Record Office show that the custom of open concubinage of white men and coloured women did not end with the abolition of slavery. The will of 'John Smith, a native of Scotland now residing at Cape Clear Pen in the Parish of Metcalfe' (formerly and subsequently St. Mary), and styling himself 'Planter' was entered at the Island Record Office on 22 January 1870 (JIRO Wills, Lib. 131, Folio 88). In it he leaves to Bridget French Kilkelly, now residing at Cape Clear, 'one hundred pounds sterling and one moiety or half share of my table knives, silver forks, silver spoons, furniture', etc. However, it is his 'natural daughter, Janet East, daughter of the said Bridget French Kilkelly' who is to be his residual legatee after various monetary bequests are made to nephews and nieces in Scotland and in Canada. This natural daughter is married to one Patrick East and is the mother of John Smith's grandchildren, John Slater East and Isabella East. The documents do not mention race, but it is unlikely that Bridget French Kilkelly was white. The subsequent career of John Smith's grandchildren is not known, but many coloured people of similar rural origin moved into the emergent urban, bureaucratic middle class, a class increasingly preoccupied with respectability.

[7] This contrasts with the situation in the United States immediately after emancipation as reported by Gutman. See Chapter 9 of his *The black family in slavery and freedom 1750-1925* where he provides evidence of the strong desire among ex-slaves to register marriages.

102

A pathetic will entered on 19 July 1870 illustrates the predicament of those whites who found it difficult to maintain a privileged and prestigious style of life (JIRO Lib. 131, Folio 122). William Robinson of Robin's Hall Plantation in the Parish of Manchester, Jamaica, leaves to Ann Robertson and Jane Lewis what is left of Robin's Hall 'as I have been selling off a considerable quantity.' He also notes that his horned stock, sheep, pigs and fowls are depleted by sales and theft. Then he leaves 50 acres of land to 'a Son of mine.' His child's mother, Ann Heron, 'deserves every encouragement for her kindness and attention during my sickness and at a previous Occasion when no one would give me a drink of water.'

The experience of the O'Sullivan family of Clarendon, Jamaica, is probably typical of the period. It is set out in letters and other material, entered in the 'diary' of Albinia O'Sullivan covering the years 1872 and 1873 (Institute of Jamaica Manuscript Collection MS 1604).[8] This small leather bound book contains little in the way of diary entries but many copies of letters sent and received by the daughter of John Augustus O'Sullivan of Highgate Park, Jamaica and formerly of Richins Park, Buckinghamshire, England. At one time Provost Marshal of Jamaica, owner of considerable acreage and two houses in St. Catherine, O'Sullivan (he notes that he was 'formerly called Sullivan only') died in June 1871 leaving three daughters and five sons by his late wife Jane, daughter of Sir Charles Taylor of Cothrell in County Glamorgan, Wales.

Albinia's 'diary' begins with an accurate and complete transcription of her father's will (entered JIRO, Lib. 131, Folio 202, 7 November 1871), which leaves 100 acres to each of the four younger sons and a grandson; a house and the income from a £5,000 life insurance policy to the daughters; and the residue of the estate – including pictures, books, family heirlooms, and the family great house at Highgate Park to his eldest son and heir, Augustus.

Subsequent letters reveal the plight of the family. Augustus, having taken holy orders, emigrated to Nova Scotia with his wife and children. He wrote from there urging his brothers and sisters to join him, rent a farm and make a new start.

Tell [the boys] to come to Canada. Put Pride in their pockets or leave it in a yam hill and go to work like 1000ds of others are daily doing in a few years they may be sure of having a thriving farm each of their own and a jolly wife apiece to churn butter make cheese too. I implore them not to waste their lives in Jamaica. (Letter dated 17 May 1872)

They declined this invitation, and indeed Gussie soon returned to Jamaica

[8] I have been informed that there is information on the O'Sullivan family in the March 1969 issue of *The Jamaica Journal*. Unfortunately I have not been able to obtain a copy of this issue.

with wife and children and with plans for revitalizing the old Highgate Park property – using the capital of his brothers and sisters. The problem was that the capital was insufficient; Albinia and her sisters had already been forced to sell the piano, and various other treasures, just to keep going. Brother Edward, who lived in Four Paths, was so hard up that he had to walk four miles to his office each day; Brother George was trying to make a go of cattle farming; the most successful brother lived in Richmond Park and had a steady job in business, but even he could not afford £40 or £50 a year to have his son Benji educated by a private tutor in Kingston.

No attempt has been made to find the living descendants of the O'Sullivans, but in similar cases the more energetic and successful family members moved to town, or migrated to north America, leaving behind a deteriorating property on which the remnants struggle along, having 'outside' children, and often marrying darker-skinned partners (see Craton 1978 for a discussion of cases of this kind).

7. Illegitimacy redefined as a class problem

Before about 1830 few slaves married, so that 'illegitimacy' was not a meaningful concept unless a slave had a rich father. As an integral part of the slave system illegitimacy could hardly be considered a special problem. In the approximately 150 years since the ending of slavery illegitimacy rates have remained high, and remarkably stable. Jamaica's rate, for example, has varied between 60 percent and 70 percent of live births since reliable records were first kept in the 1870s (Roberts 1957, p. 288). As Roberts shows, the rate is tied to the marriage rate, which is low. Many West Indians defer marriage until they have several children, but not just to accumulate resources for a proper ceremony. Economic determinist theories have made illegitimacy appear to be an exclusively lower class 'problem,' but many errors could have been avoided if Bishop Nuttall's statement of 1886 had been remembered. In Jamaica in the mid-1880s, an upsurge of sentiment favoured legislation to mitigate the evil of illegitimacy and check immorality.[9] Partly a colonial echo of the social purity and anti-prostitution movement in Britain (see Walkowitz 1980), nonetheless it addressed local issues. During 1885 the Governor of Jamaica received a number of petitions expressing concern over illegitimacy. One, from a conference led by Bishop Nuttall, Anglican Bishop of Jamaica, urged enactment of a law containing the following provisions:

---

[9] This was not new. As Roberts has shown (1957, pp. 251-4 and 1975, p. 133), there had been previous attempts to introduce registration of the father's name on birth certificates of illegitimate children. They had failed because too many of those fathers were prominent citizens.

1. That, so far as possible and practicable, registration be made of the father of every illegitimate child.
2. That some Public Officer in each district (to be defined) be charged with the duty of securing such registration, and be held responsible for the taking, or causing to be taken, the necessary steps preliminary to registration.
3. That among such preliminary steps should be the proving of such paternity before competent authority in all cases where such paternity is not acknowledged by the father.
4. That every mother of an illegitimate child be required, under penalty, to give information to such Officer with a view to the ultimate registration of the father of such child.
5. That it also be made the duty of such Officer to see to the strict carrying out of the Law for the maintenance of illegitimate children in every case where there is an attempt to evade the obligations imposed by that Law. (Minute signed by H.W. Norman, Governor: Institute of Jamaica Manuscript Collection MST 209, No. 13, p. 2)

The Governor declined to take action, saying the proposals were impossible to carry out in practice. Thus provoked, the Bishop wrote a pamphlet entitled 'Public Morality: An Appeal, by the Bishop of Jamaica' (IJMC, MST 209, No. 13). Replying to the Governor's Minute, Bishop Nuttall wrote:

Let no man drag into this debate questions of class and colour, or suspect this agitation of any class sympathies or antagonisms. It is a question of the social life of a whole people. It has nothing to do with class. The immoral lives of numerous Englishmen, Scotchmen, and Irishmen in Jamaica, for generations past, are quite sufficient to silence those who want to get rid of this subject by the convenient insinuation that the blame for our present condition of things rests exclusively upon them. (p. 4)

His warning was forgotten and marriage came to be associated with 'middle class' status while the lower classes were believed to have 'disorganized' family relations marked by unstable marriage and high illegitimacy rates. Middle class coloured women now became the most vocal critics of vice and immorality and staunch defenders of the sanctity of marriage.

In spite of this new found respectability the system itself did not change; there was a reallocation of positions within it. 'Outside' unions between high status men, and women of lower status, did not disappear; indeed they are an intrinsic part of present day life. The dual marriage system is not a faint memory from the past, but a living reality (R.T. Smith 1978a; 1978b; 1982a; 1984d). It affects relations within middle class families, but its full impact is felt by the lower class woman of limited means attempting to raise several children, forced to work if and when she can, and often passing through a series of unions with men as transitory as the white bookkeepers of slavery days. It is remarkable that social scientists should have adopted a different view of this system, attributing its major characteristics to poverty, adaptation, even African culture – anything in fact but its obvious relation to the class system.

8. Marriage among ex-slaves

Non-legal unions have to be seen in the context of relations between classes, and not as if they were a 'trait' of lower class culture. This does not mean that the internal relations of the ex-slave population, and the particularity of their system of kinship and marriage, was unimportant – even if it was conditioned by the hegemonic weight of creole culture.

A world peculiar to the black population – mysterious, saturated with occult power, vibrant with sexual passion, dangerous to, and impenetrable by, whites – has always been assumed to exist. Eighteenth- and nineteenth-century writers ridiculed the gullibility of blacks influenced by the Obeah man, but creoles of all colours believed in duppies and jumbies and old hag and rolling calf. The exotic world of the blacks was encapsulated within creole society, and the very blacks who spent their nights drumming and dancing, and being possessed by spirits, were often found singing from *Hymns Ancient and Modern* on Sunday morning. Black ex-slaves lived in a cultural world different from that of the whites; the question is how it differed, and why. To what extent was lower class, black culture, including the marriage system, part of a more general structure?

Guyana is particularly interesting. Conditions in the late 1830s facilitated, and even encouraged, development of the existing slave community structure. The fertile coastal area lies below the level of the sea at high tide, producing a constant danger of flooding from heavy rains. Plantations can be maintained only by large capital outlays; in the early nineteenth century that meant large amounts of labour. The abolition of slavery drove poorer plantations out of production and it became possible for groups of ex-slaves to pool their earnings, purchase abandoned plantations and try to work them communally (see R.T. Smith 1956, pp. 39-42). The holding and transmission of property in these communities tells us a great deal about kinship and its interaction with the legal system.

In the report of the Titles to Land Commissioners, referred to above (page 99), the evidence shows that communal ownership became transformed into fragmented individual holdings as the years went by, but it also shows that intergenerational transmission of land was based on the equivalence of siblings, and the rights of all children to a share in the inheritance. The villagers operated through the colony's legal system, even to regulate domestic and kinship activities, and even though they appear not to have always understood, or adhered to, the letter of the law. However, it is unwise to assume that they were creating their own version of the law. In the early 1950s, in a West Coast Berbice village community, it was common to acquire title to a piece of land by allowing the rates to fall into arrears, arranging with the village overseer for the land to be auctioned for recovery of rates, but also arranging to buy it back for a nominal sum at the Execution Sale. It was understood that one could lose the land if the sale got out of hand, but a vigilant and cooperative overseer would withdraw the lot before that happened.

It was tempting to see this as 'adaptation' by poor people taking advantage of the legal system without paying exorbitant lawyers' fees. But the practice has deep roots and was copied from the Europeans by ex-slaves. The Titles to Land Commissioners say that the root of every original title in the Dutch colonies was a grant, or Landbrief, but in the eighteenth century, instead of providing a means of transferring those grants, the Dutch allowed the holder to resign the grant and a purchaser could petition for a new grant. Eventually the notion of 'transporting' the grant from one person to another was developed, but the procedures for inheritance and division of property were less than perfect, and the method of conveyance by Execution Sale and Letters of Decree became entrenched.

Afro-Guyanese did not invent common law marriage either. Informal unions were frequent among the white settlers of Berbice, Demerara and Essequibo, both among themselves, and with black and coloured people. The extent of such unions becomes clear when the history of land holding is examined. In 1892 the commissioners explained that claims to land have been advanced by children born outside the pale of wedlock, who have not been legitimated by the subsequent marriage of their parents. Where the claim is through the mother there is little or no difficulty, but when the property of the alleged or putative father is the subject of the claim, the rule that an illegitimate child cannot succeed as '*hoeres ab intestato*' of the father, prevails.

They go on to explain that they have tried to be very lenient in their interpretation of cases because of the 'very peculiar ideas respecting marriage' which one finds in the country. Partly this is because the memory of slave days still exists when slaves were not allowed to marry legally, but:

Your Commissioners do not for an instant wish to suggest the idea that disregard of the marriage law in British Guiana is limited to any particular class of the population; unfortunately such is not the case, as Statistics would show; what they wish to point out is, that with regard to one class at least there may be some show of excuse for a practice which is generally considered and condemned as immoral. (Titles to Land Commissioners 1892, p. 18)

The point need not be laboured. West Indian ex-slaves lived in communities where kin ties were of great importance, but legal marriage was slow to take hold. There was a clear relationship between marriage and high status, and the dual marriage system persisted, but the lower classes were not expected fully to comply with the legal norms of marriage.

9. Conclusion

The historical materials presented in this chapter illustrate the points I have made, but they are not intended as a history of West Indian marriage. A few instances have been extracted from a still fragmentary record, mostly from secondary sources, to show that there was a developing, society wide system. There were many variations, within each colony and from place to place, but everyone lived in the presence of the contrast between legal marriage and concubinage, just as they lived by the contrasts of black and white, slave and free, creole and British. Those contrasts were built into the developing social and cultural systems; one escaped their influence only by leaving the West Indies, as did Elizabeth Price Nash. The preoccupation with marriage of the post-emancipation middle class is easier to understand once we know this background.

The writing of nineteenth-century West Indian social history will be a large but rewarding task. More differences will be revealed. For example, there are many differences between Guyana and Jamaica. Some of Guyana's elite coloured families originated in unions between Europeans and Africans or Indians after the 1840s, rather than during the slavery period. Guyana had many immigrants from Barbados, prominent coloured families among them. Bridget Brereton's work on late nineteenth-century Trinidad has revealed the continuing importance of the old French creole families (Brereton 1979). If we say that the major structural features appear to be the same throughout the West Indies, it means only that it is useful, for the time being, to assume that variations occur within limits set by that structure.

Indentured immigrants of Indian, Chinese, Middle Eastern and European origin are not discussed in detail in this book. Although separate publication of material on Indo-Guyanese kinship is planned, separate treatment does not imply social separation. It is often said that indentured immigrants were outside the institutional framework of creole society. Nothing could be further from the truth. Informal unions between Indian women and white overseers on Guyanese plantations were common until recently. Marriage was so unstable among Indian immigrants in the nineteenth century that it was a specific offence to 'entice away the wife of an immigrant.' Chinese immigrants were accompanied by so few Chinese women that intermarriage with Africans, or East Indians, became the

108

norm rather than the exception. Today, Indians and Chinese are fully involved in the dual marriage system.

In the next chapter marriage is discussed from the perspective of our informants, talking to us in the late 1960s and early 1970s. Observations from other studies dating back to the 1950s are drawn upon where necessary.

6

Modern marriage and other arrangements

[Weddings] not so plentiful with us you know. I couldn't tell you the last wedding I did go to. Now death and sickness, that more common and we all pull together then.

Jamaican Informant

There is a marked resemblance between the pattern of unions and residence we have examined for coloured women like Lizette Nash and her mother Eleanor Price (page 97 above), and many of our twentieth-century lower-class informants. It is fashionable to stress the African origin of the West Indian lower class and to look for the possible continuities in custom, but that can be as misleading as to imagine that slavery wiped clean the slate of history leaving nothing but anarchy, or anomie, in its trail.[1] Slave society or, more broadly, creole society, was created out of many historical traditions under definite social, economic and political circumstances, as was the society that succeeded it. The modern lower class does not exist in isolation; its most ardent collective desire is to escape from its class position. In the absence of any clearly formulated consciousness of how that class position is created, or of any viable alternative to it (despite some evidence of beginnings in that direction), one finds a curious blend of emulation of, and contempt for, the standards and values of the middle class. Class is a matter of relations within a social formation; in this case a dependent social formation. Therefore it is necessary to consider class differences in behaviour and social institutions from the point of view of the relation between these differences, and not as though classes were separate, discrete systems. In the first stage of this research informants were separated according to class. As the work proceeded, and other studies were undertaken (Austin 1974; DeVeer 1979; Fischer 1974; Parks n.d.), class boundaries became less easy to delineate but the structural contrasts which accompany class differences were seen to be pervasive –

---

[1] See Patterson 1982 for a useful discussion of the problems involved in studying structural continuities and discontinuities.

110

found in some form in all spheres of social life. This is particularly evident in the case of marriage.

1. Definitions

Definitions have been avoided so far. Marriage, as a category for cross cultural analysis, is out of favour with many anthropologists. As long ago as 1955 Leach pointed out that anthropologists generally treat a whole range of social institutions as though they were one. After listing ten different rights which a marriage might serve to establish, he says:

In no single society can marriage serve to establish all these types of right simultaneously; nor is there any one of these rights which is invariably established by marriage in every known society. (Leach 1955, p. 183)

Needham goes further, saying:

'Marriage' . . . is an odd-job word: very handy in all sorts of descriptive sentences, but worse than misleading in comparison and of no real use at all in analysis. (Needham 1971, pp. 7-8)

'Marriage' and 'kinship' are European concepts, and not even anthropologists appreciate their full meaning, as recent research has shown (see Goody 1983). They may have no counterpart at all in other societies and cultures. After providing examples of societies having no word corresponding to 'marriage,' Needham says:

One wonders, therefore, how many other societies make no lexical recognition of that institution which has so commonly been regarded in anthropology as categorically essential and universal. (Needham 1971, p. 7)

These problems of comparative analysis seem remote from the concerns of Caribbean scholars. The word 'marriage' is in constant use; it appears to be widely understood and capable of clear definition. Closer examination reveals conflicting views, even about the legal implications of marriage, and very few West Indians are familiar with the historical development of different forms of marriage contract. The word 'marriage' may be used differently by the same person on different occasions, or in different contexts. That range of meaning concerns us.

In this book 'legal marriage,' 'common law marriage,' and 'visiting union' mean, respectively, a legally contracted union, a coresidential non-legal union, and a union which is neither legal nor coresidential. It happens frequently that a person is legally married but also in a non-legal union, residential or not, with someone other than the legal spouse. To deal with such situations the census distinguishes between 'marital status' and 'union status;' one can be married under the former classification and common law or visiting under the latter (see Roberts 1975, pp. 103-37 for a fuller discussion of union types).

2. The incidence of different types of union

We have collected no genealogy in Jamaica or Guyana that does not show legal marriages, common law marriages, visiting unions and illegitimate births resulting from casual affairs. One cannot conclude that it would be impossible to find extensive genealogies on which 'irregular' unions did not occur, but this evidence shows no sharp dividing line between classes or segments with different institutionalized forms of mating. Status differences affect relations between kin. In the lower class, legal unions are distinguished from non-legal, but all West Indians recognize the entire range of forms that conjugal unions may take. The types form a coherent series in which each one is defined by contrast with the others. All West Indians understand these contrasting categories in much the same way, and share the valuation of their status ranking. All forms of mating are practised by West Indians of all classes, though frequencies vary in ways that are not easy to measure (see Roberts 1975, p. 105). For example, a prominent businessman may have a long-standing relationship with a woman of lower middle-class status – a union with wide community recognition. It is unlikely that this union would appear in answers to a questionnaire survey, no matter how carefully designed and executed. It may not be mentioned even in the multiple interviews of a genealogical study. Some of our genealogies under-represent the number of illegitimate, outside children, and the number of non-legal unions. In some cases the informant was ignorant of them; in others the information was suppressed. Where genealogies overlap, and they often do, one can be checked against the other for this kind of under-reporting. In one case a thirty-year-old man reported a group of first cousins as having one mother and father, while a genealogy collected from a female relative of his showed that they had two separate mothers. The same man seemed unaware that a first cousin's child had been born as the result of a premarital affair. On lower-class genealogies some informants are unaware of the distinction between different 'sets' of children born to the same woman; sometimes the information was suppressed in early interviews but revealed later.

The figures in Table 30 provide only a rough guide to the incidence of different types of union on the genealogies of informants of different classes. As expected, the proportion of common law and visiting unions increases as one moves from the established middle class to the lower class. Among lower-class informants and their kin the proportion of legal marriages is high, particularly in the case of current unions, or unions

TABLE 30 — TYPES OF UNIONS APPEARING ON GENEALOGIES

| | | Old Middle Class | | | | New Middle Class | | | | Lower Class | | | | All Cases | |
| | | Jamaica | | Guyana | | Jamaica | | Guyana | | Jamaica | | Guyana | | | |
		No	%	No	%	No	%	No	%	No	%	No	%	No	%
EXTANT UNIONS															
Legal	Male	738	98.8	154	96.3	276	84.4	244	92.1	949	79.9	317	80.1	2678	86.9
	Female	659	98.4	94	98.9	264	83.0	216	91.5	870	80.5	321	78.7	2424	86.3
Common Law	Male	6	0.8	5	3.1	43	13.1	17	6.4	185	15.6	59	14.9	315	10.2
	Female	4	0.6			48	15.1	17	7.2	163	15.1	61	15.0	293	10.4
Visiting	Male	3	0.4	1	0.6	8	2.4	4	1.5	53	4.5	20	5.1	89	2.9
	Female	7	1.0	1	1.1	6	1.9	3	1.3	48	4.4	26	6.4	91	3.2
TOTAL	Male	747	100.0	160	100.0	327	100.0	265	100.0	1187	100.0	396	100.0	3082	100.0
	Female	670	100.0	95	100.0	318	100.0	236	100.0	1081	100.0	408	100.0	2808	100.0
TERMINATED UNIONS															
Legal (divorced, separated and widowed)	Male	84	96.6	10	90.9	29	72.5	18	66.7	95	60.5	26	52.0	262	70.4
	Female	174	94.6	25	86.2	46	67.6	54	84.4	171	54.1	46	55.4	516	69.4
Common Law and Visiting (separated and widowed)	Male	3	3.4	1	9.1	11	27.5	9	33.3	62	39.5	24	48.0	110	29.6
	Female	10	5.4	4	13.8	22	32.4	10	15.6	145	45.9	37	44.6	228	30.6
TOTALS	Male	87	100.0	11	100.0	40	100.0	27	100.0	157	100.0	50	100.0	372	100.0
	Female	184	100.0	29	100.0	68	100.0	64	100.0	316	100.0	83	100.0	744	100.0

Note: Unknowns and those 'Never in a union' have been excluded from this table.

existing at the time of death. If terminated unions are included, the proportion of non-legal unions rises, reflecting the early experience of visiting and common law unions (see Roberts 1975, p. 128). Our 'lower-class' informants are not among the poorest of West Indians; if the sample were to be limited to the economically marginal, the proportion of non-legal unions on genealogies might be higher. This table does not relate union type to the present class status of the person in the union. It shows union types on genealogies of informants of a particular class; the people on their genealogies may span several class categories (see Chapter 4, page 47). Table 30 is not intended to be an accurate measure of union types. It does not include those who have never been in a union, for example. It does show that unions of all types occur on all genealogies; only the incidence of occurrence varies with the class origin of the informant and his kin (for a fuller discussion of union types see Roberts 1975, Chapter 4).

Things have changed since the eighteenth century, obviously. The general model of the marriage system is much the same; men marry status equals and enter into other forms of union with women of lower status, but legal marriage is now found more frequently among the lower class than any other type of union. Figure 1 shows the preponderance of legal marriage over other forms of union on all our genealogies, and the same picture emerges from other studies (R.T. Smith 1956, Roberts 1975, Clarke 1957, Blake 1961 and others). Does this mean that a culturally unified society was created when slavery was abolished? If so, why the high incidence of non-legal unions and high illegitimacy rates? If the general rule is that men enter into non-legal unions with women of inferior status, how does that rule work within the lower class? Have observers failed to see the status correlates of different types of union within the lower class, as is suggested by Martinez-Alier (1974, p. 127)? To answer some of these questions with more than the usual dependence on logical inference, it is necessary to appreciate how different unions are experienced, and how structural principles operate in social practice.

3. Love and marriage

In Europe by the early nineteenth century, personal feelings of love were thought to be prerequisite for marriage. In the West Indies there are few references to it as a necessary ingredient for keeper relationships. Captain Stedman's feelings for Joanna were unusual (page 99 above); the most common feeling between partners was that of gratitude. Today informants are quite insistent that love is the proper basis for marriage; at least, our middle-class informants attach a great deal of weight to it. Alexander has made a detailed analysis of this (Alexander 1978).

For his middle-class Jamaican informants, conjugal love is a prerequisite to, and an essential component of, marriage; it creates what they consider an involuntary commitment to diffuse, enduring solidarity – a commitment similar to that created by ideas of common substance, or blood (see Chapter 3, page 31). 'Being in love' is a part of courtship; after marriage, love may be conceptually transformed. He points out that 'one informant countered the fact that her husband had been unfaithful by the fact that he had always taken care of his family, and the last fact becomes the new criterion of love' (Alexander 1978, p. 11). When a couple is married there is a turning away from the inwardness of 'being in love' toward a more conscious stress on actions in the social and public world: on getting things done.

The weight attached to informants' ideas of romantic love derives, in part, from the analyst's stress on culture, or ideology, rather than organization. A middle-class Guyanese woman, discussing the possible reactions to marital infidelity, was asked whether a woman would feel betrayed if she discovered her husband having an affair with another woman.

MRS. B.   She might but she wouldn't show that.
QUESTIONER   What about love?
MRS. B.   I think that they make the worst marriages actually because they are so easily broken.
QUESTIONER   Why are they so easily broken?
MRS. B.   Because they are based on love which is so damned fragile.
QUESTIONER   What else can they be based on? What are the majority of West Indian marriages based on?
MRS. B.   Position – a lot of women get married just for that. (Case number 110)

There is nothing in this brief dialogue to contradict Alexander's contention that love is assumed to be a prerequisite for marriage. Mrs. Brown's marriage was not entirely happy and perhaps she was already transforming the 'love' of courtship into the actions it must express as the marriage continues. But she also stresses status considerations that may not always be recognized or acknowledged.

Ideas about romantic love are prevalent among the lower class. It could hardly be otherwise with the constant exposure to radio, television (but not in Guyana), films and such literature as comic books, women's magazines and the daily newspapers. However, the word 'love' is more often used when discussing consanguines and how they should be treated. The relationship between conjugal partners is certainly based on attraction, love, passion, emotion, but marriage has a lot of other elements. Joseph MacGregor, when asked how he met the woman who eventually became his wife, said:

Well, you know we saw each other – eyes – eyes is a thing that is very greedy. As you look on a person, the eyes and the mind work together and then you pick a chat, and from thence it grow until you court and marry. (Case number 602)

Mr. MacGregor would be the first to acknowledge the distance between 'picking a chat' and marriage. He and his wife each had several children by previous unions before they began to live together, and when they did marry it was for religious reasons – not because they were 'in love.' As he explained:

Well you see, um, to become married is a part of the law – of God. It's a part of Christianity. When a man will marry his wife, he will live more steady than to live – well, sometimes you run to this woman and you run to that woman, and sometimes you run until you run, you run into danger. So when you try one and marry and settle down, you are able to save more; you live a better life.

Lower-class informants do not use the middle-class 'myth of origin,' but certain recurrent themes in the discussion of marriage seem to be transformed versions of this myth. Marriage is associated with stability; it should lead to 'a steady life,' a 'clean life,' a life in which men renounce 'sporting' and outside women. Women are preoccupied with stability, focussing on a better domestic life and improvement for the children.

In a study based on field research Henrietta DeVeer has shown that working-class informants in May Pen, Jamaica, do not associate romantic love with marriage in the way that Alexander's informants do. Furthermore, men and women do not stress the same elements, although they agree that men are naturally prone to wander about, have many women, and lead a wild life. One of her male informants said:

I feel a woman can control their nature more than man. I just have that feeling. I mean, a woman will easier be satisfy with one man when a man can't be satisfy with one woman. Right? (DeVeer 1979, p. 108)

If a man sees a girl and falls in love with her, he can establish a relationship, become friends, lead a sweetheart life, and still retain a large measure of freedom. Freedom to come and go as he pleases, to be out on the street with his friends, and to have other women. Women recognize men's propensity to wander, but do not particularly admire it. Mrs. W. said:

Jamaicans love a whole lot of woman, you know. Lot of woman, not just one. They don't stick to one, they must have girls outside, that's just the way . . . They just love sport [laugh]. Married men, unmarried men, it don't matter. (DeVeer 1979, pp. 108-9)

When men are asked the reasons for getting married at all, they tend to equate marriage with being a Christian, leading a straight life, and submitting to control. But, as DeVeer points out, these things 'occur only at the end of a developmental process when a man has had a chance to play out all of his "natural" urges and desires; in other words, until the point when a man becomes more like a woman' (DeVeer 1979, pp. 108-9).

If men marry because they feel it is the Christian thing to do, women – in spite of their greater involvement in church activities – rarely give religion as a reason for getting married. For them it is a question of economic security and of getting help with raising children. The majority soon become disabused of the idea that marriage alters the behaviour of men, but they feel that it is in the interest of children to have married parents.

DeVeer explored particularly carefully the complex of ideas involved in the contrast between 'outside' and 'inside,' with the former standing for the world of men, their drinking, having outside women, outside children and failing to live a straight life. 'Inside' stands for the home and a stable home life, the church and being saved, legal marriage and being responsible for the home and child care. The same opposition had been identified earlier by Diane Austin (1974). Her middle and working-class urban Jamaicans apply the distinction to a wide range of class-linked factors: inside office work as opposed to outside manual labour; houses with inside plumbing and washing facilities as opposed to the outside communal facilities of yard living; being educated as opposed to being uneducated. Ultimately the distinction is one between classes, with the working class thought of as the excluded descendants of slaves. Many of Austin's working-class informants had a myth of origin similar to the one described by Alexander (Chapter 5, page 82), but the myth is transformed, putting them in relation not only to the primordial 'white planter' ancestor, but also to the legitimate, inside, descent lines of the middle class (see Austin 1979, pp. 500-2; also pp. 123-4 below).

4. Middle-class marriage and outside unions

The theme of male 'irresponsibility' in marriage and fatherhood is insistent and recurrent in modern West Indian social life. Attention is focussed on lower-class men and the remarkably high illegitimacy rates. It is mildly surprising to find the same theme running through interviews with middle-class informants as they discuss the particularities of their own kin. Even where men appear to be devoted husbands and fathers the same issue quickly surfaces. During her first interview Mrs. Sears misunderstood the probe for information on 'miscellaneous relatives'.

I know what you mean. No, my father is one of those unusual Jamaicans who had no illegitimate children . . . its the done thing, because the Williams set [two of her mother's sisters married to two Williams brothers], their father had two or three children before he was married . . . you'll find that this happened in nine times out of ten . . . the mother is usually a person in the lower social strata. And these children are schooled, but they're not brought into the home. (Case number 206)

A fair-skinned woman of impeccable middle-class origins, Mrs. Sears provided an extensive genealogy on which a large number of men had outside children. The treatment of these children varied in interesting ways. The two children of her mother's sister's husband were not given any special consideration by the father. They were raised wholly by their mother and entered lowly occupations. The son 'was kept uneducated, and his occupation, he was a fisherman. And he never got married. He just lived with somebody and had children. That is very much the pattern.' But just as in slavery days, an outside union with a wealthy man can bring material rewards. One of Mrs. Sears' uncles married a woman who was the outside child of a prominent landowner.

I'll tell you something interesting. She is an illegitimate daughter of one of the Joneses . . . During the days when the lord of the estate would have children by their maids – I think she was a product of that. And probably that is why there was some objection at the time of the marriage to James.

Objection or not, she made a good marriage. Her father had sent his illegitimate children to good schools, and her fair-skinned mother was a high class maid in a rich household. Mrs. Sears grew up calling this woman 'Mrs. Rogers' rather than the more familiar 'Auntie,' probably because of the objections to her origin. Mrs. Rogers inherited several valuable pieces of furniture when her father died and she made these the focus of her household.

Similar divergent fortunes are found in our Guyana cases. Mrs. Esther Brown's grandfathers were pillars of respectability; both had outside unions and outside children. The maternal grandfather acquired a lady friend only after his children were grown up and he had sold the large family house, replacing it with a series of smaller ones – for his wife, each of his married children, and his mistress. He was seventy-three years old when his outside son was born. The other grandfather had five children with his outside lady, their birth paralleling that of his legitimate children. He often fathered two in one year; one outside and one inside. The children of both grandfathers received an adequate middle-class education and are now fully accepted as part of Mrs. Brown's family circle.

James Murray lived in a part of Georgetown, Guyana, reputed to be the most squalid, dirty, dangerous and poverty stricken of several depressed sections (case number 103). Aged fifty-five at the time he was interviewed, he and his wife had been living in the same two-room apartment, in a yard containing ten such apartments, for the past eighteen years. Employed in a menial and poorly paid job he was very conscious of his mixed racial background, and was one of the few Guyanese to mention descent from a white planter.

118

Well let me tell you about the Murrays! My great-great-grandfather was the Honourable James Murray. He had slaves and many of them took the name of Murray. He had a negro slave woman. My great-grandfather was Dr. Peter Ross Murray, the first coloured doctor in British Guiana. My grandfather had slaves and they married all kinds. My father used to humiliate the darker ones because they would not pull their weight. My mother was Campbell. I understand that we are relatives to the Campbells but I don't know where they came from though they were white . . . At my father's funeral the Campbells stood at the side of the road and looked on. In fact the black section of my family was never liked by the red. Even at funerals the fair ones never had anything to do with the black ones.

Although James Murray was not himself an outside child, in class terms he is outside, and his discussion of kinship is laced with judgements contrasting the treatment given to higher status people with that experienced by the less fortunate. He is not without his own prejudices against the less fortunate. Speaking of his sister's son who had migrated to England and not bothered to write, he said that 'he too beat the tiger's track.' Asked what that meant, he said, 'He became polluted like all of them with the same wicked mind because the ego is still there; that wildness is still there. The negro's mind, crude and savage, men of the jungle.'

The genealogy of Wagner, a middle-class Jamaican living in Kingston, shows the divergence of legitimate and illegitimate lines, and their association with colour (see Alexander 1976, p. 18). This complicated case would make an interesting monograph in itself, were it not for the need to maintain confidentiality. The names, some occupations and other identifying facts have been altered, without reducing the significance of the case.

Wagner's genealogy begins with two brothers who migrated from Germany in the 1860s or 1870s. According to family tradition they were sent by a merchant uncle to work with a German import firm in Jamaica, probably to avoid military conscription. They purchased an extensive property in a remote, inaccessible, hilly part of the country. The growth of the banana industry and the expansion of the railway line at the end of the nineteenth century must have increased the value of the land considerably. The Wagners joined the ranks of the class of small planters, many of them white but increasingly intermarrying with the coloured population. In this particular part of Jamaica, development of the banana industry provided mobility opportunities for black farmers as well as coloured and white, so that the population was quite differentiated and did not fit the stereotyped image of the extremely rich planter superimposed upon a huge, impoverished rural proletariat. However, colour distinctions remained important and Wagner's ancestors attempted to maintain their status as a white family.

Wagner's father's father married a woman who, according to our informant, belonged to an English landowning family long resident in Jamaica, and who had been slave owners. Significantly, he added that this family is 'all mixed up now, they're all very coloured' (Alexander 1976, p. 30). Wagner's father's father married twice. His first wife, and mother of Wagner's father, was a Miss O'Brien, who died when her son was only fourteen. Although Wagner identifies her as being Irish, he also adds that she was 'a little coloured.' After her death Wagner's father's father married again, to a Jamaican of Irish extraction once more. This woman gave birth to two children, both of whom settled in California in the 1930s. Their mother joined them there in 1948 and Wagner has lost touch with them. They are among many of Wagner's relatives who migrated from Jamaica, settling mostly in the United States and Canada, with only a few in England, Central America and other parts of the Caribbean. Looking at the overall picture presented by Wagner's genealogy one can say that the sections of the kindred who have remained (or become) white, have done so by leaving Jamaica. Of those who stayed, most have become coloured through intermarriage, and in the countryside, around the old family property, the family has become increasingly black. As Wagner points out, in that district the people who show evidence of mixed racial descent are probably related to the Wagners – through outside unions. Many pockets of fair-skinned people are to be found in the remote hill areas of the northern parishes, usually explaining that they are descendants of some small planter who lived there in the past. The Wagner family history is not unusual.

Wagner's father married his own first cousin – his father's sister's daughter. His father's sister had married a Jamaican of Welsh descent, but at least one quarter coloured; the daughter of this couple became Wagner's mother. She had three children before they separated, and subsequently divorced. Wagner's father married two other women, both much darker than his first wife. He still lives in the country and runs a small plantation, but not the old family property. That has been subdivided over the years, with some of it being sold in parcels, some divided among heirs, and some new sections have been added through purchase. The exact disposition of the various parts of the property is complex, but the two senior male members of the old Wagner family, still resident on the property, are rapidly sliding down the status scale. They drink heavily and behave more like 'cultivators' than old time planters. Both have outside children by black women and one of them has married a black woman. Albert, our informant's father's father's brother's son, lives in the house built by one of the original German immigrant brothers. He has never married but has two children by a maid, with whom he subsequently lived, and an uncounted number of outside children in the neighbourhood. The section of the property on which he now lives is not very large, but he and another cousin manage such pieces as are still owned by family members living in Kingston or abroad. Thus Wagner's genealogy spans a spectrum of place, race and status stretching from the increasingly black rural area through the brown-skinned middle-class Kingston dwellers to the mostly white inhabitants of the United States and Canada.

5. Factors affecting middle-class marriage

What factors are considered important by middle-class informants when they contemplate marriage? Mrs. Brown mentioned 'position' as being a major consideration (page 115 above), while Alexander has provided a lengthy analysis of 'love' as a prerequisite (page 40 above). Mrs. Sears, an informant encountered already (page 118), mentioned a series of other things.

We naturally would like our children to marry people like ourselves, similar background and education, but what if she turns up with a boy who isn't? The only thing I think that I would – what would hurt me most, is that if the boy, I don't care what nationality or what colour he is, I only ask that he be, have a similar background and home and, um, education . . . the thing that would hurt me most is, say, if she went and married somebody, well say the gardener boy, with whom there could be so little in common . . . But I have to think through the other differences and put them in their proper perspective. They really don't matter.

The 'other differences' to which she refers turn out to be race.

One of my sisters married a very black man. And when I was growing up at a very impressionable age, this happened. And it was one of the reasons my father objected to the marriage . . . One of the reasons . . . but as you grow up you have to think these things through for yourself . . . it's not important really if a fellow is from a good home, well educated, and in every way could make her an admirable husband.

In point of fact her sister became an outcast in the family, even though her husband was financially and occupationally the equal of other men in her family.

Race, or colour, is not the only factor provoking disapproval. A male family member married a woman from the same town who was no darker in colour than Mrs. Sears; her shortcoming was that she did not belong to the same social circle. Mrs. Sears, in discussing the choice of a husband for her daughter, continually posed her own views against those which she thought would have been operative in her parents' generation. This was characteristic of many informants. Things are changing and colour, in itself, should no longer be a criterion of social acceptability. Similarly, it is narrow minded to object on religious grounds; the person should come from a religious home but the religion itself should not matter – provided it is not one of 'the spurious sects.' (The idea of a religion other than Christianity did not cross her mind, apparently.) It should not be the Jehovah's Witnesses for example, or one of the Jamaican revivalist sects, because 'if he were a sensible, educated boy this sort of thing would not appeal to him.' It is interesting that her mother found something objectionable in every potential spouse presented by her children.

Although the paradigmatic case of the outside union is that where a man has an affair with a woman of lower status, the incidence of premarital pregnancy among women on some middle-class genealogies was fairly high. On Mrs. Brown's genealogy there were many cases of young, middle-class women having babies that were looked after by other family members; cases of covering up premarital pregnancy by sending the girl abroad; and cases where the child is just accepted into the girl's family of orientation until she marries. All informants suggested that premarital pregnancy affects the chances of making a good marriage, but in practice it seems to make very little difference. Middle-class women who had illegitimate children married men with good occupations. These pregnancies were youthful errors; the result of affairs where the father was of the same class background. Sometimes a marriage would result, but if the child were born illegitimate it would be brought up in a middle-class milieu, acquiring all the benefits of its class, including the all-important 'good' education.

6. Making progress: the new middle class

For almost thirty years, between 1940 and the late 1960s, the West Indies experienced sustained economic growth. Although structural changes in the West Indian economy were not extensive, there was a marked expansion of the middle class, into new bureaucratic, sales and similar occupations. The urban working class grew at an unprecedented rate, with new opportunities for skilled tradesmen, lower level clerical and sales workers, police, nurses, and the like. The primary beneficiaries of this expansion were the children of urban artisans, skilled workers and small, independent farmers. These groups were best situated to take advantage of the educational reforms instituted by successive post-war governments, and to share in the worldwide economic boom. Prior to the 1940s the only escape from manual labour for such children would have been entry to primary school teaching, or perhaps the police. Now they can, or could until the economic down-turn of the 1970s, enter a wide range of occupations. Banks and stores that previously employed only white or fair-skinned people now have blacks in prominent positions. The establishment and expansion of the Universities of the West Indies and of Guyana, coupled with the increased number and widened intake of secondary schools, has done much to break the monopoly of higher education once held by the coloured middle class. In turn, higher education, rather than tion, rather than family connection, has become the key to entry to the civil service and the professions.

The genealogies of informants who were upwardly mobile into middle-class occupations show a higher proportion of non-legal unions than do those born into the middle class, as we saw in Table 30 (page 113). They also tend to have slightly smaller genealogies, perhaps due to their higher degree of geographical and social mobility. Lower-class informants sometimes express resentment against kinsmen who have done well economically and who begin to 'play poor great,' as they say. It is among people moving out of the lower class, sometimes moving from rural areas into the city, that we should expect to find a turning inward of the nuclear family if theories derived from Europe and north America were applicable; toward creating a 'haven in a heartless world' (see Lasch 1977). No such tendencies could be found. Diane Austin has drawn a vivid contrast between Selton Town, a working-class area of Kingston, Jamaica, and Vermount, one of the new middle-class housing developments ringing the city.

If life in Selton Town presents an example of the outside life of streets and tenement yards, life in Vermount presents the first steps which might be taken by the sufficiently affluent to change this life to a more privileged existence; to move from an externalized to an inside life of domestic facilities within the house, of private yards and private transport, of clerical employment and commercial transactions in glass fronted shops and offices. (Austin 1984, p. 59)

Brodber has contrasted 'communal yards' in Kingston, and the government tenements and housing schemes that also represent a step up to what she calls 'family yards' (Brodber 1975). Here the transition is within the lower class, but the opposition is similarly structured. Most of these couples are in common law unions rather than being married, but they also strive to improve status through the education of children, getting better jobs, participating in church activities. According to Brodber these families feel themselves to be on the verge of becoming middle class, and they yearn for a 'home where their children can run free' (Brodber 1975, pp. 34-5). The contrast has slightly different content and the people are lower in the occupational class scale; the structure is the same.

In Austin's middle-class area, Vermount, houses are built to a typically middle-class design. Each has a 'car-port,' (essential for what Gordon Lewis has, somewhere, called 'a motorized salariat'), hot and cold running water, inside bathroom and kitchen and an outside shower and toilet for the use of a domestic servant. The design, marketing and financing of houses in these developments is predicated on the assumption that they will be occupied by small nuclear families with a regular income. The people who live here see it as a place where one can lead a private, family-centred life very different from the open street life of neighbourhoods like Selton Town, but only a few families match the image of the isolated nuclear family. More typical is the household of a couple we can call Mr. and Mrs. Green.

As Austin describes it, the household consists of husband and wife, both of whom work, and their two teenage children; a boy and a girl. At first glance a standard nuclear family. But there is also a paying boarder, daughter of a woman who is a live-in maid in an affluent household. This girl is attending the Vermount High School. Another girl, from the rural district where Mr. and Mrs. Green were born, is a resident 'helper.' Unlike many middle-class households where the domestic servant maintains a considerable social distance from the employers, this girl lives as part of the family, sleeping in the same room as the daughter and the boarder, who share one bed. The house is not elaborately furnished and most activities, such as eating, cooking, washing clothes and dishes, or just sitting around talking, take place on the back verandah which has been extended for just that purpose.

The activities of the members of this household are closely bound up with those of friends and neighbours. There is a constant procession of neighbourhood children through the house; meat is stored in the refrigerator of a neighbour who has a more efficient freezer section; when the floor has to be polished for a big occasion another neighbour lends her electric floor polisher; the family have a car and when they drive into town for work in the mornings they give rides to other neighbours. Husband and wife have clearly separated activities and spend little time together. Mrs. Green often works late, but in any case Mr. Green spends every evening with friends in a nearby bar. If Mrs. Green gets home in time she will watch television, or visit women friends along the street. This is not an isolated nuclear family. It may be that isolated nuclear families do not exist anywhere, but that is a different issue (see Seeley, Sim and Loosely 1956 for an interesting discussion of nuclear families in an upper middle class Toronto suburb).

Although Vermount is 'middle class,' many elements of 'yard life' appear. Some houses in Vermount are occupied by renters, sometimes by more than one household. The Greens are upwardly mobile, doing everything possible to provide their children with the means for further mobility, but their married life shows a high degree of segregation of activities quite unlike the 'joint' pattern described by Bott (1957).

One of Alexander's best informants, Mr. A. Benton (case number 251), has been able to move into the middle class through teaching, and his life is bound up with the church. Both he and his wife are teachers, both were born in the rural areas, both were illegitimate and did not know their fathers beyond casual contact, and both were raised by maternal grandmothers, at least until adolescence. Mr. Benton's first job was as a motor mechanic's helper, and only good fortune enabled him to get a start in teaching. The Bentons are self-consciously dedicated to making a successful family environment for their eight children. All have been to secondary school, and are thus qualified for entry into the Jamaican middle class. The idea of 'being in love' is not a dominant theme in the Bentons' discussion of marriage. Mr. Benton says that he was shy and reserved until he was about nineteen years old.

Like everyone else I always wished that I would marry, you know, when I found the right kind of person, and have – you know – my own family, and perhaps make up, ahm, make up for those things which I personally didn't have . . . when it came to girls, although I always enjoyed their company and talked with them and so on, I had a certain sense of shyness.

He then talked about how he got to know fellow teachers when he was at teacher training college, and how, because he did well in his work there, he began to feel that he had overcome some of the disadvantages of his background. He was posted to a rural school where he made himself popular with people through his manner, his efficiency, and activities such as singing in the church choir and at concerts.

It was during this time that I became acquainted with my wife, and ahm, she, we met in a teachers' association. That's how we first met, and then ahm I didn't, it was perhaps six months later that I began to seriously think about her as a possible partner, you know, and I, eventually we had a short courtship, got married.

Perhaps it is because he is talking about events that occurred thirty years previously, but the whole tenor of the narrative suggests careful consideration rather than 'falling in love,' even though the Bentons share the assumption that marriage must be based on love and respect for each other.

   Mrs. Benton is even less romantic in her recall of the decision to get married.

When we got married I said look – I personally, I suppose he was more anxious to get married than I was to him. In fact at the time I was really interested in somebody else. Yes, that's true, that's being frank. And um, I didn't want to marry a teacher because I started out teaching and um the pattern I saw of a teacher and his wife who taught, um, didn't present itself a very favourable picture to me, you see.

She explained how she tried to discourage Benton, giving him a list of things that she did not want in a marriage: having a teacher for a husband; having in-laws living with them; having any of his outside children living with them, though he would be free to support them (so far as we know he did not have any); having to teach in Sunday School just because her husband was headmaster and a lay preacher; and so on. In spite of all this 'he was insistent and eventually I gave in and decided to get married.'

Judging by the extensive interview transcripts, the Bentons' married life has been a constant struggle to provide a proper middle-class upbringing for their eight children. Apart from some short intervals, Mrs. Benton has worked, but they had to resort to economies and supplementary money-making activities in order to make ends meet, find money for school fees, books, the right clothes, and so on. In some ways their married life has been a model of conjugal cooperation and domestic devotion – a pattern more frequent in the West Indies than is generally acknowledged. Mrs. Benton pointed out that in certain parishes of Jamaica where there is a tradition of independent small farming, children are generally pushed to do well in school. Teachers often make extra money coaching for examinations after regular school hours. She is referring to the rural, church-based, lower middle class (or upper lower class) that has been so important in the development of Jamaica, and from which many members of the teaching profession and the lower civil service have come. (To call this class 'the peasantry' is uninformative, and generally misleading.) The Bentons' family backgrounds are not the kind that they themselves would consider to be stable, but they are solidly rooted in this rural, church-based tradition, and are almost exaggeratedly respectable.

Perhaps because of their own backgrounds they are concerned about the Jamaican system of marriage. Mrs. Benton gratuitously mentioned outside children in her list of requirements for marriage. Mr. Benton explained at length the tendency for Jamaican children to disparage and belittle the father.

I have found that very often young people tend to have – young people who are progressing toward adulthood, they tend to regard their father as just a convenience . . . and this kind of general attitude makes it difficult for the father to play his role properly . . . and it also seems to me this way, that very often, ah women who are grown up in homes where they didn't have a father – I mean they didn't you know receive the care and protection of a father in a definite way – they seem to grow up without understanding the true role of the father in the home and ahm sometimes they tend, I think, to believe that everything should revolve around them.

He and his wife 'worked out a plan' to prevent this. But he was always conscious of the tendency to a matrifocal bias in the internal family relationships, a bias which he sees deriving ultimately from men.

Some of these fathers are, well, like mine, they don't live with their children, sometimes they see them, every two weeks they bring them money if they are, you know, born in concubinage, they bring some money to give him this week, and for the next five weeks you don't see them, so . . . now this aspect is something that has been a worry to me since I became conscious of the fact that I have striven as much as I could to, ahm, to make sure that my children, ahm, at least do not have cause to disparage me.

126

Benton probably talks about this carefully planned, orderly, religiously based family life from the pulpit in his role as a lay preacher. It is exactly what lower-class informants have in mind when they contrast it with the 'loose,' 'dirty,' 'careless,' 'up and down' life that is more commonly experienced. For Benton it is a contrast; a contrast with the life his mother led, that his half brother now leads, that he himself has been tempted into on occasion and that some of his children could easily fall into. The contrast is not built out of Benton's personal experience; it is an integral part of Caribbean culture, brought to a very sharp focus in the consciousness of the upwardly mobile.

7. The up and down life of the lower class

In studies of social class, part of a wider programme of research that includes this kinship study,[2] West Indian informants generally see their society consisting of two or three sections: the sufferers and the opposite sets; the big shots and we the poorer people; the rich, the comfortable and the sufferers. Consistently, whatever wording they use, they refer to a sharp dividing line between those who are regularly employed, with a good salary and the ability to buy what they want without having to think twice about it, and those who are economically insecure, have to struggle to make ends meet and are therefore unable to command respect. Economic criteria are not the only indicators of class – any informant can produce a series of other factors – but for those without a steady income, poverty and powerlessness dominate their view of society.

Lower-class people live in circumstances as varied as those of the middle class. Some are regularly employed or have enough land to provide a steady income, but this does not, in itself, set them apart as a distinct set of families. People with steady incomes or more land find themselves involved in networks of relationship with those less well placed; men may spread their income over several households, while women engage in extensive exchange and helping networks. A stable, dependable income does not necessarily become the basis of a single, nuclear family budget. We saw that lower-class women (and men) often contrast an 'up and down life' with a more desirable, orderly, planned existence in which Christian marriage, a stable home life, church membership and a better future for the children, all constitute parts of a single complex. The contrast is not made as an abstract view of what is wrong compared to what is actually done, implying a norm occasionally violated, or even a 'value stretch.' It is

---

[2] These studies include a survey of factors affecting social mobility in Guyana, and various studies in Jamaica. See R.T. Smith 1978a, 1978b, 1982b, 1984b, 1984d; Graham and Gordon 1977; Austin 1974, 1979, 1984; Robotham 1970; Fischer 1969, 1974; Foner 1973; DeVeer 1979; Prindle 1975.

a contrast between two normally occurring modes of action. The contrast has been a source of confusion for anthropologists focussing on the individual who is, supposedly, trying to reconcile social values with difficult situations. It is more productive to set aside the issue of deviance and ask how different types of union (or more general patterns of behaviour) operate in lower-class contexts.

Elizabeth David, a twenty seven year old Jamaican woman, mother of three children, lives with her common law husband as part of a complex household of twelve people (case number 401). The household includes Miss David's father aged fifty-five, her father's mother, aged seventy-six, her brother, her father's brother's son, and the three children of her father's sister's daughter. Miss David's view of the class system of Jamaica was very simple. White people and Chinese are in the top class, civil servants in the middle, and poor negroes like herself comprise the most numerous part of the population. Her father is a plumber, though he seems to get jobs infrequently and was at home a good deal during the day. Miss David's mother died when she was very young and she was raised by her father's mother.

Speaking of her common law husband Miss David suggested that although 'ah really ent married as yet, . . . you will still have to say 'mi husband'.' However, she never referred to him in that way again. She always said 'the children's father' and when asked about his relatives she was quite emphatic that 'them is the children's relatives really, I don't know them names but he have five sisters and five brothers, all Roberts [her common- law husband's name]. I know that they all Roberts. His mother alive, which is the children's grandmother, but me can't say what she name. Hey, Jill, whey yuh grandmother name?' (calling to her eleven-year-old daughter). She has known her children's father for eleven years, and lived with him for about eight, but obviously she does not think of him as part of her family, nor for that matter does she have a very close personal relationship with him. She makes a point of the fact that he is the father of all her children; she had boy friends but he was the first man in whom she was 'really interested' and he visited her at home from the time she was about sixteen. At first she had to hide from her father 'to do it' but when he saw that she was determined he reconciled himself to the match. Gradually the visiting relationship turned into a more permanent arrangement and the father of her children moved in with her. There are several buildings on the lot; she lives in the old wooden house with her 'husband' and children, while her father lives in a new concrete block cottage with his mother and sundry other relatives. She looks after her husband's food and clothing, but she also cooks for her father and her brother and insists that 'we all live as one.'

According to Miss David, being intimate friends (her phrase) with

128

someone must involve economic support on one side and the provision of cooking, washing and sexual relations on the other. When asked whether it is better to live together or be married, she acknowledged that 'to get married is the best,' but went on to explain that:

Yuh can't marry a girl and have her in her parent's house. Yuh can't marry a girl and have her living with her parents still. If you marry her you must put her in a home, whether yuh goin rent a house, or have a house, or you have a home, but ah mean you can't marry a girl and have her still livin in her parent's house. You think that wise? Ah mean, some people say that it doesn't take money but is not true. Yuh can't marry without money, man, yuh can't marry without money.

For herself she says that she has it in mind to get married but they are not actually planning it at present.

For Miss David, marriage is something that might be desirable but its absence is a matter for neither regret nor shame. She has an extremely stable union with the father of her children and she is expecting another child by him. She is also firmly embedded in her own family. Three men contribute to the expenses of this household, not counting the assistance which her father's mother gets from her other children, and the money that comes in for support of children who are being cared for there. The houses and land will, almost certainly, become 'family land' when the older people die, and Elizabeth David will almost certainly continue to live there no matter what she decides to do about getting married. It is difficult to imagine that legalization of the union would provide any greater economic security for this woman; the decision to marry is usually made for religious reasons, for the sake of the children – particularly if they are in a position to go to high school, or if they have to get a passport – and for generalized community status. The marriage of the parents does not make a significant difference to the children's chances in school, but it is believed to do so if it is part of a general increase in 'steadiness' and economic well-being.

Increasing age does not always lead to the legalization of unions. A rural Guyanese couple had lived together for over forty years, and had eleven children and a large number of grandchildren. A well-known rice farmer, this man, over the course of a long and vigorous life, fathered many outside children as well as the eleven living and four dead borne by Miss Clarice. She had two other children born before she took up with Papa John. Only after he had a stroke, and became bed-ridden at the age of seventy-three, did he offer to marry her. She refused point blank, with a few choice expletives about what he could do with his ring.

Alexander has argued that lower-class West Indians are less concerned about male marginality in domestic life than are the middle class, mainly because the long term development of the middle-class family depends upon the earning power of the husband father (Alexander 1977). It is true that the conditions of lower-class life, with unstable employment, marginal

129

farming possibilities, and few avenues for upward social mobility, make it difficult to build a stable domestic unit upon the earnings of a single husband father. Domestic relations must adjust to occupational uncertainty and diffuse income but marriage and kinship ties are not shaped directly by these functional considerations. The same concerns that underlie middle-class attitudes to marriage can be found in the discussions of lower-class informants, though they are given a different emphasis.

Nancy Rogers is fifty-two years old and lives in a rented apartment in a house that contains three other tenants (case number 307). The rundown house is in an old middle-class area of Kingston, Jamaica, where property values are declining as families move out into 'better' neighbourhoods. Nancy Rogers is not middle class. Her main income comes from hairdressing, which she does at home, and from sewing. Her adult children give her money from time to time. The other tenants are domestic servants and skilled tradesmen; Nancy Rogers' own sons are skilled workers. One is a storekeeper in a large garage, and one is a watchmaker. Her daughter is a rural schoolteacher. The youngest son, Ronald, is married to a woman who is a typist. The occupational environment in which she lives is 'working class.' In a census enumeration she would be listed as sole occupant of this apartment, but her eldest son (who is twenty-four) eats there regularly. He has a room of his own in a nearby house where he sleeps, but he also spends time with the mother of his children, Babsie, who has her own place.

Nancy Rogers was born in the country. Because her parents died when she was young she was raised by her father's father's sister, Aunt Alice. Her father was the outside child of a schoolteacher, and Nancy Rogers maintains that her parents were 'people of position in the country. Father owned plenty, plenty acres, also cows and other animals.' Both parents were humble, but she knew that they had worked themselves up to a high position because on her birth registration slip her father was listed as 'planter' and not 'cultivator.' Mrs. Rogers' preoccupation with status came out in other ways, particularly in relation to marriage.

Aunt Ellie, that's my grannie, she had a sister named Grace who married a man named Rawlings – he was a clear man [i.e. light-skinned]. So her children came out with good quality. Then two girls married to Chinese. So those children come out good. They clear and they have tall [long], straight hair. My grannie did have flat mind. She live in the bush there and just like pure black nigger man. So that's why we don't have better quality. But the sister did live in the bush too, and she choose good man. So her children come out with quality. Aunt Ellie did have flat mind man; she just go, go so with any black man. And I hear she have good quality. You know, those dark people who look like Indian? She had soft hair, cool skin and slight body. So my grandaunt told me.

It was rather surprising to find such a preoccupation with marriage – legal or non-legal – as a means of self-improvement, but Mrs. Rogers was quite vehement about the need for care in choosing a partner. She kept coming back to Aunt Ellie's lack of ambition – her 'flat mind.'

She never have any taste man. She didn't go any place where she could meet a good somebody. I don't think she did know Kingston. She just live and dead same place where she born and grow. But the sister did stay same place and get a good somebody. All the same though, my grandfather was a teacher although he was black. So my father came with good sense. But he was poor you see. It was when they were young, and it was a tief thing. Then she got pregnant for him with my father, but he was still at College. They were young you know, and he wasn't a teacher yet so he couldn't help her.

So Aunt Ellie, for all her flat mind, had her moment of ambition in having a teacher's outside child, even though the man was black. Nancy Rogers' preoccupations are very like those of Mrs. Sears discussed earlier (page 121), though Mrs. Sears was concerned with the possibility of falling away from middle-class standards, while Mrs. Rogers wants to move up. When the interviewer asked what she meant by a 'good quality man' she went on:

Yes, don't you know what I mean? She didn't look out for a man who could help up how her children come out. Right? Take all my father sister, Janice. Now her father was a next black man. Then Janice come same way. No ambition. She get up and gone married one ordinary black man too. No one coarse black man? Then they have a whole tribe of children, and they coarse and black same way. . . . Janice could a get a better man for she not bad looking. They say she want to resemble the mother, so you see is not say she was ugly that she have to tek what come. Now those children can't come to anything. They not so black; they kind of clearish like, but them face broad out (pointing to her nose), and they squat like – same like him. They have no refinement. If she wasn't so low bite and choose better man, she could have more upstanding children. She could a choose a man to mek them come out brighter and good looking.

At this point she stood up and with arms akimbo, told the young, attractive, unmarried, female interviewer:

you young people think you know plenty, but you don't know everything. You open your ears and listen, for this is a fact. You have to choose a man who can give you children good colour, and make them brighter than you and, more upstanding. If you come from black and go married black again, they no going improve. I not saying you must marry for the sake of colour alone, for there are plenty good black men – teachers and doctors and so on. They have good education, so the children born with more sense and refinement. You have to choose a husband carefully. You can't pick up any ordinary black man without anything, for you children won't come to anything. Janice's children won't come to anything, for they can't help themselves; and the husband – he don't know one thing that can help anybody.

Here she sat down again, and after all this one might have expected that she would reveal what an excellent marriage she had made for herself.

Now my husband. He was darker than me, but he had soft hair; he had sense too.

131

Then he work hard for the children, and encourage them. Now they not so badly off.

Why then did they separate? Her husband had been a policeman, but he went to England in 1957 and there he worked as a labourer. For some time before he went to England they had been living in separate houses.

He was a wild man like, he love plenty women. You know, a real police. Now I can't swallow that. I must be the only fowl in the roost. From when Ronnie was a baby I walk out and took apartment. Then after a little while he come to me and ask me to come back. But he couldn't behave himself. So one day I just pack up my things and take Ronnie and gone. But he was a nice man you know. He never treat me bad or so; you know some men like to beat up their wives. He treat me good and give me money regular; only that one fault he had, and we couldn't agree over it. So I just decide to move out. And why I really move too is because of Ronnie. If it was me one, maybe I would a stay . . . and we get on fine like that you know. He come and look for us every week, sometimes all twice and three times for the week. He bring money and give me, all help with rent, and with Ronnie too . . . He was wild you know, but he had kind spirit . . . I miss him when he die! I sibble down to nothing, till I had to catch up on meself before I take sick. He was really kind: one sensible man.

Mrs. Rogers was visibly moved when she remembered her dead husband, even though she had not seen him for eleven years and he had been dead for four. But, as in the case of Elizabeth David, she knew almost nothing about his family. She had met one sister, and heard him talk about two brothers, but all she knew about her husband's mother was that she lived in a certain community at the other end of the island.

It was not necessary to infer that Mrs. Rogers was ambitious; she proclaimed it on many occasions. It was not until the fourth interview she revealed that of her three children, the first two were not her husband's.

I have the first two when I was young; when I was sixteen I have Joan . . . Is a man named Gordon fall me. [She pleaded not to have this man's name appear on the genealogy; and of course this is not his real name]. He was quite an upstanding man, you know. But I have them too young. Then I came to Kingston and rest myself, and I didn't see anybody I like you know. Then I met my husband now, and we get married.

Her first two children were taken in by their father's family who raised them. We referred to Mrs. Rogers earlier as being 'working class,' perhaps to indicate in a tentative way that indeed she is ambitious; that she has aspirations for her children and for herself, and to some extent they have been realized. This is a useful distinction for some purposes, but firm lines cannot be drawn within the lower class, for reasons which have been stated already (page 127 above). But in moving down the status scale is there a level where the reference points change? A point at which a new stability emerges, unaffected by the dynamics of class interaction though perhaps determined by class position? Is Aunt Ellie's 'flat mind' characteristic of a much greater body of people who do not care about status, or if they do, are so discouraged that they rest tranquil in a different way of life? The evidence is to the contrary.

Censuses and surveys, when used uncritically, create an impression of discrete populations each with its own institutions. Case studies restore the living texture of social reality, revealing that even the poorest and most socially despised people retain the desire for, and the capacity to achieve, what they see as a 'clean,' 'orderly' and 'religious' life in which marriage is a central symbol. Legal marriage occurs less frequently as one goes down the class hierarchy, or as the previously cited informant said, weddings are 'not so plentiful with us,' but this has to be considered from points of view, and in contexts of action, other than the purely economic. Those other points of view, and contexts of action, are considered in the next two chapters.

7

Sex role differentiation

The sexual division of labor is nothing else than a device to institute a reciprocal state of dependency between the sexes.

Lévi-Strauss 1956

Sex role differentiation is a cultural recognition that males and females differ, but also unite to create what neither can produce alone. They are separate but cannot properly exist without each other; different but complementary; integral parts of a larger totality. In all societies these differences extend to social activity. This division of labour by sex is so pervasive, and seemingly 'natural,' that it is often taken for granted and assumed to be an inevitable consequence of physical difference. Only when dramatic inversions of normal sex roles occur is normality itself reconsidered. But 'normal' behaviour also varies between societies, and even between groups within the same society. It is now widely recognized that sexual differences impose few limits on behaviour. Sex roles are culturally constituted.

West Indians have specific ideas about the behaviour appropriate to males and females at various stages of the life cycle, at various positions within the social hierarchy, and within the occupational system. The distinctive features of sexuality are clear and unequivocal because they are physical rather than social; they do not vary from class to class, race to race, or at various stages of an individual's life cycle. Males and females are readily distinguished by the presence of male or female sexual organs, and it is by reference to these distinctive features that the sex of each individual is established at birth. Sex role is not the same thing as physical sex, any more than kinship is the same thing as reproduction. Certain aspects of sex roles are uniform within West Indian society irrespective of class or race. Men are thought to be stronger and more dominating and are expected to be more active. They should be 'providers' while women need someone to be 'responsible' for them. The nature of man is such that he needs sexual intercourse; the nature of woman is such that she needs children. Needless to say, these stereotyped ideas are very different from reality.

Sex role differentiation

In this chapter I discuss some general ideas about gender, or sex roles, in order to bring the West Indian material into a wider comparative framework.

1. The cultural dimension of sex role differentiation

Schneider and Smith (1978) distinguish two aspects of the meaning of sex in American culture. There is a relational aspect, in that the symbol of sex stands for the unification of opposites through the joining together of naturally differing elements. An attributional aspect may also be distinguished, when sex stands for the absolute separation that is believed to arise from the biological and temperamental differences of male and female (Schneider and Smith 1978, pp. 70-7).

The distinction between relational and attributional aspects of sex at the level of cultural meaning is a special application of the distinction between quality and performance, or ascription and achievement, a distinction made by Talcott Parsons (1951, pp. 58-67, 180-200). Part of the 'pattern variables' scheme for the analysis and classification of value systems, the ascription-achievement distinction is highly abstract. Here the attribute-relation distinction is more limited, and does not have the same general theoretical implications.

In the West Indies, as in the United States, both relational and attributional aspects are always present in the structuring of the meaning of sex; what varies is the relative emphasis placed upon each.

i. Attributional dominance

Where the attributional aspect of sexuality is dominant, primacy is given to the differences between the sexes over a wide spectrum of social and psychological perception. It is believed that males and females are fundamentally different, not only in physical characteristics, but also in temperament, aptitude, and ability to perform certain roles. Where these beliefs are embodied in social action they produce a sharp separation of the spheres of activity of males and females. For example, one might find that women monopolize – or are believed to monopolize – the 'female' tasks of child care, cooking, washing, sewing, cleaning, and the various extensions of these tasks such as obtaining food, firewood, shopping for clothes, and so forth. Their major social intercourse is with other women and takes place in a predominantly domestic setting. For women, child bearing and child rearing may be considered the major attribute of their sexuality; tasks for which they are uniquely fitted. These cultural emphases do not always coincide with actual behaviour. For example, it has been assumed that lower-class West Indian women dominate the 'domestic domain' while men are active in the 'outside' world of occupations, politics and status determining activities generally. This assumption is shared by informants themselves, but does not correspond with observed activities. Women have always been involved in such 'masculine' pursuits as heavy agricultural labour, road work, and animal husbandry. On slave plantations the strongest women took their place beside men in the 'Great Gang,' which did all the heaviest work (see Roughley 1823, p. 99; Craton and Walvin 1970, pp. 128, 138). Sex was not used as a major criterion in allocating labour in the most labour intensive agricultural tasks; black women were assumed to be more suited for heavy labour than lighter coloured individuals of either sex. Only at the higher, skilled, levels of the occupational scale did gender affect who would become a sugar boiler, carpenter, mason, cooper, washer or seamstress. Theories that assume a total separation of male and female activities are ill-founded, even where attributional dominance is present (see R.T. Smith 1987). Where attributes dominate ideas about sex it is found that relations between men and women are stylized and circumscribed, at least until the sex role element ceases to be the most active element in the relationship. Old age diminishes sex role differences, and eases relations between men and women. Relations between husband and wife can grow in mutuality and intimacy over time, but 'the war of the sexes' is more usual, especially where a relational element is coming to be seen as necessary or desirable, but attributional concepts still dominate. Courtship embodies a particular kind of attributional stress. In the West Indies three patterns of courtship may be distinguished, with differing frequencies of occurrence in different classes. They may be called the companionship pattern, the chaperone pattern and the uncontrolled pattern. The first is appropriate to relational dominance and will be discussed later.

The chaperone pattern is the ideal of the West Indian lower class; it assumes that if young people of opposite sex are left alone they will be carried away, intercourse will be inevitable, and pregnancy will follow. A third party must be present until they are placed in the right social situation for their sexual natures to combine. That situation is marriage. To say that this is the 'ideal' of the West Indian lower class is only approximately accurate: it is the lower-class conception of how relations between young men and women should be ordered to embody the status enhancing act of early marriage. In practice it is rare for young people to court and marry in this way, except among Indo-Guyanese where marriage is arranged at an early age. The exaggerated emphasis placed upon proof of virginity at marriage in one Guyanese village has been reported previously (R.T. Smith 1956, p. 172), and other case material has been collected on courtship carried out under very close supervision (R.T. Smith 1978a, p. 355). A man should always write to a girl's guardian if he intends to be her friend, whether the object be marriage or some other form of union. These ideals of chaperonage and close control are not accompanied by concepts of family honour comparable to those found in Mediterranean society, and this makes them difficult to understand.

In practice, the most common form of early sexual experience is an uncontrolled encounter that is generally furtive and brief. Women often claim that their first experience of sexual intercourse was shrouded in ignorance (Blake 1961, pp. 52-7). Doubtless it was; not ignorance of what sex is all about, as Blake supposes – most unlikely in a predominantly rural society where sexual reference is frequent and explicit – but ignorance of the actual experience of sexual contact and intercourse. Stress upon sexual attributes as part of the nature of males and females requires a process of learning how to manage the attributes as they develop, much as one has to learn to walk or speak. Sexual intercourse is considered to be a normal and expected activity for both men and women (the lack of which can lead to illness and even insanity); therefore the definition of maturity includes sexual intercourse. In the absence of any general concept of a relationship of friendship between young people of the opposite sex, the first sexual intercourse is likely to be thought of in retrospect as an isolated and even traumatic act, as when a woman refers to 'the man who fall me' (see page 132 above).

Further development of sexual maturation leads to parenthood; symbolic of maturity for women, and virility for men. Parenthood is an attribute of each parent separately, and not an expression of the relationship between them. It does not have to be embodied in a conjugal tie and certainly not in a coresidential union. For men, a further dimension of sex role attributes is the development of 'responsibility' but this is not expected until the man is much older, and is always modified by the supposition that economic factors may make it difficult, or even impossible. Where attributes are stressed, solidarity arises through likeness; in Durkheim's terms it is 'mechanical' and not 'organic' (Durkheim 1947, pp. 71-110). If sex roles are considered in isolation, men have nothing in common with women and everything in common with other men. Men and women are to each other only necessary objects for the achievement of their respective ends. Men need women for sexual satisfaction, to prepare food and wash clothes and do other tasks defined as being inappropriate for men; women need men for economic support, and less urgently for sexual satisfaction. No joint activities are involved necessarily, except for sexual intercourse itself. Women's joint activities are with other women in the immediate domestic and neighbourhood environment, and the women most likely to be there are mother, sisters and daughters. The specifically female tasks of child care and domestic activity constitute the core of the interaction of such groups even when the women work out for wages.

137

For men the focus of solidarity and joint activities is the peer group; not the unit of father and sons, or even of brothers. This asymmetry is interesting. There is no field of activity for closely related men comparable to the domestic life of women. Young men begin to work out for wages as soon as possible since this is the means by which they assert their independence. Rarely are farms large enough to require the labour of a large body of men, even in the rice farming areas. Among Indo-Guyanese, where the ideal of filial dependence is still strong, sons expect to be set up on land of their own as soon as they mature and get married. Jobs most readily available to young men are in large concerns – sugar plantations, bauxite mines, government projects – where fathers and sons may work side by side, but equally subordinated to higher status supervisors. The difference between solidary groups of female kin and solidary groups of male peers is not a product of functional necessity; it is produced by the way in which sex roles are defined.

Where the attributional aspects of sex roles are stressed, conjugal relations are affected. Intimate relations develop between husband and wife but they rest upon a kinship, rather than a sex role, basis. There is an interesting contrast between Indo-Guyanese and Afro-Guyanese communities. In the former it is customary to marry a woman from a different village who is then incorporated into the family of her husband. The position of the young bride is notoriously bad; she is not yet a part of the female group within the household, and her husband often ignores her. When she becomes a mother she gradually becomes a part of her husband's family, and may grow to be the dominant element in the household. Among Afro-Guyanese, and other West Indians, the stress tends to be the other way. Women who go to live with a man in a common law or a legal union are mistress in their own house from the beginning. If possible they stay close to their mother, and their sisters. Where close relationships develop between husband and wife it is because one has become absorbed into the family of the other. It is more likely that the relationship continues to be 'segregated' with the man marginal to the solidary relationships of the household, and to his wife's matrilateral group.

ii. Relational dominance

Where the relational aspect of sex role is dominant the emphasis is all the other way. Rather than stressing the separation of the sexes, rooted in their respective attributes, the focus is upon the 'unity – physical, spiritual, emotional . . . the coming together into a single whole, . . . the bringing of opposites together . . . the inseparability and interdependence of the differentiated parts . . . enduring or "eternal" solidarity, and so on' (Schneider and Smith 1978, p.73). Where this aspect of sex roles is most fully developed, attributional differences are minimized in favour of equal cooperation in whatever activity contributes to the unity of the relational whole. The unity and complementarity of the sexes is stressed, rather than their differences, and so one expects joint activities as the working out of the relationship. These joint activities can extend over a wide area of social life. They can be manifest in domestic life where each does what is necessary without reference to whether it is a 'male' or a 'female' task; they can be manifest in leisure activities where each contributes to the pleasure of the other and the compatibility of the couple is the focus of attention; they can be manifest in joint efforts to enhance the social status of the couple; and they can be manifest in sexual intercourse itself where the emphasis is upon the creation of unity and mutual transcendence by whatever means seems appropriate without reference to the orthodoxy of 'male' and 'female' actions. Companionship is stressed as the essential part of courtship during the period after the couple 'fall in love' and are getting to know each other. Neither chaperonage nor an uncontrolled relationship are deemed appropriate; the first because it interferes with the interpersonal bond and the second because it contravenes the notion of mutual regard and equality.

A stress on the relational dimension of sex role differentiation links to the symbolism of kinship in a particular way, once it is brought into conjunction with the idea of production of offspring. Schneider has dealt with this issue at length in his treatment of the components of middle-class American kinship, where he shows that the master symbol of coitus 'stands for' the creation of unity out of difference, and the holding together of parents and the children who are created and sustained by conjugal love and unity. Thus, argues Schneider, the nuclear family becomes the embodiment of both conjugal love and consanguineal love, the archetype of all kinship relations, since they are rooted either in common substance or in the relationship of diffuse, enduring solidarity. The nuclear family based on the relations between spouses is the conjunction of all these factors and represents the interpenetration of the kinship and sex role domains (Schneider 1980 [1968]).

Schneider's analysis seems to be logical, an economical interpretation of the generative elements in the symbol system, but it does not satisfy many middle-class Americans. In a review of Schneider's book remarkable for its tone of disparagement, but still forced to conclude that the essay brings many fundamental issues into focus, Wallace denies that marriage in American kinship is a relationship in law, as opposed to the relationship in nature that characterizes consanguineal kin (Wallace 1969). Wallace distorts the argument by omission of certain of Schneider's qualifying statements; for example, 'sexual intercourse is an act which is undertaken and does not just happen. Yet as an act, it is natural. Its outcome is conception, which is followed by birth, and these are natural, too' (Schneider 1980 [1968], p. 38). However, Wallace is correct in pointing to informants' uneasiness over the deriving of all kinship concepts from the master symbol of coitus, a symbol that, according to Schneider, joins the relationship in law of the conjugal partners to the relationship in nature of the parents and offspring.

Without attempting to argue from the West Indies to the American middle class (or the other way), it is interesting that West Indians are similarly uneasy. Mrs. Brown, a middle-class Guyanese of mixed racial origin, was explaining the difference between 'family' and 'relatives.' Family, she said, are related by some direct connection, while relatives are connected by marriage. As soon as we began to discuss non-legal (irregular) unions, the distinction began to break down. I asked whether her sister's husband was part of her family. 'He's a relation – he's not family – he's not a "begat".' When asked the same question about her own husband the response was different and more complex. 'He is my family but their relative.' 'Why is he your family?' 'Because I married him; he is the father of my children.' At this point she was confronted with the clear distinction she had made between family and relatives. 'I know, but you can't call your husband a relative – it is ridiculous . . . All those who are from the same grandparents will be family; the in-laws would be relatives, but the husband would be a third category. The two of us would be the beginning of another family' (case number 110).

Schneider's analysis makes more sense of these West Indian data than does Wallace, who lays primary stress on the natural quality of 'love' as a state into which one gets, or 'falls.' Alexander has made a similar point (1978, p. 7). Mrs. Brown, in the interview cited above, is not discussing 'love' in that sense at all; rather she is pointing to the fact that marriage creates a tie of natural generation which is comparable to a blood tie and in fact results in the creation of blood ties. 'Love' as a state of being is beside the point. This variability in the symbolization of kinship arises because of the differential stress upon attributes and relationship in the domain of sex role differentiation.

In Schneider's middle-class cases the relational element in sex role differentiation is dominant in the conjugal bond – or so it seems. Between 'husband' and 'wife' a relationship is actively created, leading to unity through love, expressed in mutual activity, sexual intercourse being the most complete and intimate activity. However, sexual intercourse is also a fact in nature giving rise to the generation of offspring. The American middle-class informants (and Schneider) separate these two aspects, so that Schneider interprets the master symbol of coitus as embodying and combining two separate elements – kinship as law (spouses), and kinship as nature (parents and children). In the West Indies the configuration is different because of the differing emphases in sex role definition and differentiation.

Where attributional elements dominate the domain of sex, two kinship outcomes are possible. The conjugal bond may be separated from consanguineal kinship. A woman's 'husband' becomes 'the baby father' or 'Jean's daddy'; that is, her tie to him is defined in consanguineal terms – through the child. The relatives 'in-law', such as the baby's father's mother, are classed in the same way. They are the baby's blood relatives and as such it is the duty of the mother to see that the ties of blood between them and the child are given recognition and expression.

The other possible outcome is to model marriage or common law marriage on consanguinity. One informant described how her children's father goes with her when she visits her relatives.

Yes man. For my relatives are now his like too you know. We live together long now; it is not like say the children don't have a common father. They are all for him, and he come in like one of us now. But his family different like. They don't move so close, so he come more to mine, except the mother like how I told you.

What she had said about his mother was:

Agatha Wilson – she is my husband's mother and she lives at Hermitage. I visit her regularly, but I don't know any other from his family. But his mother is different; she come in like sort of family.

Thus, sex role definitions play an important part in the constitution of kinship, even at the cultural or ideological level. As an element in the constitution of social relationships and normative structure, they are even more important.

2. Sex role differentiation in the social structure

The logical implications of stress on attributional or relational aspects of 'sex' are built into culture and norms. How do sex roles vary according to their differential positioning in social structure? More specifically, what are the class variations in sex roles, and what effects do they have on kinship and family structure? At least three patterns of conjugal relationship can be distinguished in West Indian kinship. These patterns are not 'types' into which all unions must be sorted; they are models constructed to show how a sex role component enters into the constitution of conjugal unions. Elizabeth Bott, in *Family and Social Network*, found, after a process of elimination, that the organization of family activities could be classified as 'complementary,' 'independent' and 'joint'.

In complementary organization the activities of husband and wife are different and separate but fitted together to form a whole. In independent organization activities are carried out separately by husband and wife without reference to each other, in so far as this is possible. In joint organization activities are carried out by husband and wife together, or the same activity is carried out by either partner at different times. (Bott 1957, p. 53)

All three types of activity are found to some extent in each of her families, but in some families complementary and independent types of organization predominated and in those cases she described the relationship of husband and wife as a segregated conjugal role relationship. Where joint activities predominated, the relationship was termed a joint conjugal role relationship. The revised version of her book has a chapter of 'Reconsiderations' in which she discusses the close correspondence between conjugal roles and general sex role differentiation.

Bott's terminology is widely known and will be adopted here, with the added distinction that segregated conjugal role relationships should be divided into two types, and the word 'relationship' replaced by 'pattern.' These patterns are dissociated conjugal role pattern and segregated conjugal role pattern. The introduction of a distinction between 'dissociated' and 'segregated' is not entirely satisfactory, linguistically or anthropologically, but we need to distinguish independent organization from complementarity in family activities, rather than treating them both as being segregated role patterns.

i. Dissociated conjugal role patterns

The dissociated pattern of conjugal roles has a minimal relational element; it is found in many, but not all, visiting unions, and in many coresidential unions – legal and non-legal. Where this pattern occurs it is difficult to think of activities constituting a unitary whole; the stress is on exchange between two distinct entities, male and female, which differ in certain ways. Even sexual relations are conceived as 'giving' one to the other rather than as the joint activity of a couple. Intense affect is not necessary. This does not mean that unions approximating this pattern are without love or affection; it means that intense emotional involvement is not essential. Each partner probably continues to be closely involved in a network of consanguineal relationships that provide emotional support and reciprocity.

The social arrangement embodying this pattern most completely is the short term visiting union. Each partner may be involved in more than one union simultaneously, or one partner may invest very little in the union, while the other is more committed. Most usually this is described as male 'exploitation,' but there is no necessary bias in that direction.

Alice Smith lives with her six children in a small house built on the edge of a plot of 'family land' in Kingston, land in which she acquired residence rights through her father (case number 302). In Jamaica, no member of the kindred can be denied accommodation on such land. Her parents separated when she was an infant and she spent most of her childhood with paternal relatives on this family land, supported by small contributions from her father. She first became pregnant when she was sixteen, and she now says that she 'didn't know what was happening.' Alice Smith always refers to the father of her first child as 'the chap' and says that being a boy he was more experienced than she was. When she realized she was pregnant he took her to the doctor and contributed to the expenses of the delivery. They remained friends and he fathered a second child. During this period she shared a room with her father's sister's daughter, her husband and four children. After the birth of the second child she moved out, into a small one room structure built originally by her father, but occupied recently by a cousin. She has lived there since, alone with her children. She is not really 'alone'; the family land is well populated with 'relatives.' Although she claims not to get along with them, they provide child care services (for which she pays), and this enables her to work – she began as a domestic servant and now works in a dry cleaning factory. The father of her first two children developed other ties, and he now lives with the mother of his other children. Alice Smith's next friendship resulted in the birth of two more children, a girl and a boy, but she drifted away from that man because, she says, he is not 'collective' (mentally stable). He lives with his aunt, and contributes no money to the support of his children. Alice's fifth child, a girl, is nearly three years old; the father lives with another woman. He gives Alice some money occasionally and she appears to be on good terms with him. Her youngest child was born just before the beginning of the field interviews. The father was a regular visitor to the home until about a month before the baby was born, and then he stayed away for about four months, claiming that one of Alice's children had been rude to him by not saying 'goodnight' when he arrived. This exquisite sensibility was only part of the story; it turned out that another woman had just given birth to his child – this in addition to his three children in the country and a daughter attending school in Kingston. Alice was upset about his staying away because 'it looked bad' that he had not even been to see the baby. Eventually he resumed his occasional visits, giving a small contribution now and again for the support of the child. Alice was not sure whether he was actually living with the other woman or merely visiting each of them.

Miss Smith's relationships with her gentlemen friends (the local term) are typical of many such cases. She refers to them, and addresses them, as 'Mr. so-and-so'; the absence of deep personal involvement implied in such terms is characteristic. In principle Alice Smith would like to settle into a stable monogamous relationship with one man, but she has avoided moving in with a man who might turn out to be unreliable, preferring to maintain her own job and her own house. She has great hopes for her sons. One is already working as a TV and radio repair technician, bringing in money for household expenses, while the second son is almost ready to start work. She says that she would never have had so many children had she known what she knows now, and her conversations are punctuated with yearnings for a better life. She hopes to move into a better neighbourhood before the girls get older, and is always talking about her 'ambition,' especially her desire to migrate to the United States as a domestic servant. The men with whom she has had relationships remain insubstantial. She knows them of course, and maintains contact with them and their families, but they are not now, nor do they appear ever to have been, figures of deep personal significance. How else could she have been unaware of their other, simultaneous, sexual relationships?[1] In terms of the classificatory system suggested above, it appears that the attributional aspect of sexuality is dominant in these dissociated conjugal relationships. In the following case, there seems to be less detachment, but in spite of a considerable emotional component, attributes dominate the explanation of the breakup of each of the unions.

Lester Chase, thirty-two years old, has a steady job in a biscuit factory just outside Georgetown, Guyana; he has just broken up with a 'girlfriend' with whom he has been living for the past three years (case number 108). He has two children by other women; the first was born as a result of an affair with a young girl he met through the church. She was seventeen when the baby was born and he had some idea of marrying her, but nothing came of it. His second child was born while he was in a coresidential, non-legal union with Vernel Payne, a domestic servant who already had several children. He says he got along extremely well with Vernel.

> Yes man, fine. She was what you would call a housewife. The nice type. The only difficulty I find with her was that she had these many children. I found it difficult with them. I asked her to give them to the rightful parents and so on. I would even consider marrying her. But she won't agree. She said she would give some of the children to their fathers and one girl she was going to keep because she didn't have any girl children. But I couldn't agree to that so eventually we split down the middle. It wasn't an easy task.
>
> How big were the children? From fourteen right down. The little girl was about nine. But I know that if I had kept the girl the father would have come there to see the child. In so doing conversation might have reached a stage where she might have accepted something from him.

[1] See Roberts 1975, p. 150, note 5, for evidence from Barbados of women's lack of knowledge of visiting partners.

Eventually they would be in bed and I would be the comic in the middle. Once there is that spark there's always some kind of feelings so I think it was wise.

I don't have that trust in people on the whole, because on many occasions I've tried and people let me down. Women are like rain – there's no telling when it might fall. But this girl was really great. When I say great I mean great. There wasn't a thing I wanted she won't share. Suppose I get sick – I would get great care from her. Moreover she had nice ways. But we just couldn't agree about the children. One time I struck her and the little boy she had was about ten. He said, 'Don't strike my mother. You're not her father, nor mine.' And that boy used to eat out of me. I said to myself, in years to come he would break me up, even if I talk a little harsh to her. It would be a very one-sided affair. To prevent these things from happening I thought it best for me to leave.

His most recent union was even more turbulent. Peggy is three years older than he is, has a good job as a clerk in a small business and is separated from her husband. She has three children ranging in age from nineteen to fifteen who live with her husband's family. Lester met her by chance one evening and then ran into her again a couple of weeks later.

We went into the restaurant down the road there and had a few beers. A friend of mine came in the same time and tell me about a sport [dance] up in La Penitence. I asked her if she would go. She told me she wasn't dressed and had to get home early. Anyhow I tell her to come along – we would only stay two hours or so. When we get there – I am a drinking man – I moved over with the boys – then me and a fellow put together and buy a large [a quart bottle of rum]. If you see this woman drinking down this rum! I take her out on the bicycle and we went to my room. Six o'clock next morning is when she leaving – although she had to get home!

Anyhow, I gone to Bookers and buy that bed; not even sheets. And she move in. She live there for three years until last week.

Why did you break up?

From the beginning when I see what a trickster she was I tell her straight – 'look Peggy I don't want to like you so you leave me where I am and go your way.' But she got more brains than U Thant. [He then launched into a long account of her unfaithfulness and deceit]. Any woman can come in my house but she isn't hanging up anything.

It's a bad way I know – a man needs a foundation and stability in life but you can't trust no woman.

This Peggy, I had to let her go because she was too hot. It was the same thing with her husband. She only want to know the size of every man's cock. Women are a barbarous set of people.

145

In this case, as in the last, the unions involve sex and the mutual provision of other services, but failure to adjust the practical details of that mutuality quickly leads to the break up of the union, especially if one partner has independent resources. Lester Chase's union with Vernel Jones was less dissociated but his marginal position in relation to her and her children, made it unstable.

ii. Segregated and joint conjugal role patterns

The pattern contrasting most strongly with the dissociated pattern may be termed, following Bott, the joint conjugal role relationship pattern. Here the emphasis is upon the partners doing things together with a minimum of concern about the separate attributes of each sex, and no assumption that each should have reserved activities. Either partner will do what is necessary for the common good, whether it be preparing a meal, painting a room, cleaning the house, or taking care of the children. Husband and wife share leisure activities; a visit to friends, a trip to the beach or a night at the cinema. Emphasis is placed on 'the family' meaning the family of husband, wife and their children – the unit to which primary loyalty is owed. If both partners work, their income is pooled for the common good.

This pattern has been most fully described for Europe and north America. It does occur in the West Indies, but the segregated conjugal role pattern is more frequent, and is often compared unfavourably with the joint pattern. In the segregated pattern the stress is on complementary activities; upon the meshing together of the distinctive attributes of husband and wife as male and female, with each person having a clearly defined area of competence into which the other does not venture. This pattern of conjugal role structure is found in both the lower and middle classes, but with differing consequences and content.

The cultural definition of complementary activities in segregated conjugal role patterns says that men should provide support and general protection while women engage in child rearing and domestic work. Some supplementary provisions may be added, as when rural women may be expected to market the produce of jointly operated farms.

When the male contribution to the conjugal union is defined as the provision of economic support, the occupational system must influence male familial activities. However, occupational roles do not determine family roles. The independence of conjugal role patterns was shown by Bott in her study of London families (1957, p. 111). Male familial roles are not confined to the conjugal relationship. Men play an important part in the family as sons and brothers, and occupation does not determine what that part shall be, even if it sets limits to what it can be. The occupational system in the West Indies has made it difficult for men to be reliable

146

providers, and has made it possible for women sometimes to earn as much as men – more in some cases. Historically women worked at the hardest tasks alongside men (see page 136 above), and if today women do the lighter tasks such as weeding, some may still perform the heavy labour of loading bananas, breaking rock for road building, planting and harvesting rice, carrying firewood and cultivating small farms. Domestic service has always been a source of employment for women, the numbers so engaged rising and falling as the tides of economic prosperity erode or augment male earnings. Women dominate petty trade, and even 'middle-class' women sometimes make cakes, do dressmaking, or engage in other part-time, income-producing activities.

The easy availability of low-paid domestic servants, and nursemaids to take care of children, has enabled middle-class West Indian women to have full time occupations and careers. But women of different classes work for different reasons and this throws light on the relationship between employment and conjugal roles. Middle-class married women say that they work for personal satisfaction or to help out with domestic expenses and clothes for themselves and the children. Major recurrent items, such as rent or mortgage payments, utility bills, and food, are the man's responsibility, but the exact division of payment for other things is rarely a settled matter. The idea is that both partners are contributing to the needs of the family, of which 'advancement' is a major part. In practice things may not work so smoothly; where there is segregation of conjugal roles men rarely share their income openly, usually giving the woman a fixed sum for housekeeping that she supplements through her own activities. This pattern also prevails among lower-class couples, but the husband's income is more critical in the domestic economy of the middle class. It is larger in absolute terms and essential for the maintenance of the domestic budget and the status of the family. The income of the lower-class male is smaller and more erratic; since the family does not operate on a fixed budget its income and expenditures vary from day to day.

Male roles are not defined solely in terms of economic support. When the attributional aspect of sex roles is dominant men are perceived to be strong, virile, active and domineering as well as 'responsible.' They are thought to be so by nature, not by education or effort. If a man cannot get work it does not mean that he is 'emasculated'; it is thought to be bad luck, because he 'can't do better' or because of the perversity and evil of the society as a whole. Masculinity does not depend on work performance; it is demonstrated by 'manly' activities with other men, by sexual conquest of many 'girl friends,' and by 'having children all about.' Masculine role identity is established by displaying the sexual attributes themselves. Similarly women are mothers, housekeepers, sexual partners at the appropriate stages of their social development. Conjugal relations are not entered into by calculating the cost of maintaining a household. Being 'friendly' with someone of the opposite sex, or being married, is natural for adults. This is different from the idea that marriage is active cooperation for the production of a 'family,' and for its progressive advancement in the social scale.

These varying patterns of conjugal roles are associated with class but the link is not absolute. In middle-class West Indian families conjugal roles are generally segregated, though young people are moving toward joint activities. There is a pervasive feeling that middle-class marital relations should be more joint than they are. Constant criticism of men's refusal to lift a finger in the house or help with the children, even when women go out to work, is not diminished even when domestic servants take care of the dirty work. In his discussion of the asymmetry in the division of labour within the conjugal relationship, Alexander points to two interesting aspects. Men believe that domestic chores diminish masculinity, but there is no corresponding feeling that women's employment is a threat to either partner's sexual identity. It is also commonly said that men's behaviour is an aspect of their identity as Jamaican, or West Indian, men, who are then compared unfavourably (by women) with foreigners. Yet these complaints about male indifference to family life are less strident when families are more prosperous and the burden on working wives less onerous. The middle-class preoccupation with male familial roles is projected onto the lower class in public discussion about the 'problem' of West Indian family life, as it has been for at least 100 years (see pages 104-5 above and R.T. Smith 1982a).

8
Household and family

It is but of late, that the planters have paid much attention to elegance in their habitations: their general rule was, to build what they call a make-shift; so that it was not unusual to see a plantation adorned with a very expensive set of works, of brick or stone, well executed; and the owner residing in a miserable thatched hovel, hastily put together with wattles and plaister, damp, unwholesome, and infested with every species of vermin. But the houses in general, as well in the country parts as the towns, have been greatly improved within these last twenty years. The furniture of some of them is extremely costly; and others constructed in so magnificent a style, and of such durable materials, as to shew that they were not intended for a mere temporary residence.

Edward Long 1774

This chapter draws together some of the main threads of the argument by considering the question with which we began: what is the relation between kinship, family structure and domestic relations? Concern with the 'domestic domain' has dominated the study of kinship for the past fifty years, and has exerted enormous influence on our understanding of the family in the Caribbean. In Meyer Fortes' graphic phrase it has been assumed that the household is 'the workshop of social reproduction' (1958, p. 2). Chapter 1 showed how a preoccupation with the household, motivated by method as well as theory, has diverted attention from the wide ranging networks of kin ties experienced by all, or most, West Indians. It would be a mistake to conclude that households are, therefore, of little or no importance; Goody's widening of the focus from coresidence to joint activities is a move in the right direction, relevant to West Indian materials (Goody 1972). However, our data do not support theories that equate households with family, much less with the 'nuclear family.'

Knowledge of family life, both historical and contemporary, has been broadened by studies of household composition. Censuses and household lists from the past have been subjected to new techniques of analysis and this process will continue as more material is discovered, preserved,

149

organized and made available for computer analysis. This expands knowledge and understanding, but for every step forward in the refinement of techniques their limitations have become evident. Household composition is an unreliable index to kinship and family relations and must be interpreted with care, as we saw in Chapter 5. Child rearing is at the heart of most of the discussions of household composition and domestic activities; Fortes' phrase 'the workshop of social reproduction' refers to the physical care of children but also to the transmission of moral values and the creation of the social bonds on which society rests. In this view the mother-child relationship is the core of all domestic relations, but most anthropologists also believe that paternity is a universal human need; fathers, or father surrogates, are needed to relate to the mother-child dyad. Sylvia Yanagisako has shown how difficult it is for anthropologists to move beyond these assumptions, even when they are sensitive to the need for distinguishing between families, coresidence and domestic activities (Yanagisako 1979; see also R.T. Smith 1978a).

Earlier chapters argued that kinship and family relations should be examined without preconceptions as to their biological rootedness, or functional necessity. Kinship is not just a social recognition of biology, and therefore the West Indian system of cultural concepts is central to analysis. The same considerations apply to the study of domestic life; kinship is not determined in its structure by an invariant set of functions or needs carried out by domestic groups. Sleeping, eating, sexual relations and child care need not form a single complex of activities, much less take place under the same roof, and the Caribbean data show this clearly.

1. Housing in plantation colonies

West Indians do not live in large compounds such as one finds in West Africa, nor in extended households like those in Eastern Europe. In bureaucratic jargon the majority of West Indian houses look like 'single family dwellings.' Whether rural cottages, urban villas surrounded by spacious lawns, slum shacks, apartments in yards, or the concrete boxes of new urban and suburban tracts, they appear to be the dwellings of single families. Appearances are deceptive. Large dwelling houses may be, and frequently are, divided into many separate units each housing a single domestic group; yards contain anything up to thirty separate domestic units clustered around common washing, bathing, cooking and toilet facilities; in some cases a collection of separate buildings may house a group of people who form a single housekeeping unit. The 'functions' generally asssumed to be those of domestic groups may be divided among a number of separate agencies; individuals may divide their time between a number of houses, keeping clothes in several different places and sleeping wherever is convenient; and the people who engage in cooperative cooking, washing or child care may be quite different from the elementary family of parents and children. Although these facts are well known it has proved difficult to incorporate them in any discussion of West Indian kinship except as interesting deviations from an assumed universal pattern of family relations.

2. Historical background: colonial and creole whites

Throughout West Indian history migration, transient populations and makeshift housing arrangements have played counterpoint to determined efforts to establish social stability and an ideally conceived 'normal' domestic life. Some idea of the tentative nature of domestic arrangements among the earliest settlers may be gauged from Richard Dunn's citation of two inventories from Barbados estates in 1635.

A Captain Ketteridge had five white servants, a Negro slave, and six hundred acres, yet his total household furnishings consisted of an old chest, six hammocks (the Negro slept on the ground), some empty barrels, a broken kettle, an old sieve, some battered pewter dishes, three napkins and three old books. Mathew Gibson, with four servants, possessed even less: a chest, a cracked kettle, two pots, several barrels, a sieve, a glass bottle and a pamphlet without covers (Dunn 1972, p. 54).

As late as the 1770s Edward Long could write as we saw him doing in the passage at the beginning of this chapter. Long and other eighteenth-century writers were preoccupied with what they saw as social irregularity and even debauchery, but the system of kinship, marriage, and domestic relations – in place almost from the beginning of settlement – embraced a wide range of possibilities.

Gilberto Freyre's discussion of the way in which architecture expressed the way of life of north-east Brazilian slave society has no counterpart in West Indian historical studies (but see Berthelot and Gaumé 1982; Buisseret 1980; Handler and Lange 1978). Freyre argues that the Great House, complemented by the slave huts, encompass 'an entire economic, social, and political system' (Freyre 1946, p. xxvii). The architecture, when properly understood, reveals the complexity of social relations that cut across domestic life; it is significant that Freyre's book *Casa-Grande e Senzala* is translated for a more literal minded English-speaking audience as *The Masters and the Slaves*.

In the West Indies, as in Brazil, many European settlers – and particularly those who became serious planters – were intent upon establishing family dynasties, taking as their model the way of life of the English landed classes. Long notes that 'Most of the old Creole families are allied, by the inter-marriages among their ancestors before the island [of

Jamaica] was populously settled' (Long 1774, Vol. 2, p. 266). Others had more modest ambitions and just tried to make a new life for themselves and their families, without too much thought of great wealth.

Port Royal in Jamaica was not a typical seventeenth-century West Indian town, but a detailed account has been given of its settlement and early years (Pawson and Buisseret 1975). Built upon an insubstantial spit of land commanding the entrance to Kingston Harbour, it quickly became an important shipping and mercantile centre. First settled when the British acquired the island in 1655, by 1680 it had a population of about 'two thousand "whites" and about 850 "blacks"' (*ibid.*, p. 98). Established as a fort and naval station, Port Royal's population included women and children almost from its inception; by the time the earthquake of 1692 destroyed most of the old town, the white population consisted of about 1,600 men, 1,400 women and 1,000 children. The number of slaves is not known exactly but their number had increased steadily and probably reached well above the 414 males and 431 females reported in 1680. A high proportion of the whites were indentured servants subject to sale in much the same way as slaves; many had been shipped from the prisons of London. Still, they seem to have settled into something closely resembling an English mode of domestic life.

Everyday life at Port Royal seems to have been very similar to what might have been observed in any English seaport of similar size. There was very little evidence of 'creolization' during the four decades after 1655; food, clothes, buildings and recreations all obstinately followed English norms, however unsuitable these might be . . . Mr. Pepys would have felt perfectly at home in Port Royal. (Pawson and Buisseret 1975, p. 119)

The authors provide a wealth of evidence to support this statement, from lists of furnishings of the substantial brick houses, to the names and locations of nineteen taverns, the names of a dazzling array of tradesmen – including an architect, baker, barbers, blacksmiths, bricklayers, butchers, carpenters, cabinetmakers, chandlers, surgeons, coopers, shoemakers, fishermen, druggster, glazier, goldsmiths, gunsmiths, hatmaker, ivory turner, limeburner, masons, mariners, merchants, pipemakers, pewterers, sailmakers, a schoolmaster, shipwrights, tailors – and an impressive collection of victuallers, vintners, and tavernkeepers. There is not much information on marriage and family life, though we know of at least one brothel with twenty-one white and two black women, and a contemporary observer noted that many of the drinking places were the haunts of prostitutes and strumpets (Pawson and Buisseret 1975, p. 119). One interesting feature was the dividing of dwelling houses into rented rooms, each tenant having rights to use the yard where the cook house, water storage tank and the 'house of office,' or latrine, were situated. The presence of African slaves, most of whom worked and lived in the houses of the wealthier whites, already introduced a distinctive feature of creole Jamaican social life.

In spite of its special nature as a naval, trading and privateering centre, accessible only by water and with a great many English characteristics, Port Royal contained within itself the oppositions that became more general and more fully worked out in the plantation setting. These were: the opposition between rich and poor represented by the opulent brick houses of the wealthy merchants, and the crowded yards of lesser whites and indentured servants; the contrast between religious piety (there was an astonishing variety of religious bodies and churches including a synagogue, a Roman Catholic church, an Anglican church and many Christian sects), and licentious living in the form of excessive drinking, prostitution and diversions such as bear baiting and cock fighting; an array of forms of marriage including carefully contracted unions that consolidated family fortunes, ordinary marriages, consensual unions among lesser whites, various forms of visiting union, and prostitution. Domestic life was closely interlocked with the economic life of the town. Craftsmen and tradesmen had their slaves and labourers living as part of their household, or close by. Contemporary sources refer to large numbers of children, most belonging to the lesser whites, since the wealthy sent their children to England. How many were bastards we do not know, but in Maryland at about the same time fully 20 percent of the children born to white servants were illegitimate (Carr and Walsh 1978, p. 267). Sugar planting did not gain momentum in Jamaica until the eighteenth century, though immediately after the British occupation in 1665 there was an influx of experienced planters from other parts of the Caribbean. When Francis Price, an officer in the army of Penn and Venables, arrived in Jamaica in 1655 he decided to obtain a land patent for an estate in Lluidas Vale and there he built a 'Great House' of modest proportions in which he installed a wife and raised three sons and a daughter.

The subsequent history of the estate, Worthy Park, shows the importance of carefully contracted marriages and genealogical succession in the consolidation of landed fortunes in the sugar colonies. Francis Price's third son, Charles, was the chief architect of the family's fortune; he raised thirteen children in the Great House built by his father. The house was small, with only three main rooms, a hall and a closet on the first floor, and three rooms on the second. A kitchen, wash house and coach house were separate from the main structure, and the stone basement of the house was used for storage and as a hurricane shelter. When an inventory was drawn up in 1731, soon after Charles Price died, it listed beds in every room in the house. It also showed that despite its modest size the house was equipped with good furniture, silver, looking glasses, and even a spinet (Craton and Walvin 1970, p. 56).

Similar developments were taking place in other parts of the Caribbean. The inventory of the Pinney House in Nevis for 1722 shows a level of luxury in furnishings, plate and linen that, if not great by European standards, was more than comfortable (Pares 1950, pp. 336-9). In June of 1796 Dr. George Pinckard visited the estate of Mr. Blair, across the river from New Amsterdam in the then Dutch colony of Berbice, now a part of Guyana. 'The house is a compact dwelling, neatly built of plain timber, offering in its exterior, nothing to attract the stranger's eye, nor to bespeak the many luxuries within' (Pinckard 1816, Vol. 1, p. 453). The level of luxury in the construction and furnishing of Great Houses was less important than their symbolic value, a value established and maintained by entertaining and lavish hospitality. Pinckard was most enthusiastic about the luxury and opulence of Blair's welcome and entertainment, though the estate was newly established, and the visitors were accommodated in hammocks rather than beds. The luxury lay in the profusion of things to eat and drink, along with the plate, cutlery and glassware necessary to their service, rather than in the grandeur of the house itself. Domestic hospitality of this kind has always been a West Indian value, in both city and countryside. Visitors to a plantation were assured of a place to sleep, plenty of food and drink and the attention of numerous servants. These values diffused throughout the population and have survived into the present. However, the elite responsible for their development and propagation became increasingly remote.

Charles Price was a creole; he was born in Jamaica and never left it. Of his thirteen children, eight died before they reached adolescence; in his will he provided that all his surviving children should be educated in England, and allowed to buy land and settle there if they wished. Craton and Walvin say, 'Colonel Charles Price was merely among the first of a long line of those who saw sugar wealth not as a solace for residence in Jamaica but as a means of escape; if not for them, for their sons and daughters' (Craton and Walvin 1970, p. 67). All the Price children took up residence in England, but each returned to Jamaica, if only for a short visit. Absentee ownership became a distinguishing feature of West Indian industry, contributing in no small measure to the emerging pattern of family life among the whites. The plantations were operated mostly by single men, though the number of married couples on smaller properties should not be underestimated. Just how stable was the family life of those couples is another question. The practice of married men taking black or coloured concubines and fathering 'outside' children was widespread (but less common on small estates according to Higman 1976, p. 148). Family instability was also created by early widowhood and remarriage, producing compound families. Stories of fortunes being made by a judicious marriage (or series of marriages) to a wealthy widow, or widower, were common in the eighteenth and nineteenth centuries. William Hickey, writing in the eighteenth century, describes the way in which Mr. Robert Richards acquired extensive estates in the Jamaican parishes of St. Ann and St. Mary through successive marriages to wealthy widows (Spencer 1918, Vol. 2, p. 46).

Domestic life, even among the landed elite, was transient and unstable. In a society where slavery intruded itself into the very bosom of the domestic life of the whites, the details of everyday life had to differ from that in Europe, or the settler colonies of the north. Here whites were separated from their peers and surrounded by large numbers of slaves. Children had to be sent away at an early age if they were to become 'civilized' – or so it was believed. Life took on the appearance of a drama in which the polarities of black and white represented the difference between civilization and savagery, and these polarities were copresent in each moment of everyday life – for everyone, including the slaves. As in other cases of chronic social conflict and tension, life went along peacefully enough most of the time, and within the limits set by this inherent conflict, all kinds of accommodations were made.

The sugar economy reached its peak of development in the late eighteenth century, when the importation of African slaves was at its height and the industry was so profitable that the owners could leave their properties to be run by paid staffs of Europeans supervised by attorneys. These white staff members were most often the fathers of coloured children, and the domestic life of those who lived on the sugar estates embodied the structural features of the creole system. The majority of whites did not live in families at all, and although a majority of slaves may appear to have been in nuclear families, all the elements on the plantation must be considered together – black, white and coloured, slave and free.

A definite hierarchy of housing existed on these plantations. The Great House was generally reserved for the use of the owner, or his representative attorney who was supposed to visit each plantation under his care. The resident manager, or overseer as he was called in Jamaica, had a substantial house of his own where he accommodated the single white male employees of the estate. Writing in the 1820s out of an experience going back to the late eighteenth century, Thomas Roughley – author of The *Jamaica Planter's Guide* – described the ideal arrangements for the housing of the white staff of a sugar plantation.

The overseer's house . . . should be built compact and convenient, not over roomy; and raised sufficiently high from the foundation, with good masonry work, to admit of suitable stores underneath, to keep all the plantation stores and supplies in . . . The rooms should be all on the same floor, and closely boarded with seasoned stuff. Each white man should have a small bedroom to himself, with a glazed sash window on hinges, and a shutter to it. The bedrooms should be eleven feet by nine each, of which five should be in every overseer's house on a sugar estate, leaving the overseer's room somewhat larger than the book-keepers. A large well-covered piazza, with comfortable glazed windows, (to rise and fall occasionally), will answer all the purposes of a dining and breakfast hall, and for walking in . . . A small back piazza, made comfortable by moving blinds with stops, would be proper for the servants . . . the overseer's cooking-room, washing-room, etc., should be apart from the house, though not far off, conveniently fitted up, and of a moderate size. (Roughley 1823, pp. 184-5)

The inhabitants of such a house would be attended by large numbers of domestic servants, usually drawn from the slave population, making it less like a military barracks than it otherwise might have been.

3. Historical background: slaves and free coloured

Sugar plantations were organized on bureaucratic principles, with strict accounting procedures and with a disciplined labour force marshalled for clearly defined tasks. They were among the first rational-capitalistic enterprises (but see Mintz and Wolf 1957). Since workers were recruited from abroad, a military model would have been appropriate for housing and feeding the workers. To some extent this model was adopted. In some areas workers were fed communally for at least one meal per day; medical attention was provided by the estate owner; clothing and personal items were issued to all workers; and in some places houses resembling barrack blocks were constructed. However, these seem to have been a late development. In Guyana one can still find (or could some years ago) remnants of the old 'ranges' or 'logies' in which indentured workers were housed, and on some sugar estates in Jamaica, workers' housing was built on this pattern. In Cuba, slaves were often locked up at night in the giant barrack blocks in which they, and indentured workers alike, were housed (see Montejo 1961). But for the most part the West Indian slave regime operated with a model adapted from the English country estate with its large manor house, surrounded by the villages of tenants and tied workers. Slaves were compared to English, or Irish, farm labourers, and the apologists for slavery always argued that living conditions were better in the slave colonies. Only after slavery was abolished did the barracks model gain ground in the West Indies.

The turnover of white employees on sugar estates was remarkably high; on the average sugar estate in Jamaica there was a constant procession of young, single white men passing through the estate, moving on to better jobs or falling ill and dying. The life of the white staff was organized around the overseer's house and catered to by cooks, washers and cleaning servants provided by the estate, but it was customary for white men to form semi-permanent attachments to women – slave or free – who provided services beyond those laid down in the estate code. Sexual services were probably less important than nursing through the many illnesses that beset white employees. It is no accident that John Stedman fell in love with the slave girl Joanna after she had nursed him back to health after a severe bout of fever (see page 98 above).

The strongest and most prominent Free Coloured women developed a pattern of domestic life that is a paradigm of the creole system. H.P. Jacobs (1971) discusses Couba Cornwallis (a delightful juxtaposition of African and English names), also known as The Duchess of Port Royal and referred to as such by Lady Maria Nugent. The entry in Maria Nugent's diary for 4 March 1805 (not 5 March as H.P. Jacobs has it) reads as follows:

See Martin's (the Duchess of Port Royal as she is called) daughter soon after breakfast. It is a sad thing to see even this good kind of woman in other respects, so easy on the subject of what a decent kind of woman in England would be ashamed of and shocked at. She told me of all her children by different fathers, with the greatest sang-froid. The mother is quite looked up to at Port Royal, and yet her life has been most profligate, as we should think, at least in England. (Wright 1966a, p. 222)

Jacobs believes that Couba Cornwallis was probably the model for a character in an 1836 novel, *Rattlin the Reefer*, in which the hero catches Yellow Fever in Port Royal. Rather than risk the hospital he is nursed back to health by a free mulatto woman. In the novel this woman owns a number of slaves who are rented out for work at the naval dockyard, and she herself takes in washing for naval officers. One of the points of the story is that she has been wooed by various officers but refused them all, though, like Couba Cornwallis, she has a number of children by different fathers. The household of such a woman was open, well managed, and typical of that of many Free Coloured women. A few married Europeans, but the majority were realistic enough to prefer the freedom of temporary liaisons with men whose stay was limited, and who would find it difficult to take a coloured wife back to England.

Less is known about the domestic life of the slave population than about the whites and free coloured. Apologists for slavery found life in the slave quarters compared favourably with that of European peasants. General descriptions of slave houses abound, but they often referred to houses of the head people, thus giving a false impression of the comfort and opulence of the average slave cabin. Probably more accurate are the remarks of the author of *Practical Rules for the Management and Medical Treatment of Negro Slaves in the Sugar Colonies* (1811), who noted that slaves had so little time of their own to spend on the upkeep of houses 'that they are suffered to remain in a decayed and mouldering state so long as they can hold together, to admit their owners to crawl into them; and when they are taken down and rebuilt it is in a manner, and with materials, that promise an existence of four or five years only' (Anon 1811, p. 117). We do not know how much interest was taken in the sexual and domestic life of the slaves by estate staffs. The Europeans had a vague notion that the nuclear family was natural and the most appropriate unit for the residence of slaves, but they appear to have been indifferent to activities that did not interfere with efficiency. Sexual relations between slaves from different estates were frowned upon because they involved nocturnal wanderings, but they could not be stopped. We saw in Chapter 7 (p. 136 above) that since female slaves were found in every gang, including those that required the heaviest labour, domestic activities were correspondingly fragmented and dispersed. Older women were put in charge of infants and the midday meal was often cooked communally. Referring to the Great Gang, Roughley advises that 'Their cook should be regular with their breakfast by nine o'clock in the morning, and their salt provisions constantly served to them. Keeping them in heart they will work accordingly' (Roughley 1823, p. 101). However, rations were also issued on a per capita basis for preparation at home, except in the case of men without wives.

A new synthetic view of slave family structure is emerging from the work of historians, and especially from the detailed and careful studies of B. Higman (Higman 1973, 1975, 1976, 1978; also see Craton 1979 for a summary discussion of this, and other, work). African slaves, arriving in the colonies without kin (apart from the ties between 'shipmates'), settled in what look like monogamous unions and nuclear family households; that is, small domestic units with no complex ties of kinship within them, and without apparent links to other units in the vicinity. Creole slaves, by contrast, were enmeshed in local kinship networks in spite of their liability to sale or summary transfer. As local networks grew more dense slaves sought mates farther afield, expanding the range of kinship networks. According to Craton's interpretation, 'the process tended toward matrifocality rather than the nuclear family . . .' at this stage of development. It is not entirely clear what is meant here by 'matrifocal,' but he emphasizes the coexistence of many different forms of family organization, and regards the carrying forward of African customs, modified by plantation organization and a desire to adopt European forms for status and property reasons, as the key to understanding both historic and modern forms of family life (Craton 1979, pp. 26-35).

Higman analyses data pertaining to Old and New Montpelier sugar estates and Shettlewood Pen, all situated in the western part of Jamaica, for the years from 1817 to 1832. A special report made in 1825 gives a detailed list of 'names with their families and dependants, if any' (Higman 1976, p. 157). Using Laslett's distinction between 'household' and 'houseful' (the latter referring to all persons resident in a house irrespective of assumed 'family' connection), Higman classifies the housefuls into thirteen types. Only 19.8 percent of the 252 houses in the sample contain a man, a woman and her children; 15.5 percent contain a male and a female; 11.1 percent contain males and females; and 1.6 percent contain a male, a woman, her children and her grandchildren. It is difficult – indeed impossible – to know how many of the coresident couples are conjugal partners, but Higman estimates that most of the couples living in Type 1 housefuls (man, woman and her children) were mates – a reasonable assumption. In the absence of any information on the relationships between the individuals in these houses it is impossible to say definitively how kinship relations or domestic organization were structured. Higman is impressed by the apparent dominance of what he calls (tendentiously) 'elementary families.'[1]

The modal houseful comprised a male, a woman and her children (Type 1). This was followed by Types 4 (a male and a female) and 2 (a woman, her children and others). More than half the housefuls contained consanguines (identifiable through the maternal line). The picture changes somewhat if the houseful types are analysed in terms of the number of individuals they accounted for. Almost 75 percent of the slaves lived in units containing consanguines (Types 1-3 and 6-9). Half of them lived in housefuls of Types 1 and 2, the latter being in many cases essentially a sub-type of type 1. Thus although less than 25 percent of the slaves lived exclusively with identifiable kin, almost 50 percent lived in units approximating the elementary family. This has important implications for the understanding of slave family structure. It suggests that the woman-and-children household was far from dominant, whatever the importance of the mother-child link (Higman 1976, p. 159).

The conclusions drawn from these data by Higman are both surprising and unjustified; they make sense only as an attempt to dispel the notion of total promiscuity and exclusively female-headed households – a notion so far-fetched that it needs no special repudiation (see Patterson 1969b for a view very close to this).

The material suggests a pattern of kinship relations similar to that found today. The primary emphasis on the mother-child relationship, and that between siblings, is accompanied by various types of conjugal union, from visiting unions to coresidential unions of differing degrees of stability. Higman remarks that the Africans, because of the relative lack of extensive kinship ties, seem to have lived most frequently in Type 1 housefuls (man, woman and her children), while the slaves of colour (racially mixed) – particularly those with white fathers – always lived in households 'dominated by mothers, grandmothers and aunts' (Higman 1976, p. 160). In summing up, Higman collapses thirteen categories into three that he believes have wide validity. The first consists of people living alone or with

---

[1] Higman's discussion is conditioned by his concern to refute some of Patterson's generalizations about slave family life. See R.T. Smith, 1984d for a discussion of these disputes.

friends; mainly old people, and many Africans without kin. Secondly, the 'great majority of the 70 percent of slaves who did possess family links lived in simple family households, most of them nuclear units' (Higman 1976, p. 168). The third type consisted of extended family households inhabited mostly by creole-born slaves. Although Higman says that this third category was 'relatively unimportant,' a conclusion based solely upon frequency of occurrence in the house lists, he goes on to provide important information which is not based on simple counts of who lives in what house. At Montpelier and Shettlewood 'ten of the groups of families and dependants [were] occupying two or three houses. Most of the latter were Type 2 housefuls, containing coloured and skilled slaves; they generally had the use of relatively large areas of provision grounds and possessed considerable numbers of livestock. It is evident that these slaves had more than one house not because of their numbers but because of their privileged occupations and relative prosperity' (Higman 1976, pp. 168-9). This is fascinating information, pertaining as it does to the influential and powerful elite of the slave population. Some of these privileged men may have had polygynous extended family households, but it appears that polygynous compounds were rare. Drivers, skilled tradesmen and the like more probably built up extended family units in which both men and women played important roles as the nucleus of household groups, while the dominant males established unions with women in other places, thus creating households that appeared to be both female-headed and matri-focal.

The effects of matrifocal ties were to be seen in households other than those of high-ranking slaves; most houses seemed to cluster in what can only be described as matrifocal groups of adjacent houses. This inference depends on the reasonable assumption that houses were listed systematically, so that houses next to each other on the list were physically adjacent. 'At Old Montpelier thirty slaves did not live with their mothers, but thirteen of them lived in the house listed next to their mothers' and another three were only one house further removed . . . In general, 50 percent of the slaves who did not live with their mothers were no further away than one or two houses' (Higman 1976, p. 169). Higman thinks it likely that these groups of adjacent houses formed yards or compounds, and cites independent evidence from another parish for the existence of such yards containing related households.

We have seen that 'yards' appeared very early in Jamaica in the form of urban crowding in Port Royal (see page 153 above), but the rural clusters of houses containing people linked by kinship ties did not necessarily derive from the same source. Africans and people of African descent had their own cultural models of domestic life, models that could not be implemented exactly in the new conditions of West Indian life any more than could the model of the English country estate.

4. Post-emancipation society

The most important development affecting domestic life after the abolition of slavery was the establishment and growth of church-based village communities, and the effects of accumulating economic distress as the sugar industry went into ever steeper decline. This is not the place for an extensive review of those developments; a more detailed discussion will be found in Chapter 5.

Slavery was abolished throughout British possessions in 1838, following a few years transition to wage labour. The event was experienced as a great transformation, ideologically at least, even though the change in social relations proceeded at a very slow pace indeed. The impact on domestic life was less than has generally been assumed. Missionary activity preceding and accompanying emancipation reinforced an existing ideology of respectability, sharpening the contrast between accepted colonial standards and an abstract metropolitan ideal. Emancipation also extended the involvement of the working population in the commodity market, by enlarging the population of small farmers, and creating a class of marginal cultivators dependent on the plantations for seasonal or part-time work to supplement their agricultural activity (see Hall 1978).

As we saw in Chapter 7, the abolition of all legal distinctions based on race and colour did not lead to a rapid increase in the rate of marriage or a diminution in the extent of non-legal unions. However, the growing influence of the churches began to produce a literate, devout core element from the ex-slave population, an element that constituted the 'peasantry' so often referred to at the time as the stable foundation of the new order. The actual economic position of this group varied from colony to colony, but they were generally small farmers growing 'minor' crops (as opposed to sugar) such as coffee, ginger, arrowroot, plantains, pimento – crops traded through middlemen who became prosperous produce dealers. In Jamaica, banana was to become the favoured crop after the opening of the north American market in the 1870s.

Most of the ex-slaves constituted an impoverished rural proletariat, and even those who managed to acquire some marginal cultivation land found it little different from the 'provision grounds' to which they had access as slaves. They still had to work for wages on the surviving plantations and engaged in an increasingly bitter struggle over the conditions and rewards of their labour. Those with land suitable for semi-subsistence farming appeared to be cushioned from the full force of industrial discipline but it would be a mistake to think of this as a peasant population working only occasionally for wages. These workers, whether living on the plantations or not, had their lives shaped by the plantation system; the legacy of resentment created by the whites' refusal to permit a radical transformation of the society, and its economy, is embedded in much of present-day West Indian life.

Before about 1830 few slaves married and 'illegitimacy' was a meaningful concept only for the bastard children of the rich. Since it was an integral part of the slave system it could hardly be defined as a separate social problem. As was shown in Chapter 5, illegitimacy rates have remained high, varying between 60 percent and 70 percent of live births in Jamaica since the 1870s (Roberts 1957, p. 288). West Indians often defer marriage until they have several children, but this is not just a system of deferred marriage pending the accumulation of resources for a proper ceremony. 'Economic' theories have been used to explain West Indian patterns of kinship and marriage, converting the 'problem' of illegitimacy into an exclusively lower class matter, and tying it to a supposed inability to maintain stable domestic units. Orlando Patterson, perhaps in an unguarded moment, once wrote:

The sugar industry has always undermined and continues to undermine, the institution of the family, and, by extension the entire social fabric. You are all acquainted with the way in which the the [sic] sugar plantation during the period of slavery not only destroyed the family life of the African slaves but also that of their masters. What is less known is the fact that it still continues to do so . . . if you compare a sample village of independent small farmers with a sample sugar estate village, you will find this disturbing contrast: in 7 cases out of 10, at least, within the independent village the individual is born and brought up in a stable family protected in the warmth and security of both parents who, in the majority of cases are not only faithfully living with each other, but are likely to be legally married. In contrast, no more than half of the households on the estates (at a very generous estimate) are likely to have both parents present, and what is worse, the majority of such households invariably tend to be extremely unstable. (Patterson 1969a, p. 47)

He attributes this state of affairs to low wages and lack of job security, without considering whether these forces always produce the same effects; among the East Indian estate population of Guyana they do not. Nor is he correct in assuming that rural Jamaican children living outside sugar estate villages always grow up in stable, two-parent households.

The contrast between the supposed immorality of estate life and the Christian stability of the small farmer class is embedded in the class ideology of the small farmers, an ideology forged in the latter part of the nineteenth century. Although relatively few in numbers the class of small farmers has been the matrix for the growth of an upwardly mobile population of black West Indians who have spread into teaching, the police, the civil service and the professions. It has formed the main strength of the non-conformist churches, the active elements in the educational movement that preceded and followed emancipation, and it has always been in the forefront of 'progressive' movements, such as the Jamaica Agricultural Society, the cooperative movement, and more recent nationalist and political independence movements. Many radicals have sprung from this class, beginning with Paul Bogle – the major architect of the Morant Bay Rebellion of 1865 – and including such men as Marcus Garvey. However, its orientation was conservative and deeply imbued with colonial values.

The family life of this rural middle class was modelled on the English non-conformist clergy and colonial servant class, rather than the planters, but it did not escape from the general social ambience of the colonies nor renounce entirely the creole tradition. Fernando Henriques had this class in mind when he referred to the 'Victorian' patriarchalism of much rural Jamaican family life. The ideal model of domestic life, with a strong capable father, a respectable, respectful, pious and submissive mother, and clean, well-behaved, obedient children, is widespread in the West Indies. It is sometimes referred to as 'middle class,' and acts as a pattern for the upwardly mobile. However, the pattern is not that of an isolated nuclear family. Its major elements are the stress on legal and religiously sanctioned marriage – as opposed to common law or visiting unions – the legitimacy of the children, and the financial independence of the husband-father. This model is only partially efficacious in moulding the behaviour of the middle class, and has even less effect among the generality of the population. The rural elite families are the modern counterpart of the prosperous slave households described by Higman (page 160 above). Living in well-appointed, if modest, houses they maintain more extensive households that often contain non-nuclear kin, and the men – while displaying an air of Victorian propriety – are in a position to have 'outside' unions and 'outside' children. Therefore these households cannot be considered alone, but must be placed in the total context of kinship and conjugal relations.

5. Economic development and domestic life

Between the late nineteenth century and World War II there was little change in the main outlines of social life in the West Indies. A relatively stable hierarchy had been established, not devoid of conflict but held in place by a combination of force and ideological persuasion under the guidance of the Colonial Office. Social mobility was limited, class differences were marked, poverty was pervasive and the West Indian economy continued its progressive decline.

Patterns of home life were reflected in domestic architecture and in the marketing of goods and services. Robotham's sketch of the contrast between old and new ways of living in rural Trelawny has much wider

163

application (see Chapter 1, p. 16 above). The lower classes consumed a limited range of goods, most of them imported, consisting of basic household items – cooking utensils, glasses, enamelware – and a limited range of clothing such as shoes and cloth to be made up locally. Rum, sugar, and salted fish or pork were sold by neighbourhood shops, while vegetables were either grown by the household or purchased on a day to day basis from higglers. The houses of the lower classes were small, fragile (often being constructed from wattle and daub), and minimally furnished with locally made chairs and tables, if anything. Beds generally consisted of a sleeping platform covered with mattresses stuffed with dried banana leaves or grass.

The more prosperous classes enjoyed a style of life based on the plantation Great House tradition, using large numbers of servants. Architectural styles were gracious and adapted to the climate. Spacious grounds, wide overarching verandas to provide shade and access to cooling breezes, simple but solid furnishings, mostly locally made, were set in airy rooms with highly polished floors of hardwood or locally-produced tiles. In Guyana, which is south of the hurricane belt, wooden houses were set on piers high above the flood water and open on all sides to the prevailing winds.

The inhabitants of these gracious dwellings followed certain set patterns of domestic economy. Each family had accounts with a grocer (often Chinese), and with a store from which such things as clothing and imported goods could be purchased. Accounts were settled at month-end and it was not unusual for a family to slide into increasing indebtedness. Locally grown foodstuffs would be purchased by the cook from the local market, as would meat, fish, poultry and eggs when available.

In all households, rich or poor, cooking was done on stoves burning wood or charcoal. Refrigeration was rare before the 1940s, though ice could be purchased, or was delivered daily, from large central plants. Electricity became available in the cities of the Caribbean as early as 1899, and a few plantations may have generated their own power, but candles and kerosene were the only forms of artificial lighting available to most people.

Dramatic increases in the level of consumption by all classes began in the 1950s and 1960s, a period when the rate of population growth accelerated. This was a time of increasing prosperity and far-reaching changes, even in Guyana, where political conflict was acute and sometimes violent. Social services were provided on a greatly expanded scale. Schools were built at an unprecedented rate and the rapidly swelling numbers of children were afforded greater educational opportunities than had been available to their parents. Health care improvements reduced the infant mortality rate and pushed up the life expectancy of adults. New roads, sewers, electric cables and telephone lines brought a different pattern of life into the rural areas. The revolution in the material aspects of housing and household management affected the domestic life of almost everyone.

Housing development schemes introduced new, mass production techniques in many territories. The results were not always desirable but they were appreciated by those who felt themselves to be on the way up. In Jamaica, for example, extensive tracts of low and middle income housing were built around Kingston, the capital, and in almost every small town. Based on standard designs for two and three bedroom homes these houses are constructed from prefabricated concrete sections, or poured and compacted *in situ*. Sash windows and wooden jalousies are replaced by standard size metal jalousies, and roofs frequently consist of a concrete slab designed to be hurricane resistant. Cheaper houses may be roofed with corrugated iron or aluminium panels. Even in Guyana, where neither hurricanes nor earthquakes threaten, concrete block houses are gradually replacing the graceful beauty of the old open architecture wooden houses in both city and country.

Urban housing for the more prosperous sections of the middle class is generally less grandiose than that built earlier in the twentieth century, and the major boom in building was just beginning at the time of the studies reported here. In Jamaica, 'town houses' and apartments became increasingly common during the 1970s, and resident domestic servants less frequent. The high level of unemployment ensures that domestic 'helpers' are still available, but the cost of their labour has increased and the conditions of their work have improved. However, the style of middle class living has been transformed since 1970. The ideal family life presented by consumer technology and its associated advertising campaigns is that of the north American urban middle class; small, nuclear families living in their own home surrounded by the products of modern industry: refrigerators, electric or gas stoves, floor polishers and vacuum cleaners; small appliances such as irons, toasters, electric skillets, and hair dryers; furniture made from plastics and other synthetic materials; high fidelity music reproduction systems, television sets and video tape recorders; and, of course, the ubiquitous motor car. These trends are particularly clear in Jamaica, Barbados and Trinidad where television programmes are often directly transmitted from the United States. Guyana has been shielded from these developments to some extent, but consumer interest in north American lifestyles is high. Cash retailing through large supermarkets and department stores has eroded the importance of the small grocery store or the shop at which a family kept a running credit account. Credit facilities are now more commonly provided by banks and finance companies.

The lower and working classes have also upgraded their housing, except for the most depressed of the urban slum populations. In the rural areas fewer houses are built of mud and thatch. Concrete block and tile making plants supply building materials for both urban and rural construction, while lumber – almost all imported – remains a popular material for building small houses. Like the middle classes, those with smaller incomes also have upgraded their domestic equipment. Kerosene stoves for cooking, small refrigerators, radios and television sets are all to be found in even the most modest of homes, as are beds with commercially produced mattresses. In Guyana these changes were already evident when I conducted field research there in 1975.

What changes, if any, in the structure of domestic relations have accompanied these improvements in housing and levels of consumption? This is not an easy question to answer and such observations as are made here are derived solely from the research described in Chapter 1. The genealogical study of kinship was not designed to collect detailed information on domestic organization; such information as we have is embedded in long interview transcripts. To put the matter briefly, and in a manner that will need some qualification: there has been little or no change in the pattern of domestic and kinship relations consequent upon economic development.

i. The creole elite

It is difficult to define an upper class in the modern West Indies. The relative clarity of class relations in colonial society, with Government House as the centre of social life, where English culture, speech and manners were the mark of social striving – if not acceptance – has blurred into a pattern of conflicting claims by different elites, claims increasingly contested in the political arena. In some countries, perhaps most, an elite of families involved in business has found new opportunities to expand its activities and to establish different – if not entirely new – methods of influencing national affairs. Most business activity in the Caribbean is highly dependent upon alliance with outside capital, and that capital is increasingly based in the United States and Canada. Some business families have played a leading part in modern nationalist politics, allying themselves with one or other political party and executing some of the ambitious development plans.[2] In the process they have made a lot of money and have often used part of that wealth to create new, prestigious forms of domestic life. New houses have been built, usually modelled upon the homes of the wealthy in California or Florida; expensive automobiles,

---

[2] For example, the Matalon family has been closely associated with successive Jamaican governments and has undertaken extensive construction projects in conjunction with government urban development schemes. See Nicholls 1985, Chapter 8 for some discussion of the business elites.

preferably German, have been imported; and the furnishings and equipment of houses are now patterned on those of the wealthy in the United States rather than upon those of the old planting and colonial elites. The increasing tendency to move resources, whenever possible, out of the Caribbean and into north America in order to guard against the possibility of expropriation by radical governments, is bound to modify old class patterns.

ii. Middle-class domesticity

As we have seen in previous sections, the 'middle class,' that broad and internally differentiated social element, has expanded during the past thirty years. Three of our informants are typical of this class.

The Sears family (cases number 206 and 256), interviewed in Jamaica over a period of more than a year by Jack Alexander, has been discussed in some of his publications (Alexander 1976; 1977, pp. 417-20, 424-5, 428). The husband is an educated bureaucrat, having studied in the United States and worked in the civil service as well as in business management. Although he is a 'fair' Jamaican he is much darker than his wife who might pass for white outside Jamaica. She is from a rural upper middle class family that formed part of the parish elite in the town where she was born. They now live with their two children in one of the more expensive middle-class housing areas in Kingston, in a house built in the 1960s. Like most such houses it is patterned on those of Florida and California with glass and metal jalousies, broad verandahs, a two-car garage – but the maid's quarters at the rear provide a local touch. Since the mid-1970s, such houses have been equipped with 'burglar bars.' Varying in their degree of ornamentation, depending upon the financial resources of the owner, these bars are designed to keep out the growing army of intruders who will steal, rape, maim or kill without provocation – or so it is firmly believed, and not without cause. These signs of class warfare are especially marked in Jamaica, but not unknown in other parts of the Caribbean.

The Sears are the model of the new, respectable, upwardly mobile Jamaican middle class, patterning itself upon the American urban bourgeoisie. Mrs. Sears has worked as a secretary in the past and will do so again from time to time in order to provide more money to pay for children's education, home maintenance, automobiles, and the imported consumer goods necessary to maintain a prestigious lifestyle. Domestic life revolves around the children, and hopes for their future, and in this respect they fit the description of the American urban middle class. However, the social milieu is Jamaican and this makes a great deal of difference. The Sears marriage has not yet been disturbed by outside affairs, but Mrs.

Sears is anxious that her husband will be tempted by one of the women in the office where he works. She is also concerned about the choices her children will make when the time comes for them to marry or begin courtship (see page 121 above). Similar concerns are found, of course, in the suburbs of Chicago, Philadelphia and other northern cities, where divorce is more frequent.

The pattern of domestic life described above is not new, but the domestic environment has some novel features. Resident servants are now rare except in the wealthiest Jamaican and Guyanese households, but most employ a daily 'helper' and a gardener who works at least one day a week. The chance of domestic servants becoming pregnant by male members of the household is less than in the past. West Indian women still complain bitterly about men's lack of interest in domestic affairs. Men keep out of such 'female' activities as cooking, cleaning and child care, frequently handing over to their wives all domestic budgeting including such things as negotiating mortgages, bank loans and the like.

Mrs. Joyce Cook is a middle-class Jamaican widow (case number 202). One of ten children, she married at the age of thirty after having known her husband for thirteen years. The length of time that elapsed between their meeting and marriage indicates more than caution; each was deeply involved with his and her own family and did not consider marriage until his income was enough to make a proper start.

Mrs. Cook's father was a salesman for a large Kingston firm, covering a territory in several of the northern parishes. Her first memories are of life in the country where they lived in a house next to her great grandmother and her aunt; 'as early as I can remember there was mother and father, and my sisters right down to, well I mean right down to my age, and after me there were the others – my great grandmother lived next door with my aunt; she never really lived with us.' When she was quite small the family moved to Kingston where they lived first in a series of rented houses. As the children began to work the father's income became proportionately less important in the household and the older children eventually decided that it would be sensible for them all to join together and buy a house. This they did, spending more money on remodelling, and each one then had his or her own room. Mrs. Cook, like many of her sisters, went to work as a secretary after leaving high school, earning enough to be an important contributor to family finances. She also had enough freedom to be able to go for a two-year stay in Canada and New York, where she lived with various relatives and found jobs sufficient to pay for her keep. When she and her husband finally decided to get married (they met originally at the house of a common relative), it was soon after he had secured a new and promising job with a large bank in Kingston. He decided to borrow sufficient money to buy a piece of land and build a house.

He had just started working with...so he didn't have any reserves built up, but we were one of the few who took a chance. I mean he had to borrow the money to buy the land and he had to borrow the money to build the house so when we started out I had to go back to work. It was not as usual in those days as it is now but I went back to work until just about a year – until I was expecting Angela . . . then he got a good offer to rent out the house so he said would I mind going back to live at mother's for a while until we sort of built up some little reserve you know. But we didn't know Angela was expected then when we decided that, so I said alright, so we went down to my mother's place and we had to just live in one room more or less.

It is interesting that she refers to this house as her 'mother's house.' In fact her father was still there and still nominal 'household head.' But by this time he was no longer working as a salesman; income from odd jobs, such as helping small businesses with their books, was quickly spent on drink. Mrs. Cook insists that her mother was very tolerant and never tried to dominate her father, but it is clear from the interview material that the father became a source of embarrassment to the family in general and to her in particular. The expenses of the household were being met by the children who, under the guidance and leadership of the eldest daughter, contributed in proportion to their earnings. The same principle was used in buying the house.

As each child got married they spent the first year or two living in the family home before finding a place of their own – in just the way that Mrs. Cook did. She and her husband stayed there for about two years, until their first child was about eighteen months old, and then they moved back into their own house.

Mrs. Cook's mother never went out to work, but she had many ways of making money to keep herself in clothes and small luxuries without having to depend on her husband. For example, she was a well-known cake maker, and people would commission her to make wedding cakes long in advance of the wedding. The general impression one gets from Mrs. Cook is that her mother was a strong, capable person who had to put up with a husband who was weak, irresponsible and who in later life became a burden to everyone. Nevertheless he is pictured as being popular, always surrounded by his men friends – well known and well liked wherever he went. As Alexander has pointed out, this image of the father as a carefree, popular, but essentially irresponsible person who neglects his family occurs repeatedly in interviews with middle-class informants and is probably one of the sources of the middle-class preoccupation with lower class 'illegitimacy' and male 'irresponsibility' (Alexander 1984, pp. 161-2). There is no suggestion that her father ever became redundant in the family, or ceased to be accorded a certain centrality in the formal affairs of the household or in the public status of the family. He remained the formal head of the family even though her mother was the focus of everyone's attachment and the eldest daughter became the manager of household finances and chief decision-maker in practical affairs.

Mrs. Cook's attachment to her mother and her sisters never diminished during her married life. Mr. Cook gradually prospered and by the time he died was a moderately wealthy man with considerable property, though she never knew just how much he earned. The house, built when they first married, was gradually extended piecemeal as they acquired more income and the family grew. Mr. Cook worked hard and provided his wife and children with everything they needed to maintain, and improve, their level of living. Mrs. Cook did not go back to work from the birth of the first child until after her husband's death, and then it was from choice and not necessity. By any standards he was an excellent provider and had a close relationship to his children. Yet the relationship between Mrs. Cook and her husband conformed more to the segregated than the joint role pattern. When asked what kind of expectation she had of marriage, she replied at length about the distance in her relationship to her husband.

Well you see I don't know what I expected – I suppose it was more or less companionship you look forward to, and well you see my case is sort of different, because I was never a demanding person and I know the things I put up with, I don't think the young people of today would put up with it . . . I mean they may not be big things but still. For instance as I say I never asked my husband where he was going, why he was going, or when he was going. He just say, 'I'm going out this evening' and he's gone; and now that's not going to suit most people and they want to know where he's going and why he's going. Now I never . . . I figured if he wants to tell me he'd tell me, and maybe some later date I'd hear it you know. But because he was the type . . . I don't know, I always feel that he had a . . . I don't know how to explain it. There was a sort of a reservation to him, I'd hear him telling his sister things for instance that he'd never told me, and I'd overhear them talking about it with his sister. And maybe it's just something in business but I know when he came home he always said he didn't want to be bothered with business and so I never bothered him with business you know. And I always felt that when a man came home in the afternoon they didn't want to be bothered with household things and . . . But he didn't know what was going on in the house you know. He just expected his house to be run properly and he never got any of the details. He didn't know how to open the fridge or to take out a tray of ice – and I mean for instance he would go any place he felt like going but he always had the feeling that I should be here when he came home.

At one point they were separated for some months when Mr. Cook was having an affair with one of his secretaries and 'thought he was in love' as she puts it. When this happened he bought a smaller house for his wife and children and installed them in it. Mrs. Cook made no fuss, keeping it very quiet and biding her time. He visited his wife and children regularly and made every provision for their material well-being, and she attributed the 'fizzling out' of the love affair and his eventual return to his family to the fact that he missed the children. In any case, he did come back on condition that she never mention it again. Obviously, she thought this to be a victory, considering that so long as a man continues to provide properly for his family there is no point in creating a fuss, though she recognizes that 'the younger generation' would not be so tolerant.

After her husband died, some six years before the interviews began, Mrs. Cook decided that she would go back to working as a secretary, even though she had been left a number of properties and an adequate income on which to complete her children's education. She now lives with two of her sisters who are also widows and with whom she has maintained a close relationship for the whole period of her marriage.

Mrs. Cook is not a 'typical' middle-class Jamaican but many features of her life history recur in other cases, including the pattern of segregated conjugal roles, the maintenance of close relationships between each partner and their respective kin, and the strength of the network of matrilateral ties. Also of importance in other cases is the tolerance of marital infidelity and the feeling that the men of the family are less than wholly committed to their conjugal families, despite the clear importance of the husband-father as the marker of community status. Mrs. Cook put the matter very well when she was discussing child training and the importance of keeping up standards. She and her daughter were about to go to a shopping centre on some small errand and she asked her daughter to wait a moment because she had to change her dress. The daughter said, 'Oh no, you can go as you are mummy' to which she replied, 'No, remember I am Mrs. Kenneth Cook and I must keep up a certain standard you know.' She went on to explain how important is the keeping up of standards when you are known around the place; not the standards of her parental family, though that may have been a factor, but the standards based on her husband's position in the community and her share in it as 'Mrs. Kenneth Cook.'

Middle-class domestic organization begins with the acquisition of a house in which the couple will make their family life; living with parents is seen as a temporary arrangement enabling the couple to get their finances in order. A couple will not marry without clear prospects for a home of their own, an attitude shared by all West Indians. The subsequent focus of the family is children; Mrs Cook is emphatic that it was better to stay at home with her children than go out to work, but she was not satisfied spending all her time at home while her husband was outside – and just where, she never knew. Similarly she never knew how much he earned, nor the details of his career and work, while he showed no interest in the details of housekeeping. Throughout married life she kept close contact with her mother and sisters, and now that her husband is dead she has gone back to live with her sisters. The network of matrilateral ties is strong but each woman is closely identified with her husband. Mrs. Cook always refers to her sisters as 'Mrs. Levy,' 'Mrs. Jones,' etc., indicating that both marriage and the husband are socially critical.

Almost all Mrs. Cook's close female relatives have worked at some point in their lives, and many of them have professions, but sex role differentiation remains strong and domestic affairs are still the woman's concern. All the families have maids. Maids continue to be important in middle-class West Indian domestic life, but they are not closely integrated into familial relationships. Where maid's quarters are built at the rear of houses they are separated in some way. The facilities are cramped and spartan, intended strictly for single women who are not supposed to have any social life of their own. The separation of class is stronger than the identity of common household membership; indeed, servants are not a part of the household as they were in England.

Both the Sears and the Cooks were born into the established middle class. The vast majority of the 'new' middle class are upwardly mobile from the ambitious, church-going, school-oriented levels of the upper lower and lower middle class. B. Johnson is a senior civil servant in Jamaica (case number 205). Like many other members of the Jamaican bureaucratic and educational elite he comes from a rural background – a child of that solid, rural, middle-sized farmer group discussed previously (page 163). His father was a farmer and banana-buying agent; his mother a schoolteacher. He and his sister became teachers, while his brother went to agricultural college before entering the civil service. Today, Johnson lives in a new and expensive house in a fashionable part of Kingston. His wife is also a senior civil servant and his only son went to an expensive boarding school and to university. In many ways he is typical of the successful upper middle-class bureaucrat whose income has made possible a move into one of the expensive housing areas. The family's style of life includes much entertaining, mainly of friends and colleagues, and they have a resident maid. From time to time relatives come to stay, but this family is unusual in not having any relatives living with them. Superficially, they are an isolated, urban, middle class nuclear family.

The home in which Johnson grew up was, at first glance, the kind of 'Victorian' patriarchal family discussed earlier (page 163 above). His father was respected and well liked, and the family prominent in the district. His mother had married into the area from her own rural home some thirty miles away. Johnson recalls that they always had a maid to do the housework, cooking and to look after the children, making it possible for his mother to continue teaching until the end of her life. Johnson's parents were not wealthy, and – appearances to the contrary – his mother ran the home, kept the family together and made most of the decisions. Whatever income his father made from the farm, much of it was spent with his drinking companions; his mother's small but stable income kept the domestic budget on an even keel. Johnson remembers his mother being the strength of the family and its emotional centre. His father always administered punishment, was always there if needed and, formally, made all the decisions. The family lived in its own house, but was surrounded by other members of the 'Johnson clan' as he calls them – his father's brothers and their children. When Johnson was young his father's mother lived with them and other relatives were in and out of the house all the time. He, his brother and sister all did well in primary school, but the family could not afford expensive boarding schools for them, nor were they able to win one of the limited scholarships then available. Each worked his or her way through the pupil teacher system, until Johnson and his sister gained entry to Teacher Training College, and his brother to the Jamaica School of Agriculture.

Johnson now has a good and secure income with little cause to depend on kinship ties for financial help or cooperation, a situation very different from that of the business families to whom kinship ties are crucial. However, the kinship networks of members of the bureaucratic elite are no less extensive and quite important as sources of mutual assistance. As Johnson points out, a high proportion of his kinsmen are teachers, and there is a tendency for people to marry within their own professional circle. He is closest to his brother, who now lives in the country; they visit and stay with each other frequently. His father died some years ago, but his mother still lives in the old family house which remains a focal point of family solidarity.

Not all upwardly mobile members of the rural lower middle class have done as well as B. Johnson and his siblings. Most cluster in the lower ranks of the civil service, teaching, police, nursing and the commercial bureaucracies. Diane Austin's research in a Kingston suburb, which she has named Vermount, provides a vivid portrait of the domestic life of Jamaican families of this class. Most retain close connections with rural relatives. Their urban households are supplied with the cheap labour of 'adopted' girls, essentially live-in maids, and are often populated with an assortment of relatives who are 'boarding' while working or attending school in the city.

The houses in Vermount are typical of the 'middle income' housing schemes. Constructed of concrete with two or three bedrooms, each house has a carport and usually a small maid's room with attached bathroom. Many carports have been converted into extra bedrooms while the maid's rooms have become part of the domestic living space. The living room is generally furnished with chairs, small 'cocktail' tables on which to rest glasses, perhaps a rug and certainly a television set. The dining section has chairs and table, refrigerator and a china cabinet. The pattern of domestic life often does not use space in the way envisaged by the architect. In one household described in detail by Austin, most of the preparation of food, cooking, and eating was carried out in a covered portion of the yard at the rear of the house. Instead of a lawn and flower garden many residents have planted food crops and may even keep small stock. Most families try to maintain an automobile since this is an essential component of a prestigious lifestyle, but it will not always be in running condition. Car pools and lifts from friends whose car is working are the normal means of getting to work in the city, though soaring gasoline prices force some people to use the despised minibuses.

The segregation of conjugal roles is marked in these households. When the women work, as most do, they also take care of domestic affairs when they get home. Most men spend their leisure time out of the house with friends, drinking, gambling, talking or having affairs with other women. These families are not wealthy, but neither are they poor. No economic considerations intervene to require that they 'stretch' their values because of inability to live in a proper, bourgeois, Christian way. The pattern of domestic life is that of the nineteenth-century rural elite, modified only by differences in the physical accoutrements of the home; electricity, radio, television, gas or kerosene cookers and so forth. Food is traditional creole fare consisting mainly of rice, locally grown vegetables and small amounts of meat in the form of pig tail, chicken, salt fish, and occasionally beef.

iii. The urban lower class

In the rapidly growing cities of Latin America and the Caribbean the living conditions of the working and lower classes are often described in terms of overcrowding, poverty, disease and other manifestations of social neglect. These conditions exist and should not be minimized, but considerable progress has been made in housing, feeding, clothing, educating and providing medical attention for a rapidly growing West Indian population. The housing conditions of the urban poor are no worse than they were thirty years ago, and in most cases a good deal better. But better or worse, certain aspects remain the same. The urban lower and working classes live in crowded dwellings, where the dwelling unit is likely to be a room rather than a house or apartment; where cooking, washing and bathing are carried out in shared facilities; where there is little privacy; and where women form the nucleus of domestic units.

We saw earlier that 'yards' have been a characteristic form of urban living space since the establishment of West Indian cities; they were reported for Port Royal in the seventeenth century (page 152 above), and they continue to be important today. A little known, but sensitive, work by Erna Brodber, *A Study of Yards in the City of Kingston* (1975), identifies 'yard' as 'an urban Jamaican residential unit' (p. i), but her discussion shows that the concept is of wider significance; a matrix out of which other residential forms develop. Slave quarters on plantations in many parts of the West Indies were known as yards. Handler discusses yard designations on Barbados plantations at some length (Handler and Lange 1978). In Guyana after emancipation a distinction was drawn between the 'nigger yard' and the 'coolie yard' on some plantations. In one Guyanese village that grew out of an abandoned plantation, a section is still known as the 'building yard' in reference to an area which contained the sugar factory more than sixty years ago. Most generally, 'yard' refers to a particular area where some activity takes place. Brodber's usage is more particular, referring to a dwelling area that may be an individual house lot, or an extensive assemblage of buildings.

Contemporary writers compared slaves to English peasants and implied that they lived in 'cottages' clustered in something like an English village. The urban yard is a much better model of what slave quarters were like. In eighteenth-century Kingston, Jamaica, merchants kept their slaves in a yard where a cluster of residences were surrounded by a high wall. By the late nineteenth century the number and extent of urban yards had grown as they absorbed an increasing number of migrants from the rural areas coming to town to hire themselves out for work. Thus, during slavery and afterwards, urban yards were the residences of landless labourers. In the rural areas the wealthiest and most prestigious slaves lived in extended family compounds resembling yards, and a distinction should be made between kin-based compounds of that kind and yards where diverse people are thrown together out of necessity.

The relationship between the physical constraints of housing design and the structure of domestic relations is not always clear; house patterns do not always, or even frequently, reflect domestic processes. The layout and architecture of houses in Afro-Guyanese villages is a good example.

These villages, established on abandoned plantations in the mid-nineteenth century, were generally surveyed and divided into rectangular lots (see R.T. Smith 1956; Young 1958). Houses were usually small and rectangular with wattle and daub walls and thatch roofs. More prosperous villagers built wooder houses of European design with sash windows. Even wattle and daub houses are confined by the rectangular floor plan and show none of the fluidity of African patterns. These small houses are often occupied by large numbers of people related to each other in complex ways, but house structure is rarely modified to accommodate this complexity. If a household group becomes too big, an additional rectangular house is built on the same lot. During field research in Jamaica one family was found using a method of construction that was much freer; a method that adapted design to need. The area had been a squatter settlement on land in a water catchment area. When the settlement grew, the government found

175

it more practical to grant titles than attempt a massive, and politically unpopular, eviction. Even so, some of the less regulated aspects of squatter life remained. The family in question had built a temporary wooden house on the 'captured' lot. With the prosperity of the 1960s and the granting of secure title they were able to build a permanent concrete house. The family consisted of a middle aged couple, living in a common law union, and their seven children. The two eldest daughters were working and bringing in money, though each had children of their own. At the time of the interviews the new house, only partially constructed, consisted of a long rectangular row of three rooms, occupied by the elder couple, the younger children, and one daughter and her infant child, respectively. The father of the child visited regularly. The other daughter lived in the old wooden house with her 'intended' husband, and the kitchen of that house was used by the whole family. They intended to continue building rooms around a central yard before demolishing the old wooden house. Organic growth of this kind, based on need, is difficult where building regulations are more strictly enforced, but it provides insight into the dynamics of family process.

6. Conclusion

Social science is badly in need of new analytical categories that will permit of a more precise understanding of the constellations of relationship, mutuality and reciprocity that cut across household boundaries. There is no doubt of the strength of images of nuclear family household living, and they have a considerable impact on West Indian society, but the reality of domestic relations is much more complex, even among the urban middle class. Terms such as 'extended family,' 'stem family,' and 'grand family' all suffer from a certain rigidity of definition, deriving from their origin in European common sense conceptions of kinship as biology, and household as the locus of reproduction of kin relationships. What is needed is a term with the same flexibility that 'family' once had when it meant all those – irrespective of presumed biological links – who lived under the authority of the head of a household (again broadly defined). I do not suggest a new term here, but something like 'co-family' might suffice, meaning that assemblage of persons that cooperates regularly in at least some of the presumed minimal activities of family life – child care, shelter, sexual relations – irrespective of which 'household' they belong to.

9
Conclusion

Let every female live perfectly uncontrolled by any man, and enjoying every freedom, which the males only have hitherto enjoyed; let her choose and change her lover as she please, and of whatever rank he may be. At her decease, let her possessions be divided among her children.

Every child might remain with the mother, who might superintend its education. The daughters, arrived at maturity, might follow their inclinations with so little restraint as their brothers, who might quarter themselves on the daughters of other families.

Though both sexes are equal, their employments may be different . . . Man is designed for active, woman for domestic life. Let males be their own masters, and employ themselves in public affairs; let the females be their own mistresses, and manage their own domestic concerns.

James Henry Lawrence 1976 [1811]

What are the implications for general theory of the data presented in the preceding chapters?

The supposed 'problems' that have dominated the literature on Caribbean kinship (and much of that on kinship generally), were generated in the social practice of colonial social systems. The Caribbean is a particularly useful area in which to study these processes. Three hundred years of distinguishing between 'civilized' and 'natural' sexual relations, 'legitimate' and 'illegitimate' births, 'inside' and 'outside' unions – all with the peculiar stamp of colonial racial meaning (Chapter 5) – have produced a system of categories and discriminations ideally suited to mark the hierarchical structure of class, and to embed that structure in the most intimate of social relations at all levels of the society. The remarkable thing is that social scientists followed so closely the ideological concerns of their informants in the interpretation of 'the facts' (see R.T. Smith 1982a). Once again there was congruence between the dominant theoretical paradigm of social science and the political preoccupations of the time.

The dominant theoretical paradigm of the 1950s, in social anthropology and sociology alike, was structural functionalism. British anthropologists, influenced by Radcliffe-Brown and Malinowski, had developed synchronic analysis as a powerful tool for the description and understanding of systems of social relations in small-scale societies, particularly in Africa; even those with misgivings about the theory, like Evans-Pritchard, used it (see Evans-Pritchard 1951). American anthropology, heir to the German historical tradition brought to the United States by Franz Boas and others, retained 'culture' as its master concept even when synchronic functional analysis was grafted onto it. In the early 1950s a group of young Americans, (including Fallers, Geertz, Murphy and Schneider), increasingly influenced by the work of Talcott Parsons, as well as by British anthropology and the Chicago legacy of Radcliffe-Brown, continued the development of a synthesis of cultural and social structural studies, begun by scholars as diverse as Lloyd Warner, Fred Eggan and Gregory Bateson. Parsons himself was deeply interested in both cultural and social structural anthropology, envisioning a division of labour between sociology and anthropology such that cultural analysis would become the special province of anthropology. Some of the results of that idea, and the parallel growth of transactional analysis in Britain, have been discussed in Chapter 2 and in previous publications (R.T. Smith 1978a, 1984b). These developments influenced the course of studies of kinship in the Caribbean, though their impact is generally masked by arguments more appropriate to an earlier phase (see Patterson 1982 for example).

Before the publication of Fernando Henriques's *Family and Colour in Jamaica* (1953), the discussion of West Indian kinship had been dominated either by the cultural survival theories of M.J. Herskovits and his wife, or by a concern with social disorganization. Contrasting conceptions were embodied in these points of view – of a smashed and fragmented social order built upon coerced labour, or a triumphant survival of basic cultural principles in spite of the vicissitudes of slavery. The same concepts dominated discussion of north American black communities. This debate has not diminished in intensity, nor have its terms ceased to intrude themselves into discussions driven by other theoretical concerns, but the focus of attention since the 1950s has been upon creole social forms – a focus produced by the happy conjunction of structural functional theory and the drive for national self-determination.

In the 1980s both are eclipsed by other issues. Among anthropologists, uncertainty about the limits and nature of the object of study fits well with the growing political realization that small nations are pawns in a game that is played by others. Creole systems are the typical products of open frontiers and social interpenetration, as was noted in Chapter 1 (page 2); shaped first by pragmatic considerations, they become stubbornly persistent even in the shifting tides of the modern world system. Against this background, what is the status of the concepts that have been most influential in shaping our view of Caribbean kinship?

The concept of 'the matrifocal family' was developed in the early 1950s in an attempt to explain the apparently peculiar features of family and domestic organization in the West Indies generally, and in a number of Afro-Guyanese villages in particular (R.T. Smith 1956). Clearly emergent from the theoretical milieu of that period, it took account of the literature on Afroamerican kinship, was influenced by Fortes' work on the developmental cycle of domestic groups in Africa (Fortes 1949), and relied on Parsons for a view of the societal context in which families function. The term 'matrifocal' has been widely used, and a review of that use will be undertaken in a later work (see R.T. Smith 1963, 1973, 1978a; Martinez-Alier 1974; Patterson 1982; McKenzie 1981; and Gonzalez 1984 for some general discussion). However, it is pertinent to ask how the concept relates to the data reported here.

In its original form the concept of matrifocality did not assume that women dominate West Indian family life; it assumed that women's position in domestic group organization becomes salient because class and racial differentiation act upon a basic functional entity, the domestic family, to produce a particular configuration of developmental stages. The 'functions' performed by the domestic family were seen to be, primarily, childrearing and its associated activities (see R.T. Smith 1956, 1963, 1973, and 1978a). M. J. Herskovits termed this work 'scientistic,' mainly because of its rejection of his theory of survival and reinterpretation (Herskovits 1960). A structural functional approach required synchronic closure, and to that extent was ahistorical. It did not, however, deny the importance of African culture in shaping creole social structure.[1] The 'culture historical' approach to kinship analysis, as exemplified by Herskovits himself, seemed (and seems) even less productive than structural functionalism, seeking to explain current social practice as an amalgam of traits adapted for use in a particular situation. A different approach was needed, combining the precision of a structural account with the dynamic qualities of processual analysis, a long-standing aim of social scientists, given new form in the

---

[1] The disputes over the extent and strength of African 'survivals' in the social and cultural life of the modern West Indies are grossly misplaced. It is as ridiculous to suggest that all traces of African culture were removed from the West Indies as it is to suggest that African culture persisted unmodified for several hundred years. That did not happen even in Africa, and more than modern European culture is untransformed from the seventeenth and eighteenth centuries. West Indian history must document the details of everyday life throughout the colonial period and when it does the dispute over 'survivals' will be redundant. We know, as Marx said, that 'men make their own history, but they do not make it just as they please . . . but under circumstances directly encountered, given and transmitted from the past. The tradition of all the dead generations weighs like a nightmare on the brain of the living' (Marx 1963, p. 15).

179

1950s and 1960s. Restatements of the problem have been more numerous than solutions to it (see R.T. Smith 1978a, 1982a, 1984b, 1984d).

If the concept of the matrifocal family is to have any useful meaning it must be redefined to purge it of the functionalist assumptions embedded in its earlier use. Nothing can prevent its being used to mean 'female-headed household' but if that becomes an accepted usage it would be better to abandon the term. Any refurbishing of this concept must take into account the complete reappraisal of anthropological concepts that embody European cultural assumptions. Therefore it cannot be a term that takes its meaning from its contrast with 'normal nuclear family,' since there is considerable doubt as to the 'normalcy' of nuclear family structure.

Students of the contemporary Caribbean are, understandably, concerned with problems of economic and social development, poverty and the difficulties attendant on marginality within the world economic system. These are real problems that should not be minimized, but they do not cause the West Indian family to be as it is. Matrifocality arises from the way in which kinship and family life is practised, and that practice is rooted in the cultural meaning of social life developed over several hundred years. It can and will change, not as a response to increases in the level of living, but only if, and when, there is a change in the structure of social hierarchy and a change in the definition and meaning of sex roles. Matrifocality in domestic relations arises at the conjuncture of social hierarchy and marked sex role differentiation.

It has been shown in earlier chapters that family relations are not confined within the limits of households, or domestic groups, and considerable space has been devoted to showing that widely understood systems of meaning embody within their structure the rules for differential application within the class system. Thus legal, common law and visiting unions constitute a contrasted series, each with its appropriate context of embodiment. Domesticity has a similar range of meanings and appropriate contexts, and it is within this range that we must seek an understanding of the meaning of matrifocality.

Bolingbroke was only one among many contemporary observers who noted that during the slavery period plantation owners were known for their lavish hospitality, and that if they had no wife they generally provided themselves with a mistress who 'embrace[s] all the duties of a wife, except presiding at table; so far is decorum maintained and a distinction made' (see quotation on page 86). That this was a matter of some importance may be judged by the fact that it was mentioned so often by many observers throughout the eighteenth and early nineteenth centuries, and it marks clearly the point of articulation of the domestic and class systems. For the upper class, then as now, the house is a prime marker of class, and the locus of activities establishing class position. West India planters spent considerable sums on the construction of Great Houses, not all of which were as opulent as the term sounds, though some were magnificent indeed. The Codrington house at Betty's Hope plantation in Antigua was already well furnished when Sir William Codrington was resident there in the early eighteenth century. He had no wife at the time, but the household had many female house servants, one or more of whom doubtless filled the role described by Bolingbroke (see R.T. Smith 1987). Today the Great House at Betty's Hope is in ruins but its massive stone foundations, cellars and cisterns suggest its former glory. Entertaining has always been a mark of West Indian elite culture. Balls, massive banquets, extravagant dinners with the most expensive imported food and drink were, and are, accepted activities of those at the top of the social hierarchy, and in all this the master of the house, supported and accompanied by his wife, is at the centre of attraction. A housekeeper, 'keeper,' or 'kep' miss,' would certainly be invaluable in the absence of a wife, but could not share in the status of the master. During the slavery period, white men who became absorbed into the domestic life of families generated through non-legal unions with coloured women, men such as Dr. Quier (see page 96), must have had a difficult time negotiating the niceties of colonial society. They generally remained in rural seclusion, keeping their personal and public lives sharply segregated.

No matter how important a wife, or a keeper, might have been in facilitating public displays of hospitality she was the recipient of only reflected, or at best shared, glory. Her major role was internal to the domestic domain, as mother, wife or companion, though there was a marked difference in the relative positions of wife and keeper. A wife bore legitimate heirs for her husband, with all that meant in terms of property transmission and education for position in society. Much of the work of child care was delegated to servants, and the wife became a manager of the domestic domain. As Janet Schaw remarked, 'those of the first fortune and fashion keep their own keys and look after everything within doors; the domestick Economy is entirely left to them' (Andrews and Andrews 1923, p. 113). Creole white families constituted an authentic local upper class, intimately linked to a wider, metropolitan-oriented, colonial class of property owners, so that its members were both in and out of the local social system. A coloured housekeeper, no matter what degree of intimacy she enjoyed with her patron, bore children identified with her, and not with their genitor. She became the focal point of the domestic domain, excluded as she was from a share in the public status of her non-legal spouse. She also represented an unequivocally local, creole, way of life. The creole mistress who made the mistake of accompanying her protector to England was rare (see Rhys 1966).

This situation does not exist in precisely the same form today of course.

181

Kinship and class in the West Indies

Upper class West Indians rarely have resident mistresses, and neither they nor their wives are as preoccupied with property transmission and the maintenance of family position. The term 'upper class' is hardly appropriate to any segment of the modern West Indian population, except perhaps for that small group of outsiders representing the power and status of the dominating powers (Chapter 1, p. 13). The local elite operates in a different range of the status scale.

The West Indian lower classes value home life, but use their limited means to enhance status in other contexts: by dressing well on ritual occasions; by lavish hospitality in the poor man's social club – the rum shop; or by attending dances. The poor do not use their home for entertaining friends, except on the occasion of life cycle rituals when the emphasis is upon sociability and mutuality – not the quality of the furnishings. The domestic domain is dominated by women because it is the sphere of their activities – child rearing, cooking, washing – and no consideration of family position or status intervenes. Lower class domestic organization is functionally matrifocal because of the segregation of sex roles and the salience of mothering within the domestic domain. It is magnified by the dual marriage system and the open structure of domestic relations that are not confined within household boundaries.

The way in which the elements of kinship and marriage are brought together as individuals and families move within the class system has been discussed at length (Chapters 5 and 6). A man's enhanced occupational status leads to the expectation of marriage and further upward mobility, while it also increases the likelihood that he will have outside unions. The complex ideology of class both enjoins respectable family life based on marriage, church participation and education, and at the same time embodies hierarchical ideas about race and the meaning of the inside/outside distinction. Ideology does not operate within a vacuum; it is sustained by the distribution of power and the nature of institutions, and in turn it facilitates the existence of that particular hierarchy, even forming the terms of protest discourse within it.

It is now widely recognized that poverty and deprivation do not determine family structure, except insofar as those terms contain within themselves the particular structure of class, and its cultural meaning, of the society in question. The policy implications are clear, but they do not include an abandonment of social service to the poor. The family is not the cause of poverty; its particular shape is part of the social practice of class relations.

These observations are particularly relevant to understanding the use of the term 'matrifocal' in the study of north American society, where it has been generally misunderstood and has become a peg on which to hang slogans in an ideological battle couched in sociological jargon. It began

182

with a United States government report self-consciously designed to produce controversy and social action; *The Negro Family in America: The Case for National Action*, published in March 1965 by the Office of Policy Planning and Research of the United States Department of Labor. Its opening sentence reads, 'The United States is approaching a new crisis in race relations,' and goes on to say that 'The fundamental problem . . . is that of family structure.' Written by Daniel P. Moynihan, then Assistant Secretary of Labor, in collaboration with other staff members, it became both an integral part of President Johnson's policy views and a focus of bitter debate among academics. Moynihan adopted a view, taken from Franklin Frazier (1939) and increasingly popular among social planners in the British colonies (see R.T. Smith 1982a), of the family life of Blacks as disorganized and therefore the 'cause' of 'welfare dependency.' Moynihan's argument was simple; 'the family is the basic social unit of American life' in which adult social conduct is learned. White families have 'achieved a high degree of stability' while 'the family structure of lower class Negroes is highly unstable.' The root of the problem lay, according to this report, in slavery, and the abolition of slavery did not create the right atmosphere for 'progress' toward the middle class pattern. While matriarchy may be all right in some situations it is a disadvantage in a society that 'presumes male leadership in private and public affairs.'

After twenty years of increasing struggle for women's rights and a tremendous change in the standards of acceptable social behaviour among the American middle class, these remarks appear to be grossly misplaced. However, unemployment, welfare dependence, urban crime and marital instability continue to exist – and are indeed exacerbated – in the largely black and Hispanic neighbourhoods of American cities. There is no evidence that poverty is caused by family structure, and a good deal of evidence that kinship ties continue to represent the major ameliorating factor making life bearable among the urban poor. Thus the debate about the 'matrifocal family' is largely misplaced. What is needed is a more complex study of the genesis of the patterns of kinship, marriage and family in the historical experience of Americans in the slave societies of the southern states. Such a study would need to take account of the relations between black and white, the manner in which each element in those societies defined itself in opposition to others, and the structure of the system that encompassed them all. Such a perspective is not new; in many ways it was the point of view adopted by Tocqueville in his penetrating comments on race relations in America (1954, Vol. I, Chapter XVIII) and it is embodied in Dumont's sketchy discussion of race and caste (1980, pp. 247-66).

The West Indian family is not a 'problem' to be dealt with by government action, any more than is the American family, though both societies have their share of social problems that need to be addressed by the government. Kinship has constituted the major tissue of sustaining human relations throughout a turbulent West Indian history. Its social significance is different from that in small scale societies. It has spread a network of mutuality complementing, and sometimes replacing, that of tribal affiliation, caste, and even locality, bridging the gap – no matter how tentatively – opened up by the political and class structure of a society rooted in slavery, racism and economic exploitation. In the midst of the demeaning of the human spirit inflicted on both masters and slaves, kinship humanized the life of the slaves and created some bonds of affection between white and black. From the perspective of the righteous indignation of the twentieth century it is easy to discount those ties. For West Indians of predominantly European ancestry to grow dreadlocks and adopt fierce Somali names makes a political statement but does not expunge the past.

Today West Indians maintain networks of kin that belie the notion of an anarchic family life. When they meet in London, Toronto, New York or Birmingham (either one) they experience a feeling of identity that is based not only on race or territorial affiliation, but on the common inheritance of a created, valued way of life that is creole. The depth and dimensions of that life are to be seen in the material collected through genealogical analysis of the kind described here. It serves to lay bare the complex relations that are often backgrounded in superficial discussions of 'family' but it also provides data that illuminate the structured systems of concepts concerning acceptable behaviour which seem to be highly resistant to change so long as the social matrix in which they acquire pragmatic meaning remains intact. The lower classes of the New World are not impoverished because their families are disorganized; their kinship systems were born and reproduce themselves within a particular kind of class system that links all family 'types' into a structurally related series dominated by an ideology of evaluation that serves to reproduce the class system itself. The way of life of the poor would be denigrated no matter what its content just as the actions of the 'master' in the microcosmic 'family' of the 'outside union' remain free of stigma so long as his class position is intact. Genealogies enable us to see the real links between and within classes without the preconceived limitations of a segmented view.

References

Alexander, Jack 1973. *The culture of middle class family life in Kingston, Jamaica.* Unpublished Ph.D. Dissertation. Department of Anthropology, University of Chicago.
   1976. A study of the cultural domain of 'relatives.' *American Ethnologist,* 3: 17-38.
   1977. The culture of race in middle-class Kingston, Jamaica. *American Ethnologist,* 4: 413-35.
   1978. The cultural domain of marriage. *American Ethnologist,* 5: 5-14.
   1984. Love, race, slavery, and sexuality in Jamaican images of the family. In Raymond T. Smith (ed.), *Kinship ideology and practice in Latin America.* Pp. 147-80. Chapel Hill: University of North Carolina Press.
Alexander, Jeffrey 1983. *The modern reconstruction of classical thought*: Talcott Parsons. Vol. 4 of *Theoretical logic in sociology.* Berkeley: University of California Press.
Andrews, Evangeline W. and C.M. Andrews (eds.) 1923. *Journal of a lady of quality: being the narrative of a Journey from Scotland to the West Indies, North Carolina and Portugal in the years 1774 to 1776.* New Haven: Yale University Press.
Anon (By a professional planter) 1811. *Practical rules for the management and medical treatment of negro slaves in the sugar colonies.* London.
Austin, Diane J. 1974. *Symbols and ideologies of class in urban Jamaica: a cultural analysis of classes.* Chicago: University of Chicago Ph.D. dissertation.
   1979. History and symbols in ideology: a Jamaican example. *Man* (N.S.) 14: 497-514.
   1984. *Urban life in Kingston, Jamaica: the culture and class ideology of two neighborhoods.* New York: Gordon and Breach.
Barrow, Christine 1983. Ownership and control of resources in Barbados: 1834 to the present. *Social and economic studies* 32: 83-120.
Bendix, Reinhardt 1960. *Max Weber: an intellectual portrait.* New York: Knopf.
Berthelot, J., and Gaumé, M. 1982. *Kaz Antiyé.* Paris: Editions Caribéennes.
Bickerton, Derek 1975. *Dynamics of a creole system.* London: Cambridge University Press.
Blake, Judith 1961. *Family structure in Jamaica: the social context of reproduction.* New York: Free Press.
Bolingbroke, Henry 1809. *A voyage to the Demerary, containing a statistical account of the settlements there, and of those on the Essequebo, the Berbice, and other contiguous rivers of Guyana.* London: Printed for Richard Phillips.

References

Bott, Elizabeth 1957. *Family and social network: roles, norms, and external relationships in ordinary urban families*. London: Tavistock Publications Limited.

Bourdieu, Pierre 1977. *Outline of a theory of practice*. (Translated by Richard Nice). Cambridge: Cambridge University Press.

Braithwaite, Lloyd 1953. Social stratification in Trinidad. *Social and economic studies* 2: 5-175.

    1960. Social stratification and cultural pluralism. In Vera Rubin (ed.), *Social and cultural pluralism in the Caribbean*. Pp. 816-31. New York: New York Academy of Sciences.

Brathwaite, Edward 1971. *The development of creole society in Jamaica 1770-1820*. Oxford: The Clarendon Press.

Brereton, Bridget 1979. *A history of modern Trinidad, 1783-1962*. London: Oxford University Press.

Brodber, Erna 1975. *A Study of Yards in the city of Kingston*. Mona, Jamaica: Institute of social and economic research, Working Papers No. 9.

Brown, Jennifer 1980. *Strangers in blood: fur trade company families in Indian country*. Vancouver: University of British Columbia Press.

Buchler, Ira R. and Selby, Henry A. 1968. *Kinship and social organization*. New York: Macmillan.

Buisseret, David 1980. *Historic architecture of the Caribbean*. London: Heinemann Educational Books Ltd.

Campbell, Mavis C. 1976. *The dynamics of change in a slave society: a sociopolitical history of the Free Coloreds of Jamaica, 1800-1865*. Rutherford: Fairleigh Dickenson University Press.

Cancian, Francesca M. 1975. *What are norms? A study of beliefs and action in a Mayan community*. London: Cambridge University Press.

Carr, Lois G. and Walsh, Lorene S. 1978. The planter's wife: the experience of white women in seventeenth century Maryland. In Michael Gordon (ed.), *The American family in historical perspective*.

Cassidy, Frederic G. 1961. *Jamaica Talk: three hundred years of the English language in Jamaica*. London: Macmillan & Co. in association with The Institute of Jamaica.

Clarke, Edith 1957. *My mother who fathered me*. London: George Allen and Unwin.

Cokayne, George E. 1932. *The complete peerage, or a history of the House of Lords and all its members from the earliest times*. Revised and enlarged by The Hon. Vicary Gibbs. Now edited by H. A. Doubleday and Lord Howard de Walden. 12 vols. 1910-1959. London: The St. Catherine Press.

Commonwealth Caribbean 1970. *1970 population census of the Commonwealth Caribbean*. Kingston, Jamaica: University of the West Indies, Census Research Programme.

Craton, Michael 1978. *Searching for the invisible man: slaves and plantation life in Jamaica*. Cambridge, Mass.: Harvard University Press.

    1979. Changing patterns of slave families in the British West Indies. *Journal of interdisciplinary history* 10: 1-35.

Craton, Michael and Walvin, James 1970. *A Jamaican plantation: the history of Worthy Park 1670-1970*. London & New York: W.H. Allen.

Cumper, George 1962. The differentiation of economic groups in the West Indies. *Social and economic studies* 11: 319-32.

References

Curtin, Philip D. 1955. *Two Jamaicas: the role of ideas in a tropical colony 1830-1865*. Cambridge, Mass.: Harvard University Press.

DeCamp, David 1971. Toward a generative analysis of a post-creole speech continuum. In Hymes, Dell H. (ed), *Pidginization and creolization of languages*. Cambridge: Cambridge University Press.

DeVeer, Henrietta 1979. *Sex roles and social stratification in a rapidly growing urban area – May Pen, Jamaica*. Chicago: University of Chicago Ph.D. Dissertation.

Drummond, Lee 1980. The cultural continuum: a theory of intersystems. *Man* 15: 352-74.

Dubin, Robert 1960. Parsons' actor: continuities in social theory. *American Sociological Review* 25: 457-66.

Duff, Robert 1866. *British Guiana: being notes on a few of its natural productions, industrial occupations, and social institutions*. Glasgow: Thomas Murray and Son.

Dumont, Louis 1980. *Homo hierarchicus: the caste system and its implications*. Chicago: University of Chicago Press.

Dunn, Richard S. 1972. *Sugar and slaves: the rise of the planter class in the English West Indies, 1624-1713*. Chapel Hill: University of North Carolina Press.

Durkheim, Emile 1947 [1892]. *The division of labor in society*. Translated by George Simpson. New York: Free Press.

Edwards, Bryan 1794. *The history, civil and commercial, of the British colonies in the West Indies* (2 Vols.). London: John Stockdale.

El Zein, Abdul Hamid M. 1974. *The sacred meadows: a structural analysis of religious symbolism in an East African town*. Evanston: Northwestern University Press.

Evans-Pritchard, Edward E. 1951. *Social anthropology*. London: Cohen and West.

Fallers, Lloyd 1956. *Bantu bureaucracy*. Cambridge: W. Heffer and Son for East African Institute of Social Research.

1973. *Inequality: social stratification reconsidered*. Chicago and London: University of Chicago Press.

Firth, Raymond, Hubert, J. and Forge, A. 1970. *Families and their relatives*. London: Routledge and Kegan Paul.

Fischer, Michael 1969. *Opposite sets and selected masques from a rural Jamaica point of view*. Unpublished M.A. thesis, Department of Anthropology, University of Chicago.

1974. Value assertion and stratification: religion and marriage in rural Jamaica. *Caribbean Studies* 14(1): 7-37; 14(3): 7-35.

Foner, Nancy 1973. *Status and power in rural Jamaica: a study of educational and political change*. New York: Teacher's College Press.

Fortes, Meyer 1958. Introduction. In J. Goody (ed.), *The development cycle in domestic groups*. London: Cambridge University Press.

Frazier, Franklin 1939. *The negro family in the United States*. Chicago: University of Chicago Press.

Freyre, Gilberto 1946. *The masters and the slaves*. New York: Knopf.

Furnivall, J. S. 1948. *Colonial policy and practice: a comparative study of Burma and Netherlands India*. London: Cambridge University Press.

Gonzalez, Nancie Loudon 1984. Rethinking the consanguineal household and matrifocality. *Ethnology* 23: 1-12

References

Goody, E. N. 1971. Forms of pro-parenthood: the sharing and substitution of parental roles. In Jack Goody (ed.), *Kinship*. Harmondsworth: Penguin Books.

Goody, Jack 1972. The evolution of the family. In Peter Laslett (ed.), *Household and family in past time*. Pp. 103-24. London: Cambridge University Press.

1983. *The development of the family and marriage in Europe*. Cambridge: Cambridge University Press.

Graham, Sara 1973. *Occupational mobility in Guyana*. Unpublished Ph.D. dissertation. Kingston, Jamaica: University of the West Indies.

Graham, Sara and Gordon, Derek 1977. *The stratification system and occupational mobility in Guyana*. Mona, Jamaica: Institute of social and economic research.

Gudeman, Stephen 1972. The compadrazgo as a reflection of the natural and spiritual person. *Proceedings of the Royal Anthropological Institute of Great Britain and Ireland for 1971*. Pp. 45-71.

1976. *Relationships, residence and the individual: a rural Panamanian community*. London: Routledge and Kegan Paul.

Gutman, Herbert G. 1976. *The black family in slavery and freedom, 1750-1925*. New York: Pantheon.

Guyana Handbook 1975. Georgetown, Guyana: Guyana Manufacturers Association.

Hall, Douglas 1972. Jamaica. In Cohen, D. W. and Greene, J. P. (eds.), *Neither slave nor free*. Baltimore: Johns Hopkins University Press.

1978. The flight from the estates reconsidered. *Journal of Caribbean history*. 10/11:

Handler, Jerome S. 1974. *The unappropriated people: freedmen in the slave society of Barbados*. Baltimore: The Johns Hopkins University Press.

Handler, Jerome S. and Lange, Frederick W. 1978. *Plantation slavery in Barbados: an archaeological and historical investigation*. Cambridge Mass.: Harvard University Press.

Hart, Ansell n.d. *The life of George William Gordon*. Cultural Heritage Series, Volume I. Kingston, Jamaica: Institute of Jamaica.

Henriques, Fernando 1953. *Family and colour in Jamaica*. London: Eyre and Spottiswoode.

Herskovits, Melville J. 1960. The ahistorical approach to Afro-American studies: a critique. *American Anthropologist*, 62: 559-68.

Heuman, Gad 1981. *Between black and white: race, politics and the free coloreds in Jamaica, 1792-1865*. Westport: The Greenwood Press.

Hickerson, Harold H. 1966. Review of Lewis Saum, The fur trader and the Indian. *American Anthropologist*, 68: 822.

Higman, Barry W. 1973. Household structure and fertility on Jamaican slave plantations: a nineteenth century example. *Population Studies*, XXVII: 527-50.

1975. The slave family and household in the British West Indies, 1800-1834. *Journal of Interdisciplinary History*, VI: 261-87.

1976. *Slave population and economy in Jamaica, 1807-1834*. Cambridge: Cambridge University Press.

1978. *Domestic service in Jamaica, England and the United States (1770-1970)*. Jamaica: University of the West Indies, Department of History.

Holzberg, Carol S. 1977. *Race, ethnicity and the political economy of national entrepreneurial elites in Jamaica*. Ph.D. dissertation. Boston, Mass.: Boston University.

References

Hymes, Dell H. (ed.) 1971. *Pidginization and creolization of languages.* Cambridge: Cambridge University Press.

Inden, Ronald B. and Nicholas, Ralph W. 1977. *Kinship in Bengali culture.* Chicago: University of Chicago Press.

Institute of Jamaica Manuscript Collection. Nuttall Papers, MST 209. Kingston, Jamaica

Institute of Jamaica Manuscript Collection. MS 1604. Kingston, Jamaica.

Jacobs, H. P. 1971. Port Royal in decline. *The Jamaica Historical Review* 8:34-59.

1973. *Sixty years of change, 1806-1866: progress and reaction in Kingston and the countryside.* Kingston: Institute of Jamaica.

Jamaica Population Census 1970: Preliminary Report 1970. Kingston, Jamaica: Department of Statistics.

JIRO. Jamaica Island Record Office. Wills, Lib. 131. Spanish Town, Jamaica.

Jayawardena, Chandra 1962. Family organisation in plantations in British Guiana. *International Journal of Comparative Sociology* 3: 43-64.

Jefferson, Owen 1972. *The post-war economic development of Jamaica.* Mona, Jamaica: Institute of Social and Economic Research, University of the West Indies.

Kincaid, Dennis 1973 [1938]. *British social life in India, 1608-1937.* London: Routledge and Kegan Paul.

Knight, Derrick 1978. *Gentlemen of fortune.* London.

Kruskal, William 1981. Statistics in society: problems unsolved and unformulated. *Journal of the American Statistical Association,* 76: 505-15.

Labov, William 1972. *Language in the inner city: studies in the Black English vernacular.* Philadelphia: University of Pennsylvania Press.

Lasch, Christopher 1977. *Haven in a heartless world: the family besieged.* New York: Basic Books.

Lawrence, James Henry 1976 [1811]. *The Empire of the Nairs.* A facsimile reproduction of the 1811 edition, with an Introduction by Janet M. Todd. New York: Delmar.

Leach, Edmund 1955. Polyandry, inheritance and the definition of marriage: with particular reference to Sinhalese customary law. *Man* 55: 182-6.

Lévi-Strauss, Claude 1956. The family. In Shapiro, H. L. (ed.), *Man, culture and society.* New York: Oxford University Press.

1963. *Structural anthropology.* New York: Basic Books.

1966. The scope of anthropology. *Current Anthropology* 7: 112-23.

Lewis, Gordon K. 1983. *Main currents in Caribbean thought: the historical evolution of Caribbean society in its ideological aspects, 1492-1900.* Baltimore and London: The Johns Hopkins University Press.

Lomnitz, Larissa and Marisol Pérez Lizaur 1978. The history of a Mexican urban family. *Journal of Family History* 3: 392-409.

1984. Dynastic growth and survival strategies: the solidarity of Mexican grandfamilies. In Smith, Raymond T. (ed.), *Kinship ideology and practice in Latin America.* Chapel Hill and London: University of North Carolina Press.

London Gazette 1838. *London Gazette,* Number 19656. Pp. 2004-5. London: Her Majesty's Stationery Office.

Long, Edward 1972 [1774]. *The history of Jamaica.* 3 vols. New York: Arno Press [London: T. Lowndes in Fleet Street].

Malinowski, Bronislaw 1929. *The sexual life of savages.* London.

1938. Introductory essay on the anthropology of changing African cultures. In *Methods of study of culture contact in Africa.* International Institute of

References

African Languages and Cultures Memorandum XV [reprinted from *Africa*, Vols VII, VIII and IX], pp. vii-xxxviii. London.

Marshall, Woodville (ed.) 1977. *The Colthurst journal: journal of a special magistrate in the islands of Barbados and St. Vincent July 1835-September 1838*. New York: KTO Press.

Martinez-Alier, Verena 1974. *Marriage, class and colour in nineteenth century Cuba: a study of racial attitudes and sexual values in a slave society*. London: Cambridge University Press.

Marx, Karl 1963 [1852]. *The eighteenth brumaire of Louis Bonaparte*. New York: International Publishers.

Marx, Karl and Engels, Friedrich 1965 [1843]. *The German ideology*. Revised English trans. London: Lawrence & Wishart.

McKenzie, Herman I. 1981. *The African family in the New World: some recent studies*. Unpublished manuscript.

Mintz, Sydney and Wolf, Eric 1957. Haciendas and plantations in Middle America and the Antilles. *Social and economic studies*. 6: 380-412.

Montejo, Esteban 1961. *The autobiography of a runaway slave*. Edited by Miguel Barnet, translated by Jocasta Innes. New York: Pantheon

Nadel, Siegfried F. 1951. *The foundations of social anthropology*. London: Cohen and West.

Needham, Rodney 1971. Introduction. In R. Needham (ed.), *Rethinking kinship and marriage*. Association of Social Anthropologists, Monograph 11, pp. xiii-cxvii. London: Tavistock Publications.

Nicholls, David 1985. *Haiti in Caribbean context: ethnicity, economy and revolt*. New York: St. Martin's Press.

Pares, Richard 1950. *A West-India fortune*. London: Longmans, Green and Co..

Parks Jr., Anderson n.d. *Working class kinship in Jamaica: a study of culture, social structure and the process of change*. Unpublished manuscript.

Parsons, Talcott 1947. Introduction to Weber, Max, *The theory of social and economic organization*. Glencoe, Illinois: The Free Press.

1949. The social structure of the family. In Anshen, Ruth Nanda (ed.), *The family: its function and destiny*. New York: Harper and Row.

1951. *The social system*. Glencoe, Illinois: The Free Press.

1966. *Societies: evolutionary and comparative perspectives*. Englewood Cliffs, N.J.: Prentice- Hall.

Patterson, Orlando 1969a. Social aspects of the sugar industry. *New World Quarterly* 5: 47-9.

1969b. *The sociology of slavery*. Rutherford: Fairleigh Dickenson University Press.

1982. Persistence, continuity and change in the Jamaican working-class family. *Journal of Family History* 7: 135-61.

Pawson, Michael and Buisseret, David 1975. *Port Royal, Jamaica*. Oxford: Clarendon Press.

Pinckard, George 1816. *Notes on the West Indies, including observations relative to the creoles and slaves of the western colonies, and the Indians of South America; interspersed with remarks upon the seasoning or yellow fever of hot climates*. Second edition with additional letters from Martinique, Jamaica, and St.Domingo. (2 vols.) London: Messrs. Baldwin, Craddock, and Joy, Paternoster Row; and L.B. Seeley, Fleet Street.

Post, Ken 1978. *Arise ye starvelings: the Jamaican labour rebellion of 1938 and its aftermath*. The Hague, Boston, London: Martinus Nijhoff.

References

Powell, Chilton L. 1917. *English domestic relations 1487-1653*. New York.

Prindle, Carol 1975. *Trinidad as callaloo: the East Indian feeling of belonging to a social category*. Unpublished M.A. thesis, Department of Anthropology, University of Chicago.

Radcliffe-Brown, A.R. 1952. *Structure and function in primitive society: essays and addresses*. London: Cohen and West.

Reid, Stanley 1977. An introductory approach to the concentration of power in the Jamaican corporate economy and notes on its origin. In Stone, Carl and Brown, Aggrey (eds.), *Essays on power and change in Jamaica*. Kingston, Jamaica: Jamaica Publishing House.

Rivers, W.H.R. 1968 [1914]. *Kinship and social organization*. London: Athlone Press.

Rhys, Jean 1966. *Wide Sargasso Sea*. London: André Deutsch.

Roberts, George W. 1957. *The Population of Jamaica*. Cambridge: Cambridge University Press.

   1975. *Fertility and mating in four west Indian populations: Trinidad and Tobago, Barbados, St. Vincent, Jamaica*. Jamaica: Institute of Social and Economic Research, University of the West Indies.

Roberts, George W. and Sinclair, Sonja A. 1978. *Women in Jamaica: patterns of reproduction and family*. Millwood, N.Y.: KTO Press.

Robotham, Donald K. 1970. *National integration and local community structure in Jamaica*. Unpublished M.A. thesis, Department of Anthropology, University of Chicago.

   1980. Pluralism as an ideology. *Social and economic studies* 29: 69-89.

   1982. *The notorious riot: the socio-economic and political bases of Paul Bogle's revolt*. Kingston, Jamaica: Institute of Social and Economic Research, Working Paper No. 28.

   1985. The why of the cockatoo. *Social and economic studies* 34: 111-51.

Rodman, Hyman 1963. The lower-class value stretch. *Social forces* 42: 205-15.

Rodney, Walter 1981. *A history of the Guyanese working people, 1881-1905*. Baltimore: Johns Hopkins University Press.

Roughley, Thomas 1823. *The Jamaica planter's guide*. London: Longman, Hurst, Rees, Orme and Brown.

Sahlins, Marshall 1981. *Historical metaphors and mythical realities: structure in the early history of the Sandwich Islands Kingdom*. Ann Arbor: University of Michigan Press.

Sankoff, Gillian 1980. *The social life of language*. Philadelphia: University of Pennsylvania Press.

Scheele, Raymond L. 1956. The prominent families of Puerto Rico. In Steward, Julian, *The people of Puerto Rico*. Urbana: The University of Illinois Press.

Schneider, David M. 1965. Kinship and biology. In Ansley J. Coale *et al.* (eds.), *Aspects of the analysis of family structure*. Princeton: Princeton University Press.

   1972. What is kinship all about? In Priscilla Reining (ed.), *Kinship in the Morgan Centennial Year*. Washington D.C.: Washington Anthropological Society.

   1976. Notes toward a theory of culture. In Basso, Keith H. and Selby, Henry A. (eds.), *Meaning in Anthropology*. Albuquerque: University of New Mexico Press.

   1980 [1968]. *American kinship: a cultural account*. Chicago: University of Chicago Press. [Englewood Cliffs N.J.: Prentice-Hall].

References

1984. *A critique of the study of kinship*. Ann Arbor: University of Michigan Press.

Schneider, David M. and Cottrell, C. B. 1975. *The American kin universe: a genealogical study*. Chicago: University of Chicago Studies in Anthropology.

Schneider, David M. and Smith, Raymond T. 1978 [1973]. *Class differences in American kinship*. Ann Arbor: University of Michigan Press [Englewood Cliffs, N.J.: Prentice-Hall].

Seeley, J.R., Sim, R.A. and Loosley, E.W. 1956. *Crestwood Heights: A study of the culture of suburban life*. New York: Basic Books.

Silverstein, Michael 1972. Chinook jargon: language contact and the problem of multi-level generative systems. *Language*, 48: 378-406, 596-625.

Simey, Thomas S. 1946. *Welfare and planning in the West Indies*. Oxford: Clarendon Press.

Smith, Michael G. 1953. Some aspects of social structure in the British Caribbean about 1820. *Social and economic studies* 1: 455-80.

1956. *A framework for Caribbean studies*. Kingston, Jamaica: University College of the West Indies, Extra-Mural Department.

1983. Robotham's ideology and pluralism. *Social and economic studies* 32: 103-39.

1984. *Culture, race and class in the Commonwealth Caribbean*. Kingston, Jamaica: University of the West Indies, Department of Extra-Mural Studies.

Smith, Raymond T. 1956. *The negro family in British Guiana: family structure and social status in the villages*. London: Routledge and Kegan Paul.

1963. Culture and social structure in the Caribbean. *Comparative studies in society and history*, VI: 24-46.

1966. People and change. In *New World: Guyana Independence Issue*. Demerara, Guyana. Pp. 49-54.

1967. Social stratification, cultural pluralism and integration in West Indian societies. In Lewis, Sybil and Mathews, Thomas G. (eds.), *Caribbean integration: papers on social, political and economic integration*. Rio Piedras: Institute of Caribbean Studies, University of Puerto Rico.

1973. The matrifocal family. In Goody, Jack (ed.), The character of kinship. Pp. 121-44. Cambridge: Cambridge University Press.

1976. Religion in the formation of West Indian society. In Kilson, Martin L. and Rotberg, Robert I., *The African Diaspora*. Cambridge, Mass.: Harvard University Press.

1977. Introduction to Graham, Sara and Gordon, Derek, *The stratification system and occupational mobility in Guyana*. Mona, Jamaica: Institute of Social and Economic Research, University of the West Indies.

1978a. The family and the modern world system: some observations from the Caribbean. *Journal of family history* 3: 337-60.

1978b. Class differences in West Indian kinship: a genealogical exploration. In Marks, Arnaud F. and Romer, Rene A. (eds.), *Family and kinship in Middle America and the Caribbean*. Leiden: Royal Institute of Linguistics and Anthropology.

1980 [1962]. *British Guiana*. Westport, Conn.: Greenwood Press [London: Oxford University Press].

1982a. Family, social change and social policy in the West Indies. *Nieuwe West-Indische Gids*, 56: 111-142.

References

1982b. Race and class in the post-emancipation Caribbean. In Ross, R. (ed.), *Racism and colonialism*. Pp. 93-119. The Hague: Martinus Nijhoff.

1984a. *Kinship ideology and practice in Latin America*. Chapel Hill: University of North Carolina Press.

1984b. Introduction. In Smith, Raymond T. (ed.), *Kinship ideology and practice in Latin America*. Chapel Hill: University of North Carolina Press.

1984c. The concept of social class in anthropology. *Annual Review of Anthropology* 13:467-94.

1984d. Some theoretical issues in family and household studies. A paper presented at a conference on 'New Perspectives on Caribbean Studies: Toward the 21st Century' held in New York, August 27th to September 1st 1984.

1987. Hierarchy and the dual marriage system in West Indian society. In Collier, Jane & Yanagisako, Sylvia (eds.), *Gender and kinship: essays toward a unified analysis*. Stanford: Stanford University Press.

1987. Kinship and class in Chicago. In Mullings, Leith (ed.), *Cities of the United States*. Pp. 292-313.New York: Columbia University Press.

Smith, Raymond T. and Jayawardena, Chandra 1959. Marriage and the Family amongst East Indians in British Guiana. *Social and economic studies* 8: 321-76.

Spear, Percival 1932. *The Nabobs*. London: Oxford University Press.

Spencer, Alfred (ed.) 1918. *Memoirs of William Hickey*, 4 vols. London: Hurst and Blackett.

Stedman, Captain J. G. 1971 [1806]. *Narrative of a five years expedition against the revolted negroes of Surinam in Guiana on the wild coast of South America from the years 1772 to 1777. Elucidating the history of that country and describing its productions, viz. quadrupeds, birds, reptiles, trees, shrubs, fruits and roots; with an account of the Indians of Guiana and Negroes of Guinea.* 2 vols. Barre, Mass.: The Imprint Society [London: J. Johnson and J. Edwards]

Stone, Carl 1973. *Class, race and political behaviour in Urban Jamaica*. Kingston, Jamaica: Institute of Social and Economic Research

Stone, Lawrence 1977. *The family, sex and marriage in England 1500-1800*. New York: Harper and Row.

Tambiah, Stanley J. 1973. From Varna to Caste through Mixed Unions. In Goody, Jack (ed.), *The character of kinship*. Cambridge: Cambridge University Press.

Titles to Land Commissioners 1892. *Report of the titles to Land Commissioners on claims to land in the county of Demerara*. Georgetown, Demerara: Baldwin and Co., Printers.

Tocqueville, Alexis de 1954 [1875]. *Democracy in America* (trans. Henry Reeve). London.

Trinidad and Tobago Central Statistical Office 1964. *British Guiana Population Census, 1960*. Vol. 2, Parts A and B. Port of Spain: Population Census Division, Central Statistical Office.

United States Department of Labor, Office of Planning and Research 1965. *The negro family: the case for national action*. Washington, D.C..

van Lier, Rudolf 1971. Introduction to Stedman, Captain J. G., *Narrative of a five years' expedition against the revolted negroes of Surinam*. Pp. v-xv. Barre, Mass.:Imprint Society.

Walkowitz, Judith R. 1980. *Prostitution and Victorian society: women, class and the state*. Cambridge: Cambridge University Press.

References

Wallace, Anthony 1969. Review of Schneider, D.M., *American kinship: a cultural account*. In *American Anthropologist* 71: 100-106.

Weber, Max 1968. *Economy and society* (3 vols). Edited by Roth, Guenther and Wittich, Claus. New York: Bedminster Press.

Wilden, Anthony 1972. *System and structure: essays in communication and exchange*. London: Tavistock Publications.

Wolf, Linda M. 1964. *Anthropological interviewing in Chicago: analysis of a kinship research experience*. Chicago: University of Chicago, Department of Anthropology. American Kinship Project, Monograph No. 1. Available from The University of Chicago Library, Department of Photoduplication.

Wright, Philip 1966. *Lady Nugent's journal of her residence in Jamaica from 1801 to 1805*. Kingston, Jamaica: Institute of Jamaica.

Yanagisako, Sylvia Junko 1978. Variance in American kinship: implications for cultural analysis. *American Ethnologist* 5: 15-29.

1979. Family and household: the analysis of domestic groups. *Annual Review of Anthropology* 8: 161-205.

Young, Allan 1958. *The approaches to local self-government in British Guiana*. London: Longmans.

194

Index

Index

Index

cultural account, 24, 28
cultural anthropology, as specialized study, 24
culture
  American, 40
  and American anthropology, 178-9
  analytical separability of, 23
  Bengali, 28-30
  boundaries, 2
  contact, 6
  conglomerate level, 24-6
  and consciousness, 127
  diversity, 3
  domains, 24
  erosion of, 5
  and functionalism, 6-7
  and history, 3
  integration of, 2
  and meaning of sex, 135, 141
  Parsons on, 22-3
  pure level, 24-6
  and social action, 22-3
  and social practice, 26-8
  survivals, 39
  transformation of, 4
  see also person, plural society
Cumper, George, 95
Curtin, Philip D., 93

David, Elizabeth (informant), 128-9, 132
Davis, Dalton, 10, 18
DeCamp, David, 39
DeVeer, Henrietta, 116-17, 127n
distinctive feature, concept of, 25
domestic
  credit, 165
  domain, 149-50
  group, functions of, 150
  hospitality, 154
  servants, 156, 165, 166, 168, 172, 173
domestic life
  and economic development, 163-6
  instability of, 155
  lower class, 163-4
  of prosperous classes, 164-5
  in 17th century Port Royal, 152-3
  of slaves, 157-60
domestic relations, and consumption, 166
domesticity, of middle class, 167-74
Drummond, Lee, 21, 39
dual-marriage system, 105-6
Dubin, Robert, 23
Duff, Robert, 101
Dumont, Louis, 183
Dunn, Richard S., 151
Durkheim, Emile, 137

East Indians, 6, 11, 12, 13, 14, 15, 17, 38-9, 40, 43, 44, 54, 93-4, 108-9, 137-8, 162
economic development, 14-15
  and changing family relations 166
economies, dependent nature of, 11, 12
Edwards, Bryan, 84-6, 88-9
Eggan, Fred, 178
El Zein, Abdul Hamid M., 3
elites
  racial composition of, 13-15
  white planter, 12-13
  see also intelligentsia, social class
entertaining, 181, 182
Ethiopianism, 93
Eurasians, 87
Evans-Pritchard, E.E., 178
ex-slaves
  communal ownership of land, 106-8
  marriage among, 106-8

Fallers, Lloyd, 23, 178
family
  defined by census, 8-9
  distinguished from relatives, 140
  and domestic group, 180
  'deviant' forms, 4
  forms, viability of, 4
  functions, 179
  and household, 29, 180
  instability, 154-5
  land, 60, 143
  meaning of, 41-4
  of slaves, 158-60
  and spontaneous kin lists, 41
  supposed universality of, 4
father
  as affine, 39
  attitudes toward, 126
  as genitor, 25
  minimal definition of, 25
field sites, described, 15-18
Firth, Raymond, 10, 18, 61, 72
Fischer, Michael, 15, 16, 17, 21, 127n
Foner, Nancy, 16, 17, 127n
Forge, Anthony, 10
Fortes, Meyer, 6, 150, 179
Frazier, Franklin, 183
Free People of Colour, origin of, 90
  see also Coloured population
Freyre, Gilberto, 151
fur-trade marriage, 86-7
Furnivall, J.S., 5

Garvey, Marcus, 163
Gaumé, M., 151
Geertz, Clifford, 178

197

Index

Index

Index

and missionary activity, 101-2
and occupation, 168-9
and race, 121
and religion, 116, 121-2
as start of family, 43
types of in England, 83
see also union types, common-law marriage
Marshall, Woodville, 40
Martinez-Alier, Verena, 114
Marx, Karl, 92, 179n
matrifocal
bias, 126-7
family, 7-8, 179, 183; among Free
Coloured, 157
household, in eighteenth century, 96
matrifocality, 182, 158, 160
matrilateral kin, 56-8
Mayers, Jacqueline, 16
mental experiments, 3
middle class, see social class, middle
Miller, Barbara, 17
Mintz, Sydney, 156
mixed race
numbers of, 91
see Coloured population
mobility, social, 14
Montejo, Esteban, 156
Morant Bay rebellion, 93, 102
mother-child relation, as core of domestic
group, 150
Moynihan, Daniel P., 183
multicultural societies, creation of, 3
multiracial societies, creation of, 3
Murray, James (informant), 118-19

Nadel, Siegfried, 22
national religion, 5
nationalism, origins of, 92
Needham, Rodney, 111
Nicholas, Ralph, 28-30
Nicholls, David, 13, 14
non-legal unions
and kin recognition, 79
and kinship terms, 40
and land holding, 107
emotional aspects of, 143-6
importance of, 82
see also concubinage, common-law
marriage, keeper
norms, 21
and behaviour, 22-3
and culture, 23
nuclear family, 180
and residence, 33
and structure of genealogies, 33
Nugent, Maria, 85, 157

nursing, as aspect of concubinage, 98, 145,
157
Nuttall, Bishop, 104-5

O'Sullivan family, 103-4
occupations, and race, 122
outside children, 154
see also illegitimacy, bastardy
outside unions, 117-20
see also concubinage, keeper

parenthood
and residence, 137
symbolism of, 137
Parks Jr., Anderson, 110
Parsons, Talcott, 22, 23, 26, 178, 179
patrilateral kin, 56-8
Patterson, Orlando, 110n, 178
Pawson, Michael, 84, 152
Pérez Lizaur, Marisol, 95
person, as cultural construct, 24
philosophical radicalism, 4
Pinckard, Dr. George, 154
plural society, 3
as myth, 5
theory of, 5
population growth, 164
Port Royal, 152-3
Portuguese, 12, 13, 14, 54, 87, 93, 94
Post, Ken, 11, 93
poverty, 7
and family life, 127-8; in United States,
182-3
Powell, Chilton L., 83
Price family, 94, 96-8, 153-4
Prindle, Carol, 127n
procedures, described, 10-11
'prokin' defined, 45

quantitative analysis, 8
Quier, Dr. John, 96, 181

race and intermarriage, 120-2
race mixture, classifications of, 84, 91
racial boundaries, 2
Radcliffe-Brown, A.R., 6, 178
Ragbir, Rohan (informant), 51
Rattray, R.S., 37
Reid, Stanley, 14, 94
religion, 5, 14, 22, 28
and marriage, 116-17, 121
and social mobility, 14-15
Rhys, Jean, 181
Rivers, W.H.R., 47
Roberts, George W., 28, 30, 38, 104, 112, 114

200

Index

Robotham, Don, 7n, 16, 17, 18, 163-4, 102, 127n
Rodman, Hyman, 5
Rodney, Walter, 11
Rogers, Nancy (informant), 130-3
Roughley, Thomas, 155-6, 158

Sahlins, Marshall, 86
Sankoff, Gillian, 2
Schaw, Janet, 181
Scheele, Raymond, 95
Schneider, David M., 10, 17, 18, 24, 25, 26, 27, 28, 40, 49, 61, 72, 74, 139-40
Sears, Mrs. (informant), 117-18, 121-2, 131, 167-8, 172
Seeley, J.R., 124
segregated role pattern, 170, 171
Selby, Henry A., 9
Sephardic Jews, 13
sex
    division of labour by, 134, 136
    meanings of, 135
    in organization of genealogy, 33, 38
    and rape, 84
    as survey category, 10
    and genealogical variation, 49
sex roles, 25, 26
    in constitution of kinship, 25, 26, 141
    class variations in, 141-8, 172
    cultural dimensions of, 135-48
    dissociated, 142-6
    joint, 139, 141, 142, 146-8, 170
    and matrifocality, 182
    normality of, 134
    and 'responsibility,' 137
    segregated, 138, 142, 146-8, 170-1
    and social structure, 141-8, 180
    variation of, 141-8
    West Indian beliefs about, 134-6
sexual intercourse
    beliefs about, 38, 137
    early experience of, 137
sexuality
    attributional aspects, 135-8
    distinctive features, 134
    relational aspects, 138-42
Silverstein, Michael, 2
Simey, T.S., 31
Sinclair, Sonja, A., 30, 38
Singh, Reginald (informant), 43
slavery
    abolition of, 93, 161
    effect on domestic life, 161
    and legal status, 102
slaves
    family structure, 158-60

marriage customs, 88-9
    validity of marriages, 102
small farmer class,
    family ideology of, 162-3
Small, Bertha (informant), 42
Smith, Alice (informant), 142-4
    relatives of, 60
Smith, Michael G., 5, 6, 7n
social boundaries, 2
social change, 4
social class
    categories explained, 15
    as component of roles, 26
    consciousness of, 91-4, 127
    and domestic domain, 180
    and family differences, 5
    and genealogical tabulations, 48-9
    ideology and perception of, 21, 89-94
    and informant's view, 128
    intelligentsia, 13-14, 93
    and kinship, 8
    lower: rural, 12; urban, 174-6
    and 'matrifocality', 8
    middle: domesticity, 167-74; and outside unions, 117-20; expansion of, 122; myth of origin of, 90-91, 95-101; preoccupation with marriage, 108, 148; role in social development, 90-5; rural family life, 163
    and occupations, 52-5
    problem of definition, 166, 182
    and race, 90-1; association of, 13; West Indian described, 11-15
    and racial meanings, 177
    terms for, 127
    and theories of conception, 37
    upper, 12-13, 94-5, 166, 180, 182
    warfare, 167
social mobility
    and racial prejudice, 14
    rate of, 14-15
    and religion, 13-14
social purity movement, 104
South Africa, 6-7
Spear, Percival, 87
Spencer, Alfred, 87
spontaneous kin lists, 31-37, 41-4
spouse, defined, 63
squatters, 16
Stedman, Captain John, 98-9
Steward, Julian, 95
Stone, Carl, 11
Stone, Lawrence, 83, 84
structural functionalism, 177-8
sugar estates
    organization of, 156

201

Index

Cambridge Studies in
Social Anthropology

Editor: JACK GOODY

Cambridge Studies in Social Anthropology

Cambridge Studies in Social Anthropology

   * Available in paperback